s three-part collection of essays taps the
inal thinking of one of America's foremost
ologists, a social theorist whose work has
; had what are described as 'potentials of
vance' for diverse domains of practice.

book examines the interplay between
al research and social policy with a focus
he practicing professions—medicine and
llied disciplines, the law, social services,
the clergy.

art I, Merton analyzes the structures and
esses of social scientific research, center-
on how the internal organization of the
iplines affects the choice and formulation
y problems for investigation. Part II deals
ifically with the practicing professions, ex-
ning the processes of socialization in the
ical school and the workings of institu-
alized altruism in the professions within
context of the entrepreneurial imperative
affects relationships between professionals
clients in today's society. Part III, which
oduces the concept of potentials of
vance, analyzes the connections between
ological knowledge and the formulation of
al policy, exploring both basic aids and
ediments to the use of social research. The
ussions are attuned throughout to the
ies and unanticipated consequences of
al action.

essays collected here can help members of
practicing professions, sociologists,
omists and makers of policy to under-
d themselves, their colleagues and their
ts better than before. All readers will gain
enlarged appreciation of the limits and
ntials of drawing upon sociological
wledge in trying to cope with social and
onal problems.

SOCIAL RESEARCH AND THE PRACTICING PROFESSIONS

Other Books
by ROBERT K. MERTON

SCIENCE, TECHNOLOGY, AND SOCIETY IN SEVENTEENTH-
CENTURY ENGLAND
MASS PERSUASION *(with M. Fiske and A. Curtis)*
SOCIAL THEORY AND SOCIAL STRUCTURE
THE FOCUSED INTERVIEW *(with M. Fiske and P. L. Kendall)*
THE FREEDOM TO READ *(with R. McKeon and W. Gellhorn)*
ON THE SHOULDERS OF GIANTS
ON THEORETICAL SOCIOLOGY
THE SOCIOLOGY OF SCIENCE
SOCIOLOGICAL AMBIVALENCE
THE SOCIOLOGY OF SCIENCE: AN EPISODIC MEMOIR

Editor
CONTINUITIES IN SOCIAL RESEARCH
(with P. F. Lazarsfeld)
READER IN BUREAUCRACY
(with A. Gray, B. Hockey, and H. C. Selvin)
THE STUDENT-PHYSICIAN
(with G. G. Reader and P. L. Kendall)
SOCIOLOGY TODAY
(with L. Broom and L. S. Cottrell, Jr.)
CONTEMPORARY SOCIAL PROBLEMS
(with R. A. Nisbet)
THE SOCIOLOGY OF SCIENCE IN EUROPE
(with J. Gaston)
QUALITATIVE & QUANTITATIVE SOCIAL RESEARCH:
PAPERS IN HONOR OF PAUL F. LAZARSFELD
(with J. S. Coleman and P. H. Rossi)
TOWARD A METRIC OF SCIENCE
*(with Y. Elkana, J. Lederberg,
A. Thackray, and H. Zuckerman)*
SOCIOLOGICAL TRADITIONS FROM GENERATION TO
GENERATION
(with M. W. Riley)
CONTINUITIES IN STRUCTURAL INQUIRY
(with P. M. Blau)

ROBERT K. MERTON

Social Research and the Practicing Professions

Edited and with an Introduction
by
Aaron Rosenblatt and Thomas F. Gieryn

Abt Books
Cambridge, Massachusetts

Library of Congress Cataloging in Publication Data

Merton, Robert King, 1910–
 Social research and the practicing professions.

 Bibliography: p.
 Includes index.
 1. Sociology—Research. 2. Professions—Sociological
aspects. 3. Social policy. I. Rosenblatt, Aaron.
II. Gieryn, Thomas F. III. Title.
HM48.M46   1982   301'.07'2   82–8752
ISBN 0–89011–569–9   AACR2

for
Diana Rosenblatt
A woman of valor

Contents

Contents

PREFACE AND ACKNOWLEDGEMENTS

The idea for this volume originated with Professor Aaron Rosenblatt of the State University of New York at Albany and Professor Thomas F. Gieryn of the University of Indiana. Deeply interested in the sociology of the professions, in social research and its interplay with the formation of social policy, they managed to persuade me that it might be useful to gather up these papers previously scattered in a variety of journals, symposia, and other books, most of them not easily accessible. The text of these essays remains largely as first published although the editors and, on occasion, I too have removed infelicities of expression and have updated facts and figures when this was called for.

As often before, I am obliged to Mary Wilson Miles and, now also, to Karen Ginsberg for monitoring the preparation of a manuscript and for helping to prepare the indexes. My editors tell me that I am also obliged to Pamela Fitzpatrick, Sharon Georgianna, Ingrid LaCasse and Mac Venezia for their patient assistance in getting word processors to behave and in reading proofs.

I owe thanks to the National Science Foundation and to The Commonwealth Fund for grants in aid of some of the papers in this volume but, of course, I am indebted most of all to Aaron Rosenblatt and Thomas Gieryn.

Robert K. Merton

Morningside Heights
New York City
7 April 1982

INTRODUCTION

The route between social research and social policy has always been a tortuous one. The journey from social policy to social research often ends in frustration for policymakers hoping to use sociological understanding to correct troubled institutions and organizations, or for members of the helping professions hoping to correct the troubled lives of patients and clients. Sociological knowledge sometimes appears irrelevant or impractical in the face of routinely urgent decisions. The opposite journey, from social research to social policy, is sometimes not even attempted by sociologists who measure professional success not by solutions to practical problems but by scholarly contributions to empirical and theoretical knowledge of how society works. To ease the journey for travelers in both directions is our rationale for gathering these ten essays by Robert K. Merton.[1]

The practical relevance of this collection will not be found in the recency of its essays: some were first published in the 1940s and 1950s, and incidental mention of the racist Senator Bilbo from the FDR years or of Watergate from the Nixon years seems to put distance between the concerns of those times and ours. But Merton deals with enduring themes as they are reflected in specific historical contexts. Neither will relevance be found in technical strategies: Merton rarely offers a formula for solving this or that problem. Moreover, the essays are perhaps too abstract to be included among "policy evaluation studies" or "utilization research." Instead, Merton draws on his unique skills as social theorist and as sociologist of science to explore patiently the structural contexts for the *creation* and potential *application* of sociological knowledge, as a set of problems deserving their own attention.

Merton's exploration has three parts, and these neatly summarize our organization of the ten essays. In Part I he analyzes the structure and process of social scientific research, in particular how its internal organization affects application of its fruits by those engaged with social policy or the helping professions. In Part II he turns his attention to the helping professions, with an eye on how their institutional arrangement facilitates or resists application of sociological knowledge. In Part III Merton analyzes the link between social research and the formation of social policy, focusing on impediments which have so far made this link less than effective. In reading these essays, sociologists, members of the helping professions, and guardians of social policy will come to know more about themselves and about each other, perhaps better appreciating the perils *and* potentials in applying sociological knowledge to the solution of urgent social and personal problems.

Those who turn to sociology for practically useful information have various expectations. Some social workers or experts in public policy, for example, seem to hold an image of sociology that overstates its achivements. For them, sociological theory and research findings are expected to be objective truth, easily translated into recipes for action. Some doctors or lawyers, on the other hand, may underestimate the achievements of sociology. For them, sociological knowledge is merely an ideological reflection of investigators' politics or common sense, or so theoretically abstract as to be worthless for practical ends, or fragmented into competing theoretical orientations with few signs of consensus.[2] With either set of expectations, these potential consumers of sociological knowledge may come away frustrated. The four essays in Part I offer an insider's reflections on social research and help correct these inflated and deflating caricatures of sociology.

We chose to reprint Merton's classic paper on the normative structure of science (Chapter 1) because it succinctly states the goal of social science research (to extend certified knowledge) as distinct from the goal of "social technology" (to apply sociological knowledge in the solution of practical problems). Merton argues that the extension of certified knowledge is best served by institutionalization of a set of values—universalism, communism, disinterestedness, and organized skepticism—that prescribe for scientists certain patterns of behavior.[3] The institutionalization of this ethos of science, as a standard for evaluation and reward of scientific performance, facilitates (though does not guarantee) production of the kind of knowledge most trustworthy and historically most effective when used in concrete applications.

These institutional values of science are not the only ones affecting the production of sociological knowledge. In the process of "problem finding" (Chapter 2), Merton observes that sociologists are guided by another set of personal values—intellectual, social, political, or moral. For example, a detached, theoretical interest in how social structures generate conformity as well as deviance may lead sociologists to investigate gangs of delinquent youths. Other sociologists may investigate the same sociological problem not because of an abstract interest, but because they feel the need to do something useful about crime rates. These diverse motives for selecting problems for sociological research offer no guarantee that results will be useful to those working to solve social problems. The intellectual development of sociological theory has often pushed inquiry into directions with no immediate practical payoff, even as a concern for the social problems of crime and delinquency, sexism and racism, has sometimes led to productive agendas of social research.

And this, in Merton's view, is how it should be. In the happy case, practical and theoretical interests coincide, but they should not be forced to do so by design. To restrict sociology to research squarely aimed at urgent social problems will result in ideas and information less useful for members of the helping professions or shapers of public policy. Academic sociologists—sheltered as well as circumscribed by their ivory tower—might offer fresh conceptualizations by locating a specific case in a general pattern, and so suggest new strategies for help. Merton provides examples throughout the collection: perhaps *only* a social theorist would recognize the seemingly far-fetched connection between Malinowski's ethnography of the Trobriand Islanders and Abraham Flexner's ethnography of turn-of-the-century medical education. Both illustrate a common pattern, usefully appreciated by movers and shakers: *public* announcements of deviance often serve as needed catalysts for correction.

Efforts to apply social theory to practical problems are often thwarted by the quick discovery that there is no single theory of deviance, for example, but several theories of deviance. How can policies or helping strategies be informed by social theorists who do not agree on the definition of the problem, on the most effective investigative technique, or on the best explanation of what all agree to be so? Sociological understanding of deviance is enhanced by "theoretical pluralism," even if this frustrates those forced to choose a single best ameliorative strategy. The sources and consequences of this pluralism are examined by Merton in Chapter 3.

Perhaps outnumbering those who even try to apply sociology in practical settings are those who dismiss it as mere common sense. The apparent bit of whimsy on sociological vernacular (Chapter 4) is directed to them. Merton offers examples of popularized language that originated as precise sociological concepts before diffusing to a broader public: "minority group," "youth culture," "ethnocentrism," and "charisma." Sometimes public appropriation of sociological concepts makes it difficult to retain technical meanings, as Merton illustrates in his discussion of the several meanings of "socialization" (Chapter 6). Ironically, those who define sociology as mere common sense would be at a loss to describe their opinion were it not for the linguistic contribution of sociologist and social critic Walter Lippmann: "stereotype."

The three essays in Part II investigate the institutional structure of the helping professions, and they nicely illustrate two themes which characterize Merton's theoretical orientation. First, Merton's analysis of the helping professions draws attention to the *diverse consequences* of institutional structures for all parties concerned: patients and clients; individual social workers, doctors, lawyers, and nurses; the profession as a collective; and society at large. Consider, for example, the professional association as an institutional feature of most helping professions (Chapter 6). To examine its "functions" is to identify the consequences of existing social arrangements and proposed alternatives, with a recognition that these may be differently evaluated by members of the profession and by those they serve. Upgrading the standards of nursing education may be viewed by the American Nurses' Association as necessary to improve health care, while consumer advocate groups might consider such upgrading an effort to increase the wages of nurses by restricting their supply. Thus, Merton distinguishes the consequences of a professional association from its organizational goals and from the motivations of members. Sociologists will go beyond an accounting of desired and intended consequences to reveal unanticipated and sometimes unwanted consequences of an institutional arrangement—in Merton's terms, the "latent functions and dysfunctions."

One other example must suffice. Merton suggests that a norm of altruism has been institutionalized in the helping professions, one that encourages the provision of *more than* adequate care even at the short-run expense of the provider (Chapter 5). Of course, some doctors and lawyers may violate the norm by taking every advantage of their patients and clients, but the incidence of exploitation is reduced by institutionalization of competent altruism as a standard by which professionals evaluate the behavior of peers. The manifest (or intended and recognized) functions of the norm of altruism are to protect vulnerable patients and clients and to enhance their chances of receiving satisfactory care at equitable rates. Other latent consequences are important for maintaining privileges now enjoyed by the helping professions. If rates of exploitation increased, the prestige now accorded doctors and lawyers would diminish, and calls for their regulation by government or citizens' watchdogs would grow louder.

The second theoretical theme suggests that diverse motives and

interests of individuals can be translated by institutional or social
structural contexts into common patterns of behavior. In order to
be effective, for example, the institutional arrangement of the helping
professions should be able to harness both egoistic motives for career
success and altruistic motives for helping others, and to channel them
into professionally competent behavior. Merton suggests that the
"good will of good men and women" is not sufficient to insure the
desired behavior: the dominant pattern of altruism among doctors
and lawyers is not the result of an instinctual or psychological need
to provide help. Rather, the helping professions have institutionalized
an evaluation and reward structure to insure that short-run benefits
of exploitation are usually outweighed by long-run benefits of altruism. Thus, whether their motives are egoistic or altruistic, doctors
and lawyers are *constrained* to act in the interest of the client, even
though not all of them actually do so. There is an important message
here for those seeking solutions to enduring social and personal problems: institutional structures, not the idiosyncratic motives of individuals, are the pressure points for reform of patterns of behavior.

This is not to say that Merton restricts his sociological attention
to institutional arrangements. In keeping with his interest in diverse
consequences of social structures, Merton moves easily among levels
of analysis: the individual, the collective, the group, the organization,
and the society are all considered. For example, the decision to enter
medical school is for the individual a matter of personal choice and
achievement; for the medical school, it is a matter of recruitment;
and for the society at large, it is a matter of allocating talent and
resources (Chapter 7).

The three essays in Part III shift attention to the application of
sociological knowledge in the formation of public policy. In the powerful essay, "Basic Research and Potentials of Relevance" (Chapter
8), Merton deepens our understanding of the idea of "relevance" by
taking a fresh look at the differences between basic and applied
research. The distinction has never been satisfactorily drawn by those
who emphasize the subjective intention or purpose of scientists. Despite the best laid plans of applied sociologists, the consequences of
their studies may have important implications for theoretical sociology. Similarly, the consequences of theoretical sociology may have
important latent consequences for solving practical problems. Merton
points out, however, that different kinds of basic research have different probabilities of yielding results that can prove effective.

Although Merton remains optimistic about the potential relevance of sociology for social policy, these last essays are discouraging
in their long lists of impediments which have stalled the effective
utility of sociological knowledge (Chapter 9). One difficulty results

from the fact that social research and public policy proceed at different tempos. Policy issues are invariably raised in times of trouble, and a sense of urgency surrounds their resolution. Social research proceeds at a leisurely pace by comparison: often the time needed to collect data (to say nothing of their analysis and interpretation) is longer than the tenure of a government commission charged with formulating a new policy. Merton suggests that this temporal disjunction is the source of much impatience on both sides. Sociologists ask, "If Washington wants that information *now,* why didn't they provide funds ten years ago so that we would have had time to investigate the problem thoroughly?" And policymakers in Washington lament, "Since our commission expires in six months, we'll have to rely on whatever material the sociologists now have available, even though so little seems pertinent." The problem can be alleviated: both government and the sociological community can work to anticipate future demands for useful sociological knowledge and set in motion programs of study well before the midnight hour.

Another constraint is hinted at in Merton's classic paper on the "self-fulfilling prophecy" (Chapter 10), perhaps the best-known of the several concepts Merton has introduced into the language. A self-fulfilling prophecy is a shared belief that is false initially, but the consequences of people acting consistently with that belief result in its coming true. The essay is included here because many social problems—racism, anti-Semitism, and other forms of prejudice—are perpetuated by self-fulfilling prophecies. But there is another application even more to the point. So long as sociologists regard applied research or policy studies as beneath their status as scholars, and so long as members of the helping professions and creators of social policy define sociology as mere common sense distorted by hopeless abstraction, the behavior of both groups will prevent effective use of sociological knowledge to solve practical social problems. Only an enlightened understanding of the relationship between social research and social policy can permit escape from these self-defeating images, and that is what we think Merton provides in this collection.

Thomas F. Gieryn
Bloomington, Indiana

Aaron Rosenblatt
Albany, New York

NOTES

¹A bibliography of Merton's writings to 1975 will be found in Mary Wilson Miles, "The Writings of Robert K. Merton," in *The Idea of Social Structure: Papers in Honor of Robert K. Merton*, Lewis Coser, ed. (New York: Harcourt Brace Jovanovich, 1975), pp. 497–522.

²Merton considers an assortment of images of sociologists in his essay, "The Canons of the Anti-Sociologist," in his *Sociological Ambivalence and Other Essays* (New York: Free Press, 1976), Chapter 10.

³Merton's analysis of the institutional norms of science has given rise to an enduring debate among sociologists of science. A helpful review is provided by Nico Stehr, "The Ethos of Science Revisited: Social and Cognitive Norms," *Sociological Inquiry* 48 (1978):172–196.

PART I

Sociology of Social Research

CHAPTER 1

The Normative Structure of Science*

Science, like any other activity involving social collaboration, is subject to shifting fortunes. Difficult as the notion may appear to those reared in a culture that grants science a prominent if not a commanding place in the scheme of things, it is evident that science is not immune from attack, restraint, and repression. Writing some time ago, Veblen could observe that the faith of western culture in science was unbounded, unquestioned, unrivaled. The revolt from science which then appeared so improbable as to concern only the timid academician who would ponder all contingencies, however remote, has now been forced upon the attention of scientist and layman alike. Local contagions of anti-intellectualism threaten to become epidemic.

SCIENCE AND SOCIETY

Incipient and actual attacks upon the integrity of science have led scientists to recognize their dependence on particular types of

*Copyright by Robert K. Merton. Originally published as "Science and Technology in a Democratic Order," *Journal of Legal and Political Sociology* 1 (1942): 115–126. Reprinted in Robert K. Merton's *The Sociology of Science* (Chicago: University of Chicago Press, 1973), pp. 267–278.

social structure. Manifestos and pronouncements by associations of scientists are devoted to the relations between science and society. An institution under attack must reexamine its foundations, restate its objectives, seek out its rationale. Crisis invites self-appraisal. Now that they have been confronted with challenges to their way of life, scientists have been jarred into a state of acute self-consciousness: consciousness of self as an integral element of society with corresponding obligations and interests.[1] A tower of ivory becomes untenable when its walls cave in under prolonged assault. After a long period of relative security, during which the pursuit and diffusion of knowledge has risen to a leading place if indeed not to the first rank in the scale of cultural values, scientists are compelled to vindicate the ways of science. Thus they have come full circle to the point of the re-emergence of science in the modern world.

Three centuries ago, when the institution of science could claim little independent warrant for social support, natural philosophers were likewise led to justify science as a means to the culturally validated ends of economic utility and the glorification of God. The pursuit of science was then no self-evident value. With the unending flow of achievement, however, the instrumental was transformed into the terminal, the means into the end. Thus fortified, scientists came to regard themselves as independent of society and to consider science as a self-validating enterprise which is in society but not of it. A frontal assault on the autonomy of science was required to convert this sanguine isolationism into realistic participation in the revolutionary conflict of cultures. The joining of the issue has led to a clarification and reaffirmation of the ethos of modern science.

Science is a deceptively inclusive word which refers to a variety of distinct though interrelated items. It is commonly used to denote (1) a set of characteristic methods by means of which knowledge is certified; (2) a stock of accumulated knowledge stemming from the application of these methods; (3) a set of cultural values and mores governing the activities termed scientific; or (4) any combination of the foregoing. We are here concerned in a preliminary fashion with the cultural structure of science, that is, with one limited aspect of science as an institution. Thus, we shall consider, not the methods of science, but the mores with which they are hedged about. To be sure, methodological canons are often both technical expedients and moral compulsives, but it is solely the latter which is our concern here. This is an essay in the sociology of science, not an excursion in methodology. Similarly, we shall not deal with substantive findings of the sciences (hypotheses, uniformities, laws), except as these are pertinent to standardized social sentiments toward science. This is not an adventure in polymathy.

THE ETHOS OF SCIENCE

The ethos of science is that affectively toned complex of values and norms which is held to be binding on scientists.[2] The norms are expressed in the form of prescriptions, preferences, permissions, and proscriptions.* They are legitimatized in terms of institutional values. These imperatives, transmitted by precept and example and reenforced by sanctions, are in varying degrees internalized by scientists, thus fashioning scientific consciences or, if one prefers the latter-day phrase, superegos. Although the ethos of science has not been codified,[3] it can be inferred from the moral consensus of scientists as expressed in use and wont, in countless writings on the scientific spirit, and in moral indignation directed toward contraventions of the ethos.

An examination of the ethos of modern science is only a limited introduction to a larger problem: the comparative study of the institutional structure of science. Although detailed monographs assembling the needed comparative materials are few and scattered, they provide some basis for the provisional assumption that "science is afforded opportunity for development in a democratic order which is integrated with the ethos of science." This is not to say that the pursuit of science is confined to democracies.[4] The most diverse social structures have provided some measure of support to science. We have only to remember that two Medici sponsored the Accademia del Cimento; that Charles II claims historical attention for his grant of a charter to the Royal Society of London and his sponsorship of the Greenwich Observatory; that Louis XIV, on the advice of Colbert, founded the Académie des Sciences; that, urged into acquiescence by Leibniz, Frederick I endowed the Berlin Academy; and that Peter the Great instituted the St. Petersburg Academy of Sciences (to refute the view that Russians are barbarians). But such historical facts do not imply a random association of science and social structure. There is the further question of the ratio of scientific achievement to scientific potentialities. Science develops in various social structures, to be sure, but which provide an institutional context for the fullest measure of its development?

The institutional goal of science is taken to be the extension of certified knowledge. The technical methods employed toward this end provide the relevant definition of knowledge: empirically con-

---

*At the time of the first publication of this paper in 1942, these "4 P's" to describe the spectrum of social norms were 3; "preferences" were interpolated a decade or so later to provide a finer differentiation.

firmed and logically consistent statements of regularities (which are, in effect, predictions). The institutional imperatives (mores) derive from the goal and the methods. The entire structure of technical (cognitive) and moral norms implements the final objective. The technical norm of empirical evidence, adequate and reliable, is a prerequisite for sustained true prediction; the technical norm of logical consistency, a prerequisite for systematic and valid prediction. The mores of science possess a methodologic rationale but they are binding, not only because they are procedurally efficient, but also because they are believed right and good. They are moral as well as technical prescriptions.

Four sets of institutional imperatives—universalism, communism, disinterestedness, organized skepticism—are taken to make up the ethos of modern science.

UNIVERSALISM

Universalism[5] finds immediate expression in the canon that truth-claims, whatever their source, are to be subjected to *preestablished impersonal criteria,* consonant with observation and with previously confirmed knowledge. The acceptance or rejection of claims entering the lists of science is not to depend on the personal or social attributes of their protagonist; race, nationality, religion, class, and personal qualities are as such irrelevant. Objectivity precludes particularism. The circumstance that scientifically verified formulations refer in that specific sense to objective processes and relationships militates against efforts to impose particularistic criteria of validity. A Nuremberg decree cannot invalidate the Haber process nor can an Anglophobe repeal the law of gravitation. The chauvinist may expunge the names of alien scientists from historical textbooks but their contributions remain incorporated in science or technology. However *echt-deutsch* or hundred-percent American the final increment, some aliens are accessories before the fact of every new scientific advance. The imperative of universalism is rooted deep in the impersonal aspects of science.

However, the institution of science is part of a larger social structure with which it is not always integrated. When the larger culture opposes universalism, the ethos of science is subjected to serious strain. Ethnocentrism is not compatible with universalism. Particularly in times of international conflict, when the dominant definition of the situation is such as to emphasize national loyalties, scientists are subjected to the conflicting imperatives of scientific universalism and of ethnocentric particularism.[6] The structure of the situation in which they find themselves determines the social role that is called into play. The man of science may be converted into a man of war—and act accordingly. Thus, in 1914 the manifesto of ninety-three German scientists and scholars—among them, Baeyer, Brentano, Ehrlich, Haber, Eduard Meyer, Ostwald, Planck, Schmoller, and Wassermann—unloosed a polemic in which German, French, and English men arrayed their political selves in the garb of scientists. Dispassionate scientists impugned "enemy" contributions, charging nationalistic bias, log-rolling, intellectual dishonesty, incompetence, and lack of creative capacity.[7] Yet responses to this deviation from the norm of universalism presupposed the legitimacy of the norm. For nationalistic bias is opprobrious only if judged in terms of the standard of universalism; within another institutional context, it is redefined as a virtue, patriotism. Thus in the process of condemning their violation, the mores are reaffirmed.

Even under counter-pressure, scientists of various nationalities adhered to the universalistic standard in more direct terms. The international, impersonal, virtually anonymous character of science was reaffirmed.[8] (Pasteur: "Le savant a une patrie, la science n'en a pas.") Denial of the norm was conceived as a breach of faith.

Universalism finds further expression in the demand that careers be open to talents. The rationale is provided by the institutional goal. To restrict scientific careers on grounds other than lack of competence is to prejudice the furtherance of knowledge. Free access to scientific pursuits is defined as a functional imperative. Expediency and morality coincide. Hence the anomaly of a Charles II invoking the mores of science to reprove the Royal Society for their would-be exclusion of John Graunt, the political arithmetician, and his instructions that "if they found any more such tradesmen, they should be sure to admit them without further ado."

Here again the ethos of science may not be consistent with that of the larger society. Scientists may assimilate caste standards and close their ranks to those of imputed inferior status, irrespective of capacity or achievement. But this provokes an unstable situation. Elaborate ideologies are called forth to obscure the incompatibility of caste mores and the institutional goal of science. Caste inferiors must be shown to be inherently incapable of scientific work, or, at the very least, their contributions must be systematically devaluated. "It can be adduced from the history of science that the founders of research in physics, and the great discoverers from Galileo and Newton to the physical pioneers of our own time, were almost exclusively Aryans, predominantly of the Nordic race." The modifying phrase, "almost exclusively," is recognized as an insufficient basis for denying outcastes all claims to scientific achievement. Hence the ideology is rounded out by a conception of "good" and "bad" science: the realistic, pragmatic science of the Aryan is opposed to the dogmatic, formal science of the non-Aryan.[9] Or grounds for exclusion are sought in the extrascientific roles of men and women of science as enemies of the state or church.[10] Thus, the exponents of a culture which abjures universalistic standards in general feel constrained to pay lip service to this value in the realm of science. Universalism is deviously affirmed in theory and suppressed in practice.

However inadequately it may be put into practice, the ethos of democracy includes universalism as a dominant guiding principle. Democratization is tantamount to the progressive elimination of restraints upon the exercise and development of socially valued capacities. Impersonal criteria of accomplishment and not fixity of status characterize the open democratic society. Insofar as such restraints do persist, they are viewed as obstacles in the path of full democratization. Thus, insofar as laissez-faire democracy permits the accumulation of differential advantages* for certain segments of the population, differentials that are not bound up with demonstrated differences in capacity, the democratic process leads to increasing regulation by political authority. Under changing conditions, new technical forms of organization must be introduced to preserve and extend equality of opportunity. The political apparatus may be required to put democratic values into practice and to maintain universalistic standards.

*Barely introduced in this early paper, the principle of accumulative advantage has become a major theme in the sociology of science, where it refers to the process of transforming rewards for prior role performance into enlarged facilities and recognition for later role performance, thus contributing to the observed marked disparities in scientific productivity. For a sequence of writings on accumulative advantage as social process, see Merton, "The Matthew Effect in Science," *Science* 159 (5 January 1968):56–63; Harriet Zuckerman, "Stratification in American Science," in *Social Stratification*, E. O. Laumann, ed. (Indianapolis: Bobbs-Merrill, 1970), pp. 235–257; Jonathan R. and Stephen Cole, *Social Stratification in Science* (Chicago: University of Chicago Press, 1973), pp. 119–122, 145–149, 237–247; Paul Allison and J. A. Stewart, "Productivity Differences Among Scientists: Evidence for Accumulative Advantage," *American Sociological Review* 39 (1974):596–606; Derek J. de S. Price, "A General Theory of Bibliometric and Other Cumulative Advantage Processes," *Journal of the American Society for Information Science* 27 (1976):292–306; R. Mittermeir and K. D. Knorr, "Scientific Productivity and Accumulative Advantage," *R & D Management* 9 (1979):235–239; Paul D. Allison, "Inequality and Scientific Productivity," *Social Studies of Science* 10 (1980):163–179; Stuart A. Kirk and Aaron Rosenblatt, "Women's Contributions to Social Work Journals," *Social Work* 25 (1980):204–209.

"Communism"

"Communism," in the nontechnical and extended sense of common ownership of goods, is a second integral element of the scientific ethos. The substantive findings of science are a product of social collaboration and are assigned to the community. They constitute a common heritage in which the equity of the individual producer is severely limited. Eponymous laws or theories do not enter into the exclusive possession of the discoverers and their heirs, nor do the mores bestow upon them special rights of use and disposition. Property rights in science are whittled down to a bare minimum by the rationale of the scientific ethic. Scientists' claims to their intellectual "property" are limited to those of recognition and esteem which, if the institution functions with a modicum of efficiency, are roughly commensurate with the significance of the increments brought to the common fund of knowledge. Eponymy—for example, the Copernican system, Boyle's law—is thus at once a mnemonic and a commemorative device.

Given such institutional emphasis upon recognition and esteem as the sole property right of scientists in their discoveries, the concern with scientific priority becomes a "normal" response. Those controversies over priority which punctuate the history of modern science are generated by the institutional accent on originality.[11] There issues a competitive cooperation. The products of competition are communized,[12] and esteem accrues to the producer. Nations take up claims to priority, and fresh entries into the commonwealth of science are tagged with the names of nationals: witness the controversy raging over the rival claims of Newton and Leibniz to the differential calculus. But all this does not challenge the status of scientific knowledge as common property.

The institutional conception of science as part of the public domain is linked with the imperative for communication of findings. Secrecy is the antithesis of this norm; full and open communication its enactment.[13] The pressure for diffusion of results is reenforced by the institutional goal of advancing the boundaries of knowledge and by the incentive of recognition which is, of course, contingent upon publication. A scientist who does not communicate important discoveries to the scientific community—thus, a Henry Cavendish—becomes the target for ambivalent responses. He is esteemed for his talent and, perhaps, for his modesty. But, institutionally considered, his modesty is seriously misplaced, in view of the moral compulsive for sharing the wealth of science. Layman though he is, Aldous Huxley's comment on Cavendish is illuminating in this connection: "Our admiration of his genius is tempered by a certain disapproval; we feel that such a man is selfish and antisocial." The epithets are particularly instructive for they imply the violation of a definite institutional imperative. Even though, as in the case of Cavendish, it serves no ulterior motive, the suppression of scientific discovery is condemned.

The communal character of science is further reflected in the recognition by scientists of their dependence upon a cultural heritage to which they lay no differential claims. Newton's remark—"If I have seen further it is by standing on the shoulders of giants"—expresses at once a sense of indebtedness to the common heritage and a recognition of the essentially cooperative and selectively cumulative quality of scientific achievement.[14] The humility of scientific genius is not simply culturally appropriate but results from the realization that scientific advance involves the collaboration of past and present generations. It was Carlyle, not Maxwell, who indulged in a mythopoeic conception of history.

The communism of the scientific ethos is incompatible with the definition of technology as "private property" in a capitalistic economy. Current writings on the "frustration of science" reflect this conflict. Patents proclaim exclusive rights of use and, often, nonuse. The suppression of invention denies the rationale of scientific production and diffusion, as may be seen from the court's decision in the case of *U.S.* v. *American Bell Telephone Co.:* "The inventor is one who has discovered something of value. It is his absolute property. He may withhold the knowledge of it from the public."[15] Responses to this conflict situation have varied. As a defensive measure, some scientists have come to patent their work to ensure its being made available for public use. Einstein, Millikan, Compton, Langmuir have taken out patents.[16] Scientists have been urged to become promoters of new economic enterprises.[17] Others seek to resolve the conflict by advocating socialism.[18] These proposals—both those which demand economic returns for scientific discoveries and those which demand a change in the social system to let science get on with the job—reflect discrepancies in the conception of intellectual property.

DISINTERESTEDNESS

Science, as is the case with the professions in general, includes disinterestedness as a basic institutional element. Disinterestedness is not to be equated with altruism nor interested action with egoism.* Such equivalences confuse institutional and motivational levels of analysis.[19] A passion for knowledge, idle curiosity, altruistic concern with the benefit to humanity, and a host of other special motives have been attributed to scientists. The quest for distinctive motives appears to have been misdirected. It is rather a distinctive pattern of institutional control of a wide range of motives which characterizes the behavior of scientists. For once the institution enjoins disinterested activity, it is to the interest of scientists to conform on pain of sanctions and, insofar as the norm has been internalized, on pain of psychological conflict.

The virtual absence of fraud in the annals of science, which appears exceptional when compared with the record of other spheres of activity** has at times been thought to result from the personal qualities of scientists. By implication, scientists are recruited from the ranks of those who exhibit an unusual degree of moral integrity. There is, in fact, no satisfactory evidence that such is the case; a more plausible explanation may be found in certain distinctive characteristics of science itself. Involving as it does the reproducibility and verifiability of results, scientific research is under the exacting scrutiny of fellow experts. Otherwise put—and doubtless the observation can be interpreted as lese majesty—the activities of scientists are subject to rigorous policing, to a degree perhaps unparalleled in any other field of activity. The demand for disinterestedness has a firm basis in the public and testable character of science, and this circumstance, it may be supposed, has contributed to the integrity of scientists. There is competition in the realm of science, competition that is intensified by the emphasis on priority as a criterion of achievement, and under competitive conditions there may well be generated incentives for eclipsing rivals by illicit means. But such impulses can find scant opportunity for expression in the field of scientific research. Cultism, informal cliques, prolific but trivial publications—these and other techniques may be used for self-aggrandizement.[20] But, in general, spurious claims appear to be negligible and ineffective. The translation of the norm of disinterestedness into practice is effectively supported by the ultimate accountability of scientists to

*Chapter 5, "Institutionalized Altruism: The Case of the Professions," elaborates upon this point—editors' note.

**See Harriet Zuckerman, "Deviant Behavior and Social Control in Science," in *Deviance and Social Control,* Edward Sagarin, ed. (Beverly Hills: Sage Publications, 1977), pp. 87–138; also Deena Weinstein, "Fraud in Science," *Social Science Quarterly* 59 (1979):639–652; Morton Hunt, "A Fraud that Shook the World of Science," *The New York Times Magazine,* November 1, 1981, *Passim,* pp. 42–75.—editors' note.

their compeers. The dictates of socialized sentiment and of expediency largely coincide, a situation conducive to institutional stability.

In this connection, science differs somewhat from other professions. The stance of the scientist toward lay clientele differs from that of the physician and lawyer, for example. The possibility of exploiting the credulity, ignorance, and dependence of the layman is thus considerably reduced. Fraud, chicane, and irresponsible claims (quackery) are less likely than among the "service" professions. To the extent that the scientist-layman relation does become paramount, there develop incentives for evading the mores of science. The abuse of expert authority and the creation of pseudo-sciences are called into play when the structure of control exercised by qualified compeers is rendered ineffectual.[21]

The reputability of science and its lofty ethical status in the estimate of the layman are probably due in no small measure to technological achievements.[22] Every new science-based technology bears witness to the integrity of the scientist. Science seemingly realizes its claims. However, its authority can be and is appropriated for interested purposes, precisely because the laity is often in no position to distinguish spurious from genuine claims to such authority. The presumably scientific pronouncements of totalitarian spokesmen on race or economy or history are for the uninstructed laity of the same order as newspaper reports of an expanding universe or wave mechanics. In both instances, they cannot be checked by the man-in-the-street, and in both instances, they may run counter to common sense. If anything, the myths will seem more plausible and are certainly more comprehensible to the general public than accredited scientific theories, since they are closer to common-sense experience and to cultural bias. Partly as a result of scientific achievements, therefore, the population at large becomes susceptible to new mysticisms expressed in apparently scientific terms. The borrowed authority of science bestows prestige on the unscientific doctrine.

ORGANIZED SKEPTICISM

Organized skepticism is variously interrelated with the other elements of the scientific ethos. It is both a methodological and an institutional mandate. The temporary suspension of judgment and the detached scrutiny of beliefs in terms of empirical and logical criteria have periodically involved science in conflict with other institutions. Science which asks questions of fact, including potentialities, concerning every aspect of nature and society may come into conflict with other attitudes toward these same data which have been crystallized and often ritualized by other institutions. The scientific investigator does not preserve the cleavage between the sacred and the profane, between that which requires uncritical respect and that which can be objectively analyzed.

As we have noted, this appears to be the source of revolts against the so-called intrusion of science into other spheres. Such resistance on the part of organized religion has become less significant as compared with that of economic and political groups. The opposition may exist quite apart from the introduction of specific scientific discoveries which appear to invalidate particular dogmas of church, economy, or state. It is rather a diffuse, frequently vague, apprehension that skepticism threatens the current distribution of power. Conflict becomes accentuated whenever science extends its research to new areas with deep-seated institutionalized attitudes or whenever other institutions extend their control over science. In modern totalitarian society, both antirationalism and the centralization of institutional control serve to limit the scope provided for scientific activity.

NOTES

[1]Since this was written in 1942, it is evident that the explosion at Hiroshima jarred many more scientists into an awareness of the social consequences of their work.

[2]On the concept of ethos, see William Graham Sumner, *Folkways* (Boston: Ginn, 1906), pp. 36 ff.; Hans Speier, "The Social Determination of Ideas," *Social Research* 5 (1938):196 ff.; Max Scheler, *Schriften aus dem Nachlass* (Berne: Francke, [1933] 1957, pp. 225–262). Albert Bayet, in his book on the subject, soon abandons description and analysis for homily; see his *La morale de la science* (Paris: Les Presses Universitaires, 1931).

[3]As Bayet remarks: "Cette morale [de la science] n'a pas eu ses theoriciens, mais elle a eu ses artisans. Elle n'a pas exprimé son idéal, mais elle l'a servi: il est impliqué dans l'existence même de la science" (*La morale de la science*, p. 43).

[4]Tocqueville went further: "The future will prove whether these passions [for science], at once so rare and so productive, come into being and into growth as easily in the midst of democratic as in aristocratic communities. For myself, I confess that I am slow to believe it" (*Democracy in America* [New York: Knopf, [1835] 1945, II, 48]). See another reading of the evidence: "It is impossible to establish a simple causal relationship between democracy and science and to state that democratic society alone can furnish the soil suited for the development of science. It cannot be a mere coincidence, however, that science actually has flourished in democratic periods" (Henry E. Sigerist, "Science and Democracy," *Science and Society* 2 [1938]:291).

[5]For a basic analysis of universalism in social relations, see Talcott Parsons, *The Social System* (New York: Free Press, 1951). For an expression of the normative belief that "science is wholly independent of national boundaries and races and creeds," see the resolution of the Council of the American Association for the Advancement of Science, *Science* 87 (1938): 10; also "The Advancement of Science and Society: Proposed World Association," *Nature* 141 (1938):169.

[6]This stands as written in 1942. By 1948, the political leaders of Soviet Russia strengthened their emphasis on Russian nationalism and began to insist on the "national" character of science. Thus, in an editorial, "Against the Bourgeois Ideology of Cosmopolitanism," *Voprosy filosofi*, no. 2 (1948), as translated in the *Current Digest of the Soviet Press* 1, no. 1 (1 February 1949):9: "Only a cosmopolitan without a homeland, profoundly insensible to the actual fortunes of science, could deny with contemptuous indifference the existence of the many-hued national forms in which science lives and develops. In place of the actual history of science and the concrete paths of its development, the cosmopolitan substitutes fabricated concepts of a kind of supernational, classless science, deprived, as it were, of all the wealth of national coloration, deprived of the living brilliance and specific character of a people's creative work, and transformed into a sort of disembodied spirit . . . Marxism-Leninism shatters into bits the cosmopolitan fictions concerning supra-class, non-national, 'universal' science, and definitely proves that science, like all culture in modern society, is national in form and class in content." This view confuses two distinct issues: first, the cultural context in any given nation or society may dispose scientists to focus on certain problems, to be sensitive to some and not other problems on the frontiers of science. This has long since been observed. But this is basically different from the second issue: the criteria of validity of claims to scientific knowledge are not simply matters of national taste and culture. Sooner or later, competing claims to validity are settled by universalistic criteria.

[7]For an instructive collection of such documents, see Gabriel Petit and Maurice Leudet, *Les allemands et la science* (Paris: F. Alcan, 1916). Félix de Dantec, for example, discovers that both Ehrlich and Weismann have perpetrated typical German frauds upon the world of science. ("Le bluff de la science allemande.") Pierre Duhem concludes that the "geometric spirit" of German science stifled the "spirit of finesse": *La science allemande* (Paris: A. Hermann, 1915). Hermann Kellermann, *Der Krieg der Geister* (Weimar: A. Duncker, 1915) is a spirited counterpart. The conflict persisted into the postwar period; see Karl Kherkhof, *Der Krieg gegen die Deutsche Wissenschaft* (Halle, 1933).

[8]See the profession of faith by Professor E. Gley (in Pettit and Leudet, *Les allemands et la science*, p. 181): "il ne peut y avoir une vérité allemande, anglaise, italienne ou japonaise pas plus qu'une française. Et parler de science allemande, anglaise ou française, c'est énoncer une proposition contradictoire à l'idée même de science." See also the affirmations of Grasset and Richet, ibid.

[9]Johannes Stark, *Nature* 141 (1938):772; "Philipp Lenard als deutscher Naturforscher," *Nationalsozialistische Monatshefte* 7 (1936):106–112. This bears comparison with Duhem's contrast between "German" and "French" science.

[10]"Wir haben sie ['marxistischen Leugner'] nicht entfernt als Vertreter der Wissenschaft, sondern als Parteigaenger einer politischen Lehre, die den Umsturz aller Ordnungen auf ihre Fahne geschrieben hatte. Und wir mus-

sten hier um so entschlossener zugreifen, als ihnen die herrschende Ideologie einer wertfreien und voraussetzungslosen Wissenschaft ein willkommener Schutz fuer die Fortfuehrung ihrer Plaene zu sein schien. Nicht wir haben uns an der Wuerde der freien Wissenschaft vergangen. . . ." Bernhard Rust, *Das nationalsozialistische Deutschland und die Wissenschaft* (Hamburg: Hanseatische Verlagsanstalt, 1936), p. 13.

[11]Newton spoke from hard-won experience when he remarked that "[natural] philosophy is such an impertinently litigious Lady, that a man had as good be engaged in lawsuits, as have to do with her." Robert Hooke, a socially mobile individual whose rise in status rested solely on his scientific achievements, was notably "litigious."

[12]Marked by the commercialism of the wider society though it may be, a profession such as medicine accepts scientific knowledge as common property. See R. H. Shryock, "Freedom and Interference in Medicine," *The Annals* 200 (1938):45. "The medical profession . . . has usually frowned upon patents taken out by medical men. . . . The regular profession has . . . maintained this stand against private monopolies ever since the advent of patent law in the seventeenth century." There arises an ambiguous situation in which the socialization of medical practice is rejected in circles where the socialization of knowledge goes unchallenged.

[13]Cf. Bernal, who observes: "The growth of modern science coincided with a definite rejection of the ideal of secrecy." Bernal quotes a remarkable passage from Réaumur (*L'Art de convertir le fer forgé en acier*) in which the moral compulsion for publishing one's researches is explicitly related to other elements in the ethos of science. For example, "il y eût gens qui trouvèrent étrange que j'ueusse publié des secrets, qui ne devoient pas etre revelés . . . est-il bien sûr que nos découvertes soient si fort à nous que le Public n'y ait pas droit, qu'elles ne lui appartiennent pas en quelque sorte? . . . resterait il bien des circonstances, où nous soions absolument Maîtres de nos découvertes? . . . Nous nous devons premièrement à notre Patrie, mais nous nous devons aussi au rest du monde; cêux qui travaillent pour perfectionner les Sciences et les Arts, doivent même se regarder commes les citoyens du monde entier" (J. D. Bernal, *The Social Function of Science* [New York: Macmillan, 1939] pp. 150–151).

[14]It is of some interest that Newton's aphorism is a standardized phrase which had found repeated expression from at least the twelfth century. It would appear that the dependence of discovery and invention on the existing cultural base had been noted some time before the formulations of modern sociologists. See *Isis* 24 (1935):107–109; 25 (1938):451–452. [Merton traces the history of the aphorism in his playfully serious book, *On the Shoulders of Giants: A Shandean Postscript* (New York: Harcourt Brace Jovanovich, 1965)—editors' note.]

[15]167 U.S. 224 (1897), cited by B. J. Stern, "Restraints upon the Utilization of Inventions," *The Annals* 200 (1938):21. For an extended discussion, cf. Stern's Temporary National Economic Committee Monograph no. 31 (Washington: U.S. Government Printing Office, 1941) and further studies cited therein; also Walton Hamilton, *Patents and Free Enterprise*.

[16]Hamilton, *Patents and Free Enterprise*, p. 154; J. Robin, *L'oeuvre scientifique: sa protection-juridique* (Paris: Impr. de Montparnasse, 1928).

[17]Vannevar Bush, "Trends in Engineering Research," *Sigma Xi Quarterly* 22 (1934):49.

[18]Bernal, *The Social Function of Science,* pp. 155 ff.

[19]Talcott Parsons, "The Professions and Social Structure," *Social Forces* 17 (1939):458–459; cf. George Sarton, *The History of Science and the New Humanism* (New York: Henry Holt, 1931), p. 130 ff. The distinction between institutional compulsives and motives is a key, though largely implicit, conception of Marxist sociology.

[20]See the account of Logan Wilson, *The Academic Man* (New York: Oxford University Press, 1941), p. 201 ff.

[21]Cf. R. A. Brady, *The Spirit and Structure of German Fascism* (New York: Viking, 1937), Chapter 2; Martin Gardner, *In the Name of Science* (New York: Putnam's, 1953).

[22]Francis Bacon set forth one of the early and most succinct statements of this popular pragmatism: "Now these two directions, the one active the other contemplative, are one and the same thing; and what in operation is most useful, that in knowledge is most true" *(Novum Organum,* Book 2, Aphorism 4).

Notes on Problem-Finding in Sociology*

At first appearance, it would seem easy to see and to pose a problem in a branch of science. Surely the raising of questions presents no great difficulty; children do it all the time. And yet, the experience of scientists is summed up in the adage that it is often more difficult to find and to formulate a problem than to solve it.

The substance of this now-familiar saying has been periodically lost to view only to be rediscovered through hard-won experience. In the seventeenth century, it was enough of a commonplace to be known to that genial columnist and London man-about-town, John Aubrey, who reported that "Dr. Pell was wont to say that in the So-lution of Questions, the Maine Matter was the *well-stating of them;* wch requires mother-witt, & Logick. . . ; for let the question be but well-stated, it will worke almost of itselfe." Yet, two centuries later, even so great a scientist as Darwin had to discover this for himself. Reminiscing about the course of his inquiries into the origin of species, he wrote: ". . . you would be surprised at the number of years

*From *Sociology Today: Problems and Prospects,* edited by Robert K. Merton, Leonard Broom, and Leonard S. Cottrell, Jr. Copyright © 1959 by Basic Books, Inc. By permission of Basic Books, Inc., Publishers, New York. This essay serves as an introduction to the twenty-five essays in *Sociology Today.* Numbers in brackets refer to page numbers in that collection—editors' note.

it took me to see clearly what some of the problems were which had
to be solved. . . . Looking back, I think it was more difficult to see
what the problems were than to solve them, so far as I have succeeded
in doing, and this seems to me rather curious." What Darwin thought
strange, if not singular, present-day scientists take as thoroughly familiar and typical. As the biologist Agnes Arber says, the current
"difficulty in most scientific work lies in framing the questions rather
than in finding the answers."

This scientific opinion is paradoxical in the sense that it runs
against popular opinion. But the discord can be resolved by recognizing that, in science, the questions that matter are of a particular
kind. They are questions so formulated that the answers to them will
confirm, amplify, variously revise, or refute some part of what is
currently taken as knowledge in the field. In short, although every
problem in a science involves a question, or series of questions, not
every question qualifies as a scientific problem.

This would scarcely need to be said were it not that, in the
discipline of sociology at least, it is often forgotten. At times, it is
neglected by the very sociologists who most emphatically urge the
undoubted importance of focusing sociological inquiry upon significant problems. On the face of it, this judgment is as impeccable as
the bland remark that one is against sin. Few sociologists today would
join with Herbert Spencer, who in his unbounded self-confidence
could report that "it has never been my way to set before myself a
problem and puzzle out an answer," that instead he lay hold of "cardinal truths" not "as solutions to questions raised" but as the ultimate
outcome of meditating upon an evolving body of thought. Indeed,
the doctrine that inquiry should be centered on problems has been
used as a stick to belabor even those who assent to it. For example,
one sociologist expressed his displeasure over the alleged fact that
contemporary sociology has "largely dispensed with that prime impulse of all science and scholarship, with the puzzlement over specific,
concrete, and—if this word must be used—empirical problems. Many
sociologists have lost the simple impulse of curiosity, the desire to
solve riddles of experience, the concern with problems."[1] When this
critic comes down to particulars, he inadvertently provides useful
clues to what is not entailed in the instituting of problems for sociological investigation. He presents a disarmingly simple formula: sociologists have only to select one or another social fact, declare
themselves puzzled by it, and then ask "Why is it so?" Consider these
instances of the routinized procedure:

> What I mean [by a problem] is that at the outset of every scientific
> investigation there has to be a fact or set of facts that is puzzling
> the investigator: children of businessmen prefer professional to

business occupations; workers in the automobile industry go on strike; there is a higher incidence of suicides among upwardly mobile persons than among others; Socialist parties in predominantly Catholic countries of Europe seem unable to get more than 30 per cent of the popular vote; Hungarian people revolt against the Communist regime. There is no need to enumerate more of such facts; what matters is that every one of them invites the question "Why?" and it is this question, after all, which has always inspired that noble human activity in which we are engaged—science.[2]

If routinely affixing an inquisitive "Why?" to an established fact or event were all that is needed at the outset to institute a significant problem in science, then Darwin and the many other scientists who have testified to the difficulty of seeing a problem would stand self-condemned as hopelessly opaque and slow-witted. On the evidence, this hypothesis has little to commend it. Furthermore, if this formula were sound, problems for sociological investigation could be multiplied at will by turning to any compendium of social data—say, the many volumes of the U.S. Census—and routinely putting the question "Why?" to each set of facts reported there. Happily, the finding of significant problems is not quite as simple as all this. It is not a matter of dull routine but a difficult task that taxes the trained imagination. To be sure, as Piaget has shown and as any parent can testify, young children delight in asking "Why?" about much of what they see. But though the biblical promise may on occasion be fulfilled, a little child will not ordinarily show the way to adult scientists.

Little is known, in any systematic way, about the conditions and processes that lead investigators to find problems of consequence for science. The experience remains obscure. Although psychologists and philosophers of science have been hard at work investigating the process of problem-solving, only a small part of their inquiries has been devoted to that phase of the process that can be described as problem-finding. Indeed, the design of experiments on problem-solving is often such that the problem, the puzzle, is, so to say, ready-made. It is provided; only the solution is contingent. The experimenter poses the problem and then observes how people go about trying to solve it. But because, as we have seen, the finding and formulation of a significant problem are basic to sociological investigation as to scientific inquiry generally, problem-finding provides a theme that may serve as a useful, though limited, introduction to the twenty-five papers that make up *Sociology Today.*

The intent here is to identify some of what is involved in seeing and formulating a sociological problem, so far as this is exhibited in the many cases supplied by the articles in that book. What is going on as these sociologists come to pose a problem for investigation?

How do they achieve a sense of instructive perplexity before grappling with it? Such an inquiry will not of course result in a collection of recipes for problem-finding, but it may move us a short distance toward understanding how problems come to the focus of attention.

The first and most detailed part of this essay draws upon materials in *Sociology Today* to identify the principal ingredients of a sociological problem. It notes how questions are initially raised and then so restated that the problem can be investigated. It will become apparent that this section provides only a beginning statement. The other two parts are even more cursory, largely owing, I should like to think, to limitations of space. The second identifies a few of the occasions arising within the course of sociological inquiry itself that make for the finding of problems. It directs the reader to some cases in point as presented in *Sociology Today*. The third and final part is even more severely limited, but because sociological inquiry, like the rest of science, is variously affected by its social environment, some notice should be given to these effects upon the selection of problems for investigation, so far as they are examined in that volume.

INGREDIENTS OF SOCIOLOGICAL PROBLEMS

No one road leads to the posing of problems for sociological investigation. The inquiry may begin by questioning the evidence for alleged social facts. It may begin by examining the relationship between classes of sociological variables within a single department of social life. Or it may begin by clarifying a sociological idea that, having served a heuristic purpose for a time, seems no longer adequate to the range of facts to which, in its earlier formulation, it should be expected to apply.

Following ample precedent,[3] we can distinguish three principal components in the progressive formulation of a problem. First is the originating question,[4] a statement of what one wants to know. Second is the rationale, stating why one wants to have the particular question answered. And third are the specifying questions that point toward possible answers to the originating question in terms that satisfy the rationale for having raised it.

Originating Questions

An important class of questions, often undervalued in sociology, calls for discovering a particular body of social fact. It might at first seem needless to say that before social facts can be "explained," it is advisable to ensure that they actually are facts. Yet, in science as in everyday life, explanations are sometimes provided for things that never were. We need hardly review the long list of notorious episodes of this kind. Consider only Seneca explaining why some waters are so dense that no object, however heavy, will sink in them or explaining why lightning freezes wine; Descartes explaining why the pineal gland could exist only in man just a short time before Niels Stensen discovered it in other animals; Hegel solemnly explaining why there could be only seven planets and none between Mars and Jupiter just as Piazzi was discovering Ceres in that very region; the talented physiologist Johannes Müller explaining why the rate of transmission of the nerve impulse could never be measured just a few years before Helmholtz proceeded to measure it; J. S. Mill explaining why it was impossible to conduct sound statistical studies of human behavior long after Quetelet and others had done so. Episodes of this kind no doubt prompted Claude Bernard to insist on the obvious and compelling truth that "if the facts used as a basis for reasoning are ill-established or erroneous, everything will crumble or be falsified; and it is thus that errors in scientific theories most often originate in errors of fact." Many more comparable episodes in everyday life, we may suppose, lay behind the remark by Tristram Shandy: "How finely we argue upon mistaken facts!"

Recognition that social facts are not always as they seem leads sociologists to raise questions aimed at discovering a particular body of fact. From present indications, for example, it would be premature to ask "why" the rate of mental illness has been increasing in the United States and to search for sociological factors that might help account for the rise. This is one of the cases in which the fact itself has yet to be established. A meticulous inquiry by Goldhamer and Marshall, limited though it is to a century of experience in Massachusetts, is at least enough to put the fact in question, although, as the authors make plain, the matter is far from settled [488]. Or again, a sizable number of investigations are designed to explain differences in "national character," even though "No one has ever tested a national population or even a major sub-population using either an adequate sample or adequate psychological instruments. All assertions or denials of national, sub-national, regional, or class differences of major magnitudes [in personality types], therefore, remain mere statements of faith" [267–268]. So, too, it would seem premature to ask why "urbanization is . . . accompanied by destruction of the social and moral order" inasmuch as evidence is accumulating to suggest that this consequence is often a matter of assumption rather than of fact [342].*It is also too soon to explain why "social conformity" is far more rampant among Americans today than it was, say, two or three generations ago, inasmuch as the fact remains to be demonstrated.

One class of questions, then, is directed toward ascertaining social facts. This does not yet constitute the formulation of a problem, although it is an essential step in that direction. Such questions are typically prompted by efforts to "explain" social patterns that the investigators conclude have yet to be satisfactorily established as genuine patterns. Too often, though sometimes of course with justice, this kind of inquiry is described as "mere fact-finding." Indeed, this phrase is so thoroughly stereotyped that the term "fact-finding" is almost always prefaced by that adjective of disparagement "mere." The hackneyed phrase often expresses an unexamined and impatient philosophy of investigation. It reflects the compelling urge to arrive directly at an explanatory idea. Yet practiced investigators tell us that often a fruitful idea can be adequately formulated only after reasonably sound data have brought it to mind. In sociology as in other disciplines, pseudofacts have a way of inducing pseudoproblems,[5] which cannot be solved because matters are not as they purport to be. It is only when tedious recitations of unrelated fact are substituted for the absent idea that inquiry declines into "mere" fact-finding.

As a phase in instituting a problem, fact-finding seems to have a particular force in sociology. This is so because people are apt to assume that they know the facts about the workings of society without special investigation, because society is, after all, their native habitat. True, sociology is not alone in facing this difficulty. Carl Becker once remarked that everyman is tempted to become his own historian. But relatively few exercise this franchise, for they sense their ignorance of the multitude of historical facts needed to form an opinion. Not so with sociology. Here, everyman, confident in his acquaintance with the society of which he is inevitably a part, develops firm opinions about how it works. All this heightens the importance of fact-finding as a frequent prelude to the statement of a genuine sociological problem. For contrary to widespread assumption, not all plausible beliefs about society are necessarily true.

Consider briefly the relations between the socially plausible, in which appearances persuade even as they deceive, and the socially true, in which belief is confirmed by appropriately controlled observation. The independence of the two confronts sociologists (like other

*For more recent evidence that this might have been a presumptive phrasing of the sociological question, see Claude S. Fischer, *The Urban Experience* (New York: Harcourt Brace Jovanovich, 1976)—editors' note.

social scientists) with uncomfortable options. Should their systematic inquiries only confirm what had been widely assumed—this being the class of plausible truths—they will of course be charged with "laboring the obvious." They become tagged as bores telling only what everybody knows. Should investigation find that widely held social beliefs are untrue—the class of plausible untruths—they are heretics, questioning value-laden verities. If they venture to examine socially implausible ideas that turn out to be untrue, they are fools, wasting effort on a line of inquiry not worth pursuing in the first place. And finally, if they should turn up some implausible truths, they must be prepared to find themselves regarded as charlatans, claiming as knowledge what is patently false. Instances of each of these responses have occurred in the history of many sciences, but they seem especially apt to occur in disciplines, such as sociology and psychology, that deal with matters about which people have firm opinions presumably grounded in their own experience.

Questions of descriptive fact are of course only one among a variety of originating questions. Another type directs attention to the search for uniformities of relations between classes of sociological variables. Consider only these few instances:

How can a society incorporate continuous conflict among its members and social groups and yet maintain social cohesion and the legitimacy of authority [81]?

What is it about the structure of social systems that determines the kinds of criminal acts which occur in these systems [462]?

How do sociocultural modes of defining and dealing with forms of individual psychic disturbance . . . influence the course and consequences of the deviance [501]?

Originating questions of this kind call for more than the establishment of a social fact, just as they do more than ask, without suggesting clues to an answer, why an observed state of affairs exists. They are formulated in terms of broadly delimited *classes* of sociological variables; they do not indicate, then and there, the *particular* variables in each class that may be germane to the matter in hand. The first question, for example, invites a search for types of social mechanisms that regulate but do not eliminate social conflict. The second partly delimits the inquiry by directing attention to attributes of social systems without yet indicating the particular structural attributes that may be pertinent, just as it does not yet indicate how kinds of criminal acts are to be conceived. And the third, in like manner, is preliminary to indicating how "sociocultural modes of defining psychic disturbance" are to be construed, just as it does not yet supply categories for describing "the course and consequences of the deviance."* At this stage of moving toward the definition of a sociological problem, the questions stem from a general theoretical orientation rather than from a definite theory. They suggest classes of variables to be taken into account but do not yet suggest the particular variables to be considered. This, it appears, is a frequent stage in the search for a significant problem.

Originating questions differ in their scope as well as in the degree of their specificity. Some of these questions address the relations between sociological variables within one or another institutional sphere of society. This class of questions can be readily identified by the descriptive concepts employed in the question. Social categories of teacher and student, of school administrator and school board, are of course appropriate only in the sphere of education, just as the social categories of judge and jury, husband and wife, pastor and congregation, political party and industrial organization, have their distinctive institutional reference. On occasion, the question is at first deliberately restricted to a particular institutional sphere and only later restated in a form that has broader bearing. The sociologist of education asks:

"Does the pattern of relationships that the administrator of a school establishes tend to 'spill over' into the classroom?

Does the degree to which administrators take the teacher's views into account in their decision-making affect the degree to which the teacher takes students' views into account in . . . the classroom?" [143].

These questions are at first restricted to the school system. Yet it is plain from what is later said about them that they have potential bearing on other comparable organizations in which people may reproduce in their behavior vis-à-vis a subordinate what they are experiencing in relation to their own superior.

Or the sociologist of religion might ask:

"How does the religious bureaucracy deal with pressures to adapt the interpretations of scripture to real or perceived changes in the social world?" [163].

Raised initially with respect to the adaptations of religious organizations to secular society, this question can of course be generalized,

---

*This type of sociological question, raised here by John A. Clausen (in *Sociology Today*, pp. 501–504) was given special force by Edwin M. Lemert, initially in his *Social Pathology* (New York: McGraw-Hill, 1951). It has since given rise to the theoretical orientation known as "labelling theory" or "the societal reaction approach to deviance"; see, for example, Edwin M. Lemert, *Human Deviance, Social Problems and Social Control* (Englewood Cliffs, N.J.: Prentice-Hall, 1972).

as its author implies, to deal with the adaptations of organizations of every kind to their respective environments.

In short, questions initially restricted to a particular institutional sphere have a double objective. On the one hand, they direct attention to what may be distinctive to the particular class of institutions or organizations under study. These distinctive characteristics are not at once swallowed up in generalities that deliberately neglect them. On the other hand, these questions of restricted scope can often be extended to wider classes of situations. Neither the general nor the specific version of the originating questions claims exclusive value; each has its use in augmenting knowledge of differing kind. The focus on a particular institutional sphere, with its characteristic statuses, social structure, and value system, results in findings that illuminate its distinctive character; it curbs that kind of premature generalization that loses sight of what is peculiar to an institution by attending only to what it shares with other institutions.

Another kind of originating question is put in such form that, with little or no revision, it can be addressed to a variety of institutional spheres. Or, if phrased in more restricted fashion, it has only to be juxtaposed with others of like kind to appear as different versions of a single, more general question. One example of such consolidation may be enough for illustration. Questions raised in several papers converge on the concept of the status-set,* the complement of social statuses simultaneously occupied by each of a plurality of individuals. Seemingly diverse, these questions are at one in assuming that the status-set, as distinct from the several statuses of individuals considered one at a time, helps explain variations in the behavior of people and the consequences of this behavior for the social systems in which they are involved.

> The sociology of politics comes upon this question in the following form: How do multiple-group affiliations . . . help to sustain the stability of political systems by reducing the strength of participation for unlimited goals [113]? Or it is noted that partisan conflict in politics may be counteracted by allegiance to groups with diverse and often conflicting political interests [23].

> In the sociology of education, it is noted that much investigation has been centered on the relation of a single status—that of social class—to the behavior of students, for example,

*For a detailed discussion of the concept of status-set and the companion concept of role-set, see Robert K. Merton, *Social Theory and Social Structure* (New York: The Free Press, 1968, enlarged ed.), pp. 422–438—editors' note.

in "academic achievement, level of aspiration, participation in extracurricular activities, and the dropout rate" [144]. Yet, since the "educational behavior" of children in the same social class varies, there arises the question of how the composite of their multiple statuses, not merely each of these statuses taken up one at a time, affects their behavior.

Precisely the same question crops up in the sociology of religion and for much the same reason [170].

Sociologists focusing upon social stratification and upon race and ethnic relations are led to the same consideration: " 'people in any class may vary with respect to their other social roles and . . . these may have consequences more important for their personalities than do their class positions' " [394].

And, to take a final instance of the same question, this time in the sphere of collective behavior, it is asked how the multiple (and sometimes conflicting) group affiliations and reference groups of recipients of mass communications affect their responses to those communications [552].

In all these instances, specialists have been led to substantially the same question by observations in their own field. Others, dealing with problems of social structure that cut across the various institutional fields, come upon the same question. The paper on social differentiation [429–441] is devoted entirely to exploring questions about the behavioral consequences of varying degrees of consistency in the social rank of the multiple statuses occupied by individuals. And the student of formal organization brings the same question into focus by developing the notion of " 'latent social identities,'— that is, identities which are not culturally prescribed as relevant to . . . rational organizations" but which nevertheless help shape organizational behavior [412]. Questions originating within a particular institutional sphere can thus be seen to converge with more general questions about social structure.

Originating questions can no doubt be construed in other ways. But this sketchy review may be enough to indicate that they are of different kinds and that they have different sources. Some are questions about sociological facts; others are questions about the adequacy, for given purposes, of sociological concepts. Some are questions about observed empirical generalizations; others are social uniformities derived or conjectured from some underlying ideas. Some deal with the sources of observed patterns of social organization, others with their consequences. The essential point is that originating questions, comprising a prelude to the formulation of a problem, stem from a great variety of circumstances. They do not uniformly ask "Why?" an observed social phenomenon is as it is.

Rationale of the Question

Although any of a great variety of questions may begin the formulation of a problem in science, the bare question does not constitute the problem. It is only one component. Another is the rationale of the question, the statement of the reasons for its being worth asking. The rationale states what will happen to other parts of knowledge or practice as a result of answering the question. In this way, it helps to distinguish between the scientifically consequential and the scientifically trivial question. In short, the rationale states "the case for" the question in the court of scientific opinion.

In conferring upon scientists the right to claim that a question deserves the concerted attention of others, the social institution of science exacts the obligation that they justify the claim. Otherwise, each science would be swamped by an excess of questions, for, as we have seen, questions can be readily multiplied. The requirement of a rationale may curb the flow of scientifically trivial questions and enlarge the share of consequential ones.

In suggesting this function of the rationale, I do not imply that we can state exact criteria of the scientific worth of questions. Nevertheless, judgments of the relative significance of questions, ideas, and findings are inherent in the everyday life of each science.[6] Editors of scientific journals, referees of papers sent to the journals, investigators deciding upon lines of inquiry, teachers deciding what is to be taught—all these continually make such judgments. They must decide whether a scientific paper is worth publishing, whether, once published, it is worth reading, or whether a question will probably justify the effort required to try to answer it.

Historically, the fundamental case for the entire enterprise of science has been "idle curiosity," the disinterested wish to know. Under this mandate, scientists declare that they want to know and admit no need to justify this urge further. When used to qualify "curiosity," the adjective "idle" is of course intended to convey the opposite of its ordinary meaning; it is a piece of Veblenian irony. Men and women possessed by idle curiosity, men and women in whom it "runs at a higher tension," are anything but indolent or lazy. It requires hard work to satisfy idle curiosity. As a rationale for learning and science as a whole, it refers simply to knowledge as a self-contained end. It ignores, rather than denies, the possibility that a new bit of knowledge will contribute to power, comfort, or pecuniary gain, to health, or repute, or anything other than knowledge itself. Within any branch of science, idle curiosity may serve as its own justification, but only for a time. Scientists may regard their deep interest in a question as reason enough for pursuing it. But sooner or later, if the question and its answers are to become part of the science rather than remaining a personal hobby, they must be shown to be relevant to other ideas and facts in the discipline.

Idle curiosity is often supplemented and sometimes replaced by the rationale of practical curiosity. Here the case is made for a question by indicating that its answers will help society achieve values other than knowledge itself: values of health, comfort, safety, efficiency, and the like. But the intent of a question need not, of course, coincide with the consequences of answering it. In sociology as in other disciplines, a question raised only because its answer promises to extend knowledge may nevertheless have practical consequences. The sociology of science, for example, is exploring the question of the extent and character of interdependence between systems of ideas and of social organization [218]. The question is raised in its own right as a special case of the connection between the forms in which individuals and groups organize their activities and the kinds of ideas they evolve. Yet this same question can be and has been put in an effort to find out how differences in research organizations affect the flow of ideas and the creativity of scientists at work within them [67], a practical matter of more than slight concern to many.

Conversely, a sociological question may be raised with an eye to the social value of finding an answer to it and still have important consequences for a set of sociological ideas, considered apart from practical implications. Sociologists are trying to discover, for example, how far and under what conditions legislative and judicial actions can affect current patterns of racial and ethnic relations [390]. Newspaper headlines attest the practical importance of this effort. The same question, in more general form, appears in the sociology of law as the problem of establishing "the limits of law as an instrument of social control" [121]. Its practical import is recognized here as well, but it is raised, not because of this, but because its answer will help advance the understanding of mechanisms of social control. The long and checkered history of this particular problem is one in which partial answers have been periodically taken, for a time, as full answers. In the Sumnerian phase, it was held, without serious reservations, that laws running counter to the mores cannot prove effective means of social control, and cases in point were not hard to find. Both before and after this phase, it was often held that it is enough to enact a law in order to change a prevailing social pattern. The competing doctrines, with their illustrative cases, serve notice on the sociologist of law that the problem has yet to be posed in a way that will provide for a sound answer, by indicating the conditions under which law results in a change of mores.

Once the objective consequences and the intent of an inquiry are distinguished, it becomes evident that the same question may have import both for systematic knowledge and for practical use. The authors in *Sociology Today* repeatedly indicate this double relevance of the questions they raise [120]. One such set of questions centers on the processes of adult socialization, the processes through which people become able and willing to carry out their roles in society. Because all groups face this functional task of having a sufficiency of prepared and motivated personnel, this is plainly a practical concern of great generality. It is also a basic theoretical problem, linked up with sociological ideas about "levels" of social organization [31] and the interrelations between parts of a social system [329]. So it is said, or implied, that inquiries into the processes of adult socialization for occupations generally [456] have both a practical and a theoretical rationale, just as they have, in particular, for the occupations of the teacher [149], the clergy [165], and the physician [243].

A practical rationale and a theoretical rationale for a sociological question may be, and indeed often are, quite consistent. But this double relevance for practice and theory can easily get out of balance. Because society provides a place for both kinds of rationale and because interest in one or the other differs from person to person and from group to group, it is not surprising that each kind of imbalance has been heavily criticized as vitiating one or another social value. In some cases, it is said that primary or exclusive concern with the practical purposes of a sociological inquiry has held up the advancement of sociology. Episodes of this kind are cited, for example, in medical sociology [239], rural sociology [366], and demography [322]. But telling criticism has also been leveled at imbalance of the second kind,[7] in which a problem originally having import for social values and social practice becomes wholly lost to view as it is transformed in the course of sociological investigation.

The claim that a question is worth asking because its answer will enlarge systematic knowledge takes various forms.[8] In one, the theoretical rationale holds that existing ideas can be instructively used to understand regions of phenomena, or aspects of them, that have not been examined before in terms of these ideas. In another, it begins by focusing on perceived inconsistencies in currently accepted ideas or findings and proposes to reconcile these by showing that the inconsistencies are apparent rather than real. There will be occasion to touch upon sociological examples of these two types later, but here I move on to a third, which directs attention to gaps in existing ideas that do not account for aspects of phenomena to which they should in principle apply. In some cases, it is proposed to fill the gap by ideas that are consistent with preexisting theory, which is then seen as incomplete but not mistaken. In other cases, the new theoretical proposal requires some revision, drastic or slight, of the earlier theory.

One of the wide-ranging examples of this type of problem involves the question of how to account for regularities of social behavior that are not prescribed by cultural norms or that are even at odds with those norms. It casts doubt on the familiar assumption that uniformities of social behavior necessarily represent conformity to norms calling for that behavior. It identifies a gap in that narrowly cultural theory of behavior that, expressly or tacitly, sees social regularities as culturally mandated. Yet many social regularities need not, of course, have this relation to culture. Men tend to have higher suicide rates than women, for example, even when cultural norms do not invite males to put an end to themselves. Or again, the patterned hostility of sons to fathers (or, as the case may be, to maternal uncles) occurs without being culturally prescribed. The importance of the general theoretical problem, rather than interest in the particular subject, is no doubt part of the reason why Durkheim's work on suicide has for so long exerted a profound influence on sociological thought. It was his idea that designated properties of groups (such as the degree of their social cohesion) determine the rates of culturally unprescribed behavior.

Many of the questions in *Sociology Today* aim at developing this idea further. The problem is assigned special importance in the study of socially deviant behavior, where it can be strategically investigated. However much they differ in detail, questions about varying rates of crime inquire into those attributes of social structure that indirectly result in culturally unprescribed regularities of behavior. Similarly, great cultural emphasis upon particular goals is seen as indirectly subverting conformity with cultural norms among those social strata largely barred from access to the goals—what is described as anomie-and-opportunity-structure theory.

Once the theoretical gap is identified, it leads almost as a matter of course to further questions, each with its distinctive rationale. Although cultural norms do not fully account for regularities of behavior within groups and differences between groups, it is nevertheless the case that much of patterned social behavior is culturally prescribed and socially sanctioned. This is, after all, what is meant by institutionalized behavior. Juxtaposing this fact with the developing theory of social regularities as the indirect outcome of properties of social structure leads at once to questions about the formation of social norms and the emergence of subcultures. How does a social structure produce new cultural norms prescribing behavior that was previously an unprescribed resultant of that structure? Thus, inquiry becomes focused on the formation of norms in groups similarly situated in the social structure: in the professions, which are given a mandate to "deviate in some measure from some common modes of behavior" [447]; by workers differently located in society who develop greater or less propensity to strike and who then develop norms calling for them to adopt this pattern of behavior [51–52]; in criminal and delinquency gangs, which evolve distinctive subcultures [526].

Another problem of the same kind concerns the sources of disinterested conduct and the legitimacy of institutions. This is, of course, a problem of ancient vintage. In recent generations, Durkheim, Freud, and Weber are only a few of the more distinguished minds to have tried to make theoretical sense of a familiar fact: people often act without concern for the consequences of their actions for themselves. They engage in conduct opposed to their self-interest. Moreover, when this conduct is required by social institutions, it is often felt not to be coercive, because the requirements are regarded as legitimate.

Nineteenth-century utilitarians tried to bring this recalcitrant fact under control by declaring that disinterested conduct is found, upon full analysis, to be ultimately self-interested. Another type of theoretician took the tack that disinterested conduct is simply the result of conditioning. Still others have ascribed it to ignorance: people simply do not know that the action is opposed to their self-interest. Again, this ignorance has itself been seen as the result of fraudulent persuasion or powerful coercion by those who stand to gain from the disinterested conduct of others while they themselves uniformly engage only in self-interested behavior. As is often the case, each of these theoretical proposals seems to have got tenuous hold of some part of the truth. But the still unconsolidated condition of this collection of possible partial truths indicates a major gap in theory. Various efforts to deal with the problem involve questions about the conditions making for the withdrawal of allegiance from institutions so that they lose legitimacy; the conditions under which a balance between self-interested and disinterested action is maintained or upset; the social processes through which self-interest is harnessed to the requirements of an institution.

Questions having the kind of rationale in which a gap in theory is identified have particular force when it appears that the gap can be filled only by recasting earlier assumptions. A case in point begins by examining the assumption that "group equilibrium is a function of the extent to which group members . . . conform with each other's expectations" [423]. This widespread idea, it is suggested, in turn assumes that each act in "a sequence of identical conforming acts will yield either the same or an increasing degree of appreciation or satisfaction" to the actor and to the other participants in a social system. The pair of assumptions is put in question. It is argued, instead, that the same act will have quite different consequences according to the phase of the system of social interaction in which it occurs. For example, the longer the sequence in which one person conforms to another's expectations, the more will that conformity be taken for granted and the less will others be moved to reward it. On this view, successive acts of conformity are occasions for smaller increments of reward. Whatever further investigation may find to be the case, it appears that a far-reaching issue is being raised. A study of consensus seems to accept the assumption we have just seen disputed, saying that "the rewards of actual consensus in facilitating coordinated activity" are enough to motivate people to continue their successful communication [281]. Nevertheless, since this is an inquiry into the formation of groups, it becomes necessary to wrestle with the question whether agreement in values between interacting persons has the same rewarding effect at each stage of group formation.

The study of small groups also finds it essential to investigate the varying effects of the same kind of act, according to its place in the history of interaction, as when it is observed, "An assertion made for the first time has a meaning different from that of one made after the content has acquired a history" [298].

The same idea becomes central to the analysis of deviant behavior. This analysis also begins with the assumption that the outcome of deviation or conformity is "a cumulative and collective product, and the history of the deviant act is the history of an interactional system, not of the actor who happened to author the act" [467]. This then gives rise to the same problem, almost in the very language employed in the other papers:

> How does the significance of an event for deviant behavior depend upon the stage of the interaction process? Since the stimulus value of any event depends upon the perspectives on which it impinges, and since the perspectives of participants in a system change with their experience in the system, we cannot say that certain kinds of events or circumstances are pressures for or against deviant behavior without reference to the stage of the interaction process. The rebuke which brings the incipient deviant back into line may further alienate the deviant who is somewhat further advanced [467–468].

That the same general question is evoked by a variety of observations of different forms of behavior in differing social contexts supplies one criterion of its probable theoretical importance. This is further reinforced by its bearing on competing sociological assumptions, which at the moment remain unreconciled, although each has had some heuristic value.

Specifying Questions

As we have seen, originating questions vary in degree of specificity. In their most diffuse form, they simply register a dimly felt sense of ignorance, asking what might have brought about an observed state of affairs. In somewhat more focused form, they refer to a class of variables that may be involved, without specifying the pertinent variables in that class. At this stage, the problem has yet to be fully instituted. The originating question must still be recast to indicate the observations that will provide a provisional answer to it. Only then has the problem been definitely posed.

This objective typically requires a search for empirical materials through which the problem can be investigated to good advantage. Sometimes, investigators come upon these materials by happy accident, recognizing their strategic character only after they have begun to work with them; sometimes, they select them by design. We are told, for example, that it was the unique properties of red oxide of mercury, which Lavoisier happened to choose for study, that made it possible for him to solve some of the then-current problems in the chemistry of combustion, just as T. H. Morgan's deliberate choice of the fruit fly proved particularly strategic for his studies in genetics.

The history of sociology has its own complement of cases in which long-dormant problems were brought to life and developed by investigating them in situations that strategically exhibit the nature of the problem.* Inquiry into the modes of interdependence between disparate social institutions was greatly advanced by Weber's decision to study the general problem in the particular instance of the connections between ascetic Protestantism and modern capitalism. The problem of the social bases of moral indignation, integral to an understanding of mechanisms of social control, required the finding of situations in which people react strongly to violations of social norms even though they are not directly injured by them. George Mead and Durkheim clarified the problem by proposing the study of systems of punishment, not with respect to the traditional question of their effects in curbing crime, but with respect to their other functions for

*For further discussion of the concept of "strategic research site," see Robert K. Merton, *The Sociology of Science* (Chicago: University of Chicago Press, 1973), pp. 60–61, 371–382—editors' note.

the community. William F. Ogburn and Dorothy S. Thomas seized upon the occurrence of simultaneous multiple discoveries and inventions as a peculiarly strategic point of departure for clarifying the role of cultural factors in innovation. Robert Park focused on the behavior of immigrants as providing strategic materials for investigating the problem of the marginal man, who is oriented toward the competing values of different groups in which he fails to find full acceptance, a problem integral to current work on reference groups. In instances of this sort, a decisive turn was taken by the location of strategic materials for specific inquiry into a general problem.

The prime importance of this phase in the definition of a problem is widely recognized. It presents difficulties all its own, as is implied, for instance, by Kardiner when he asks: "What features of a given society will best show how psychological forces operate in a culture?"

Consider only a few examples. The problem of how a consensus of social values develops and how this affects the formation of groups is effectively investigated by observing people who, initially strangers to one another, find themselves in a situation calling for some degree of repeated social interaction [283]. This inquiry gives rise to further suggestions about other types of situations that should exhibit elements in the process of forming consensus and groups not found in the reported investigation [292]. Again, observations of the behavior of college professors variously subjected to the stress of political pressures afford an occasion for investigating problems of social perception. Such perception is found to be a resultant both of the individual's own state of mind and of the objective social situation in which he is involved [63–64]. Racial and ethnic desegregation in housing developments is identified as a subject that can clarify the general problem of the conditions under which social policies become self-defeating in practice [391]. The study of school systems is also seen as strategic for discovering the circumstances in which organizations designed for a particular purpose give rise to unpremeditated effects. Here, the originating question asks: What are the unintended consequences of the present "rational," organizational structure of schools for the socialization of the child [134]? The author recognizes that not even the beginnings of a solution can be found so long as the question remains in this undifferentiated form. He proposes, therefore, to single out particular aspects of the organization of schools and to trace their consequences for learning. For example, how does the effectiveness of learning differ among elementary school pupils taught by one teacher and by several? How do differences in the sex composition of the teaching faculty affect the acceptance by pupils of the formal authority structure of the school?

The original question becomes determinate as it is converted into a series of such prosy but specific questions.

As a final instance of such specification, consider the general idea, briefly examined in the preceding section, that the same act has different probabilities of occurring and different social and psychological consequences when it does occur, depending upon the phase in the system of social interaction. This broad version of the idea will remain fallow until it is recast into more specific questions [467–468]. For example, the general idea was forced upon the attention of demographers concerned with improving their forecasts of reproduction rates in human populations. A precise distinction between current fertility and cumulative fertility was designed to take note of the fact that "One birth is not just like another: a couple's reproduction at the moment is influenced by whether or not they already have children, and how many." Once such variables as birth order are put "into the forefront of investigation," it becomes possible to assess how the probability of future births in families is affected by past events [317–318]. The essential point here is that demography affords a strategic site for effectively investigating a problem of wide scope. The formally comparable problem will presumably not be clarified in other domains of sociology until they too develop tools of analysis that permit it to be investigated in similarly specific terms.

OCCASIONS FOR PROBLEM-FINDING IN SOCIOLOGY

The foregoing review has barely touched upon occasions that bring one or another problem to the attention of sociologists. But since much has been said in *Sociology Today* about developments within sociology that have evoked or curbed interest in particular kinds of problems, even a quick listing of cases in point may help orient the reader.

Specialization

The division of sociology into a growing number of specialties has affected the flow of problems needing inquiry. In one form, a specialty can be seen as affording a strategic site for investigating problems of general import for sociological theory. In another, and perhaps more frequent, form, general theory can be seen as a source of problems that require solution to advance special fields, such as the sociology of law, cities, race and ethnic relations, criminology, and mass communications.

Corrective Emphases

Sociology and its specialties have been moving through various stages. Each stage evokes interest in distinctive kinds of problems and neglect of others. When, for example, early modern sociologists were engaged in trying to establish a distinct intellectual identity, they placed great emphasis upon the autonomy of the field and largely ignored the methods, ideas, and data of related disciplines. Durkheim in particular bred a race of conscientious objectors to the systematic use of psychology. As the deficiencies of this position became cumulatively evident, there developed a counteremphasis on linking psychological and sociological conceptions.

Similarly with the specialties. Stages of growth can be traced, for instance, in the sociology of law, race and ethnic relations, art, science, and medicine. In each stage, sustained emphasis on one range of problems evokes, after a time, corrective emphasis upon inadvertently neglected problems. On occasion, this calls for the revision of "analytical models" that have led sociologists to concentrate on a restricted range of problems at the expense of other problems that the model neglects. This can be seen in the sequence of models for analyzing organization, from Weber's original model of rational organization, through the "natural system" model, to a proposed synthesis of the two that takes cognizance of problems neglected by each [404–408]. Similar revisions of current models of analysis lead to the identification of new problems.

As each specialty has its distinctive history, the sequence of countervailing emphases sometimes leads to opposed recommendations for investigation of problems. Unlike many of the other specialties that are held to have neglected the study of social conflict, political sociology, for example, is said to have centered heavily on political cleavage at the expense of finding out how political consensus is achieved among people of differing social status and interests and how this helps maintain the political system.

Prevailing theoretical emphases also result in potentially productive stores of sociological data being lost to view, as has been the case with the largely unexamined data on city planning [338], data on social change that are central to the "new empirical theory of population" [327–328], and the interrelations of census and survey data in rural sociology [371].

Recurrence of Long-Standing Problems

As corrective emphases of theory develop, attention is redirected toward problems once in the forefront of inquiry and temporarily muted or put aside. The century-old problem of how individual wants are transformed into socially necessary values provides one such instance. Another is the relation of population growth to human welfare, "the oldest problem of population theory" that has been periodically reformulated to accord with new concepts and new methods of investigation [325].

Conceptual Obstacles to Inquiry

Periodically, investigation of a range of problems is found to have gone about as far as it can with the use of existing concepts. Useful for a time, the concepts now prove to be insufficiently differentiated, thus typically introducing the problem of devising appropriate classifications.

The major concept of role, for example, proves inadequate to deal with many problems as long as it falls back on the vernacular for the depiction of social positions—for example, father, judge, leader, or physician. The felt inadequacy gives rise to the problem of devising a "standard set of concepts or categories which could be used to describe *any* typical role or set of roles in a way that . . . does some justice to its complexity, and permits systematic comparison with other roles" [267]. What gives this problem special importance is that its solution is a precondition for getting on with a broader program of investigation.

Comparable circumstances lead to comparable statements of this problem. Inadequate classifications of types of community are holding up investigations in rural sociology; many kinds of criminological inquiry wait upon a satisfactory classification of criminal behavior and of gangs; there is announced need for classifying the forms of anomie and the "mechanisms by which one kind of deviant behavior generates others" [473]. So, too, a long-standing deficit in classification limits the generalizability of experimental findings, for "In spite of something like fifty years of research on individual *versus* group problem-solving, in which many concretely different kinds of tasks have been used, there is still no very good classification of tasks" [301].

The same kind of problem is instituted by those who note the use of implicit classifications, which remain unsystematic and incomplete. This seems to be the source, for example, of the question whether social institutions can be ranked according to the degree to which they integrate or divide people in a society.

Inconsistencies and Contradictions

The finding of facts at odds with experience or theoretical expectations imposes its own brand of perplexity. It invites reexamination of the ideas that led to the expectation in the first instance. Are the ideas faulty, or the inferences from them? Is the discrepancy between idea and data only apparent rather than real? Do the contravening data fail to represent what they were assumed to represent? Or must the antecedent idea be revamped to make sense of the data inconsistent with it? If so, how can this be kept from devolving into a succession of ad hoc hypotheses designed to "save" the original theory—that form of "rationalization" which has a notoriety all its own in the history of thought.

In many cases, inconsistent results lead to the posing of new problems. To take only one example, "Research studies that have attempted to examine the impact on learning of 'authoritarian' *vs.* 'democratic' social climates yield contradictory findings" [141]. This invites a redefinition of the problem: it is no longer a question of which type of social climate makes for more effective learning but rather a question of the extent to which the behavior of the teacher lives up to the expectations of students, irrespective of whether these are expectations of "authoritarian" or "democratic" behavior.

Because such inconsistencies set the stage for instituting new problems, many of the authors in *Sociology Today* search actively for "deviant cases"[9]—cases that depart from a prevailing pattern. In part, this is designed to account for more of the observed variance in the data at hand. Deviant cases are examined in order to arrive at a single interpretation of the prevailing regularity and of departures from it. Appropriately investigated, the exception can improve the rule.

In other instances, a focus on deviant cases leads to the posing of new problems, not envisaged at the time the inquiry was begun, and leading in directions removed from the course of the initial inquiry. In experiments on social pressures toward conformity, for example, primary attention may thus shift from the compliant majority to the intransigent few. The problem can then center not so much on the personal qualities of these autonomous people but on the social bases of individual autonomy, a problem of long standing that awaits further study.*

These are of course only a few of the types of occasions arising within sociology itself that make for the finding of particular kinds of problems. New tools of inquiry, for example, characteristically lead to the formation of problems that either went unnoticed before or could not be effectively investigated. A plethora of still dispersed findings gives rise to emphasis on their theoretical consolidation. Almost all authors, examining the frontiers of their own field, indicate points at which the comparison of data drawn from different societies would help clarify the formulation of a problem. But this short review may be enough to direct attention to these and other intradisciplinary sources of problems.

SOCIAL DETERMINANTS OF SOCIOLOGICAL PROBLEMS

Only some sociological problems are generated by developments internal to the field. Many others are brought into focus by influences external to the discipline itself, as we momentarily noted in considering the practical rationale of certain sociological questions. Here, in quick conclusion, are a few cases in which social influences are examined.

Changes in patterns of social life are found to give new or renewed significance to a broad subject for sociological inquiry. It has been suggested, for example, that American sociologists became disposed to turn from the study of religious institutions as long as the authority of these institutions was apparently waning. But the much-advertised revival of religion in American life seems to have brought about a renewed interest in the sociology of religion. Similarly, the marked "change of balance between work and leisure has given new emphasis and a new turn to studies of leisure" [445].

But it cannot be assumed that all social and cultural changes will automatically and promptly induce or reinforce interest in a particular field of inquiry. Usually only when changes in a society have become defined as a "social problem" and are the occasion for acute social conflict does the interest arise. For example, sociologists long paid little attention to the social institution of science, even though

---

*Which it has since received, notably in Rose Laub Coser, "The Complexity of Roles as a Seedbed of Individual Autonomy," in Lewis A. Coser, *The Idea of Social Structure* (New York: Harcourt Brace Jovanovich, 1975), pp. 237–263—editors' note.

it was evident to all that advancing science had become one of the major dynamic forces in society. A limited renascence of interest in this field occurred only when a complex of historical events subjected the institution of science to conspicuous stresses—among them, the efforts to subordinate science to political control in Nazi Germany and Soviet Russia and the imposition of secrecy upon scientific work in many societies, all violating the values of science and curbing the flow of scientific informatior This can be likened to circumstances that brought about the beginnings of political sociology, when the breakdown of forms of traditional authority brought into focus the differences between the society and the state, between man and citizen, and directed the attention of observers to problems of consensus and conflict. Or, specifically, as noted before, the ruling of the Supreme Court on desegregation gave new impetus to study of the problem of relations between law and custom.

Historical events can affect the value commitments of sociologists and lead them to work on a restricted range of problems. As a case in point, the social strains of the 1920s and 1930s in the United States, resulting from the Great Depression and from culture conflict induced by the preceding mass immigration, led many American sociologists to preoccupation with problems of social disorganization.

The social organization of sociological inquiry itself also affects the selection of problems. For example, patterns of recruitment and the working conditions of rural sociologists, especially in the landgrant colleges, have influenced their choice of subject matter and the ways in which problems are construed.

Social influences of these and comparable kinds are summed up in the observation that "Innovations in demography, or in other social sciences, are determined mainly not by the inner development of the science itself but by the impingement of historical events" [316]. The author goes on to supply much evidence of changes in secular trends of population that force the attention of demographers upon the need for new concepts and methods as well as upon new problems for sociological investigation.

All this is only prologue to the understanding of problem-finding* (as emphatically distinguished from the far more familiar subject of problem-solving). That prologue dealt with three aspects of the genesis and development of scientific problems. It began by identi-

---

*As can be seen from recent work on the subject: Harriet Zuckerman, "Theory Choice and Problem Choice in Science," in J. Gaston, ed., *Sociological Perspectives on Science* (San Francisco: Jossey-Bass, 1979), pp. 65–95; Thomas F. Gieryn, "Problem Retention and Problem Change in Science," in ibid., pp. 96–115—editors' note.

fying key ingredients in the formulation of problems: (1) originating questions, (2) specifying questions (entailing the associated concept of "strategic research sites"), and (3) types of rationale for both kinds of questions. The analysis went on to identify the varied circumstances, both those internal to the discipline and those external to it, which focus the attention of scientists on certain problems at the expense of others: (1) successive specialization, (2) counter-emphasis to redress cumulating imbalances in the foci of scientific attention, (3) reactivation of problems in the discipline, (4) conceptual frameworks as blinders to certain kinds of inquiry, (5) the prod to new formulations deriving from newly experienced inconsistencies and contradictions among and between ideas and data. Finally, this analytical account touched upon processes and events external to a discipline which affect scientists' choices of problems for investigation, a matter which had been examined in detail for another time, place, and array of sciences.[10] It was proposed throughout that problem-choice and problem-formulation are coordinate with problem-solving in the practice of scientific inquiry.

NOTES

[1]Ralf Dahrendorf, "Out of Utopia: Toward a Reorientation of Sociological Analysis," *American Journal of Sociology* 64 (1958):123.

[2]Ibid., p. 123.

[3]See, for example, John Dewey, *Logic: The Theory of Inquiry* (New York: Holt, 1938), Part II.

[4]The phrase "originating question" is adapted from Lazarsfeld [48].

[5]The preceding pages on pseudofacts and pseudoproblems have been widely drawn upon in social science writings. For example, in Herbert G. Gutman, *The Black Family in Slavery and Freedom, 1750–1925* (New York: Pantheon Books, 1976), p. 462ff.; Thomas Sowell, "Assumptions Versus History in Ethnic Education," *Teachers College Record* 83 (1981):37–71, esp. 59ff.

[6]Michael Polanyi, *Personal Knowledge* (London: Routledge & Kegan Paul, 1958), pp. 134–142. This general formulation was followed up two decades later in an empirical study of editorial and refereeing processes in the leading journal of contemporary physics, the *Physical Review*, conducted by Harriet Zuckerman and Robert K. Merton, "Patterns of Evaluation in Science: Institutionalization, Structure and Functions of the Referee System," *Minerva* 9 (1971):66–100, reprinted in Merton, *The Sociology of Science,* Chapter 21—editors' note.

[7]Most notably by Robert S. Lynd, in *Knowledge for What?* (Princeton, N.J.: Princeton University Press, 1939), and by Lawrence K. Frank, "Research for What?" *Journal of Social Issues,* Supplement Series No. 10 (1957):5–22.

[8]A rewarding account of this is found in F. C. Bartlett, *Thinking: An Experimental and Social Study* (New York: Basic Books, 1958).

[9]The logic of this procedure, described as "deviant case analysis," has been fairly well worked out. See, for example, Paul F. Lazarsfeld and Morris Rosenberg, eds., *The Language of Social Research* (New York: Free Press, 1966), pp. 167–174.

[10]Robert K. Merton, *Science, Technology and Society in Seventeenth-Century England* (New York: Howard Fertig, [1938] 1970), Chapters 7–10.

CHAPTER 3

Social Problems and Sociological Theory*

In the modern world, the visibly practical accomplishments of a science affect the social value placed upon it. For example, now that the utility of mathematics has become evident even to those in places of political power, mathematicians are being accorded vastly enlarged social support and probably heightened public esteem. To record the fact is not necessarily to applaud it. Indeed, within the subculture of science, things often stand quite the other way, with greatest value attached to new knowledge that has no directly apparent practical outcome. Expressing this sentiment is that often quoted, though possibly apocryphal, toast at a dinner for scientists in Cambridge: To pure mathematics, and may it never be of any use to anybody!

It is plain to see why many scientists assess scientific work apart from its use for purposes other than the enlargement of knowledge itself. For only on this ground can the institution of science become fairly autonomous and scientists remain free to investigate what they, instead of only what others, consider significant. Correlatively, if

From *Contemporary Social Problems,* Fourth Edition, edited by Robert K. Merton and Robert Nisbet, © 1976 by Harcourt Brace Jovanovich, Inc. Reprinted by permission of the publisher. We have borrowed freely from the 1961, 1966, 1971, and 1976 editions in constructing this composite form of Merton's essay—editors' note.

practical utility becomes the sole measure of significance, then science becomes only a handmaiden—of industry or theology or polity. Its autonomy becomes undermined. That is why many scientists today regard with misgivings the doctrine propounded three centuries ago by Francis Bacon that helped establish science as socially valuable because it had valued practical applications. But we should remember that Bacon, undeniably the great apostle of the utility of science, distinguished between what he called experiments of fruit, which could be put to use to help achieve various human purposes, and experiments of light, which brought into being new knowledge much to be sought, even though it had, then and there, no evident other uses than an enlarged understanding. Bacon was not addicted to the nothing-but fallacy that science must be *nothing but* a guide to action or that it must be *nothing but* self-contained knowledge, entirely insulated from the world of action and social values.

There is, then, this basic duality in science: it can provide greater understanding of how things happen to be as in fact they are, just as it can provide understanding that enables us to change things from what and where they are. As with most dualities in society and culture, this one has given rise to ambivalent attitudes. And since we find it hard to tolerate ambivalence, we periodically deal with such indecision by swinging violently to one extreme position or the other, emphatically denying the worth of the alternative that is being forcibly suppressed.[1] We become extreme advocates of the position that knowledge not put to practical use is not true knowledge at all or of the position that applied knowledge is at best an inferior sort of knowledge. Some become votaries of pure science, others of applied science; disciples of Plato, badly understood, or disciples of Bacon, badly understood. And so we find Macaulay writing that he greatly prefers the error of Bacon to that of Plato for "we have no patience with a philosophy which, like those Roman matrons who swallowed abortives in order to preserve their shapes, takes pains to be barren for fear of being homely."

To quote Macaulay on this matter is not to consider him a sound exponent of the technical philosophy of science. His unforgettable essay on Bacon,[2] from which this passage is drawn, is every bit as defective in its philosophical part as it is perceptive in its biographical part. But though Macaulay often errs when he attempts to write of philosophical notions, this is not one of those times. Through the use of an adroit and deliberately damaging simile, he has exposed the excessive purism of those thinkers who pride themselves on the absence of practical outcomes of their thought, thus confusing practical uselessness with theoretical worth. Yet it is at least possible that a pragmatically useless idea is not, on that account, a theoretically valuable one. The two aspects of claims to knowledge—the pragmatic and the theoretical—are partly independent of each other, authentically coinciding on occasion, turning up severally, and sometimes being altogether groundless. It is this latter case against which Macaulay has directed his fire. Among those who set great store upon speculative theory for its own sake, it is a short step to the fallacy of assuming that all which is not useful is therefore scientifically important and sound. Yet, as Macaulay (after Bacon) wants us to see, the sterile idea may be pretty because it is not laden down with the burdens that come with the pragmatic test.

The long-standing ambivalence toward pure and applied science is no less current among social scientists than among other scientists. It is particularly expressed in the orientation toward the sociology of social problems or toward applied social science in general. Applied sociology is regarded by some as having distinctly less value than theoretical sociology, if indeed it is not put entirely beyond the pale. In contrast, others hold that theoretical explorations in social science which do not bear directly upon the major social problems of our time are explorations of the trivial and that the pure theorists are, in effect, exploiting their position in society merely to satisfy their own idle curiosity rather than returning to the society that supports them the kind of knowledge that can be used to help solve social problems and to achieve social purposes.[3]

If we entertain the hypothesis that these alternative positions are not imposed upon us, that they are, rather, the results of an ambivalence toward the dual aspects of all science, theoretical and applied, we can be a little more relaxed about the matter. We can then consider that in sociology, as in the other sciences, physical, biological, and social, there is an intellectual division of labor rather than an all-or-none commitment to an orientation toward one or the other of these dual aspects. Some scientists, both by temperament and capacity, are no doubt better suited to the exclusive pursuit of one or the other of these paths of inquiry; some may move back and forth between both paths; and a few may manage to tread a path bordered on one side by the theoretical and on the other by the practical or applied. This last path is, in the main, the one I have followed in these essays, thus exhibiting my agreement with the position set forth by Whitehead:

> Science is a river with two sources, the practical source and the theoretical source. The practical source is the desire to direct our actions to achieve predetermined ends. . . . The theoretical source is the desire to understand. I most emphatically state that I do not consider one source as in any sense nobler than the other, or intrinsically more interesting. I cannot see why it is

nobler to strive to understand than to busy oneself with the right ordering of one's actions. Both have their bad sides; there are evil ends directing actions, and there are ignoble curiosities of the understanding.[4]

To draw upon both theoretical and practical sources of sociological knowledge does not mean that we make use of a single comprehensive theory of social problems—of social disorganization and deviant behavior—for there is, in truth, no such overarching theory to draw upon. No qualified sociologist holds that the discipline has evolved a single, strictly formulated theory that fully encompasses the wide range of social problems, and so enables us to account for every significant aspect of all these problems. That sort of claim must be reserved to those pseudo-sociologists who turn up in quantity whenever trouble is brewing in society and announce their quickly designed cures for everything that ails us socially. Yet in matters so complex and obscure as much of social organization and human behavior, we are wise to be on our guard against "explanations" that profess to account for every facet of that organization and behavior. For, as the ancients knew, those who try to prove too much prove next to nothing. In no sphere of systematic knowledge—whether mechanics, biology, linguistics or sociology—do specialists go on the fool's errand of explaining every aspect of concrete phenomena. Instead, particular aspects, structures, and processes of the phenomena are singled out, under the guidance of some general ideas, and methodically investigated, while other aspects are conscientiously neglected as no part of the problem in hand. This responsible, well-attested, and effective frame of mind has become so definitely established in the older scientific disciplines that it is soon taken over by novices as a firm implication of their training; it is seldom taught in explicit and didactic fashion. But the need for dealing with selected aspects of concrete events is not so widely or immediately sensed in the newer social sciences, particularly, perhaps, in psychology and sociology (since everyman considers himself a psychologist by virtue of being human and a sociologist by virtue of living his life in society). The didactic emphases in these fields upon methodology and the role of theory can be understood in part as a collective effort to keep their practitioners from falling into the trap of explaining little by trying to explain too much. The tidy and seemingly complete explanation of every aspect of human behavior and organization includes a mess of unrelated and specially concocted assumptions that are to be fitted to each distinct aspect of the complex whole under study.

But if sociologists have nothing remotely resembling a single, rigorous, all-encompassing theory of social problems, they do have a general theoretical orientation toward social problems. Similar sociological ideas and similar procedures of sociological analysis are put to work in the study of the most varied kinds of social problems. If there is no one theory unifying all the significant questions that can be raised about social problems, there is a sociological perspective from which similar kinds of questions have been raised and, in some cases and in some degree, tentatively answered. The rest of this chapter will consider a few—far from most—of the theoretical questions to be kept in mind in the investigation of social problems.

THE SOCIOLOGICAL DIAGNOSIS OF SOCIAL PROBLEMS

Just about everyone has at least a gross conception of "social problems." Unsought but undeniable troubles in society, social conflicts and confusions usually described as the "social crisis of our time," the victimizing of people by social institutions that put them at a disadvantage in life, crime, presently curable but uncured disease, the socially unauthorized use of violence—all these and more are caught up in what most of us ordinarily mean by the term "social problems." Nor is this general understanding far removed from the technical sense in which the sociologist employs the term. But since the popular and the technical senses of social problem are not identical, although they overlap, it will be useful to consider what enters into the sociologist's diagnosis of a social problem. In considering this, we must recognize that there is not a strict identity in the conception of a social problem held by all sociologists.

In examining the sociological notion of a social problem, we must treat at least eight connected questions: (1) the central criterion of a social problem: a significant discrepancy between social standards and social actuality; (2) the sense in which social problems have social origins; (3) the judges of social problems, those people who in fact principally define the great problems in a society; (4) manifest and latent social problems; (5) the social perception of social problems; (6) the ways in which belief in the corrigibility of unwanted social situations enters into the definition of social problems; (7) the hazards of "subjectivism" as an orientation toward social problems; and finally, (8) the muddle surrounding the question of a "value-free" sociology.

Social Standards and Social Actuality

The first and basic ingredient of a social problem consists of a substantial discrepancy between widely shared social standards and the actual conditions of social life. Such discrepancies vary in extent and in degree of importance assigned them, so that social problems are regarded as differing in magnitude as well as kind. In referring to social standards, we do not mean to imply that they are uniformly shared throughout the sectors of a society. Quite the contrary. As we shall see in some detail when we turn to "the judges of social problems," these standards and their implementation differ, to a degree, among the several social strata and social segments. Nevertheless, we can begin by considering certain aspects of the gap between social standards and social actuality, for this provides a useful way of thinking about widely diversified kinds of social problems.

It takes no great knowledge or effort of mind to realize that the extent of the disparity between what is and what people think ought to be varies from time to time in the same society and from place to place among societies. But it is more difficult to devise acceptable measures of the varying extent of this disjunction between social standards and social reality. I do not refer here to the notorious inadequacies in the statistics officially registering the frequency of various types of deviant behavior and symptoms of social disorganization. All sociological authorities agree that the statistics of mental illness and suicide, of crime and juvenile delinquency, or prostitution and divorce are subject to all manner of bias owing to difficulties in obtaining a thorough count of comparable units. (It is ironic, perhaps, that the most nearly faultless and most informative social statistics available in American society deal with performance in professional baseball and football, indeed, in sports generally; among statistics dealing with social problems, those of traffic accidents and casualties are perhaps the most adequate.) Beyond these technical shortcomings of the statistics of social troubles lie further difficulties in devising apt measures of the extent of the discrepancy between social standards and social actuality.

In dealing with extremely simplified cases of social casualties—as Bredemeier and Toby describe the people who signally fail to meet social standards[5]—we can adopt simple measures that serve, up to a point. One such measure would be provided, for example, by a full record of the number of homicides in a society, thus indicating the extent of the gap between the norm forbidding homicide and the way things actually are in this respect. But even in this seemingly simplest of instances, instructive ambiguities remain. Some, indeed many, moralities hold every human life to be sacred. For people subscribing to this value, the sheer number of homicides would be the appropriate indicator of the extent of this particular social problem. Since each unlawful killing—unlawful because only a fraction who hold to the general value of the sanctity of human life apply this value to the legally authorized killing of human beings, individually or en masse, in war—violates the value placed on human life, the absolute number of homicides becomes central, entirely apart from the differing probabilities of homicide in populations of widely differing size. For other observers, intent on making standardized comparisons of the scale of the problem among different societies, the absolute number of homicides no longer holds as a measure. Instead, they would use standardized rates of homicide—say, homicides per 100,000 of the population or per 100,000 of the adult population. (For the specimen case of homicide, any other form of deviant behavior can be substituted without change in the logic of the argument: for people holding fast to a value, it is the absolute numbers of violations of that value which register the scale of the problem; for the sociological investigator, intent on ferreting out the sources and consequences of social problems, it will ordinarily be the relative numbers—the rates or proportions—that are used to estimate the magnitude of the problem.)

Furthermore, the frequency of deviant acts—whether counted in absolute or relative numbers—is of course not enough to measure the social significance of the discrepancy between standards and behavior. Social values and their associated standards differ greatly in the importance people assign to them. They are not all of a kind. Everyone knows that petty theft—the very term includes an evaluation of significance—differs in its moral and social significance from homicide, this difference being partly registered in the currently[6] different punishments meted out to the two classes of offenders. But how are these two classes of deviant behavior to be compared as to the degree to which they constitute social problems? Is 1 homicide to be equated to 10 petty thefts? 100? 1,000? We may sense that these are incommensurables and so *feel* that the question of comparing their magnitude is a nonsense question. Yet this feeling is only a prelude to our recognizing the more general fact that we have no strict common denominator for social problems and so have no workable procedures for comparing the scale of different problems, even when the task is simplified by dealing with two kinds of criminal acts.

When we try to compare the magnitude of very different kinds of social problems, the issue of course becomes all the more difficult to resolve. Shall we conclude that the 20,000 murders in 1978 represent about two-fifths as great a social problem in the United States as the approximately 50,000 deaths from vehicular accidents in that year? And, in turn, how are these to be compared in order of magnitude with the approximately 6 million unemployed Americans, the nearly as many known alcoholics, or the unnumbered millions who are seriously alienated from their jobs, finding little joy and small purpose in them and at best being resigned to using only part of their capacities in work that is for them little more than a necessary evil?

In short, there are no agreed-upon bases of rigorously appraising the comparative magnitude of different social problems. In the end, it is the values held by people occupying different positions in society that provide the rough bases for the relative importance assigned to social problems and, as we shall see later in this chapter, this sometimes leads to badly distorted impressions of the social significance of various problems, even when these are judged in the light of reigning values.

Social Origins of Social Problems

It is sometimes said that social problems must have social origins. It is not always clear whether such a statement is offered as a partial definition or an empirically testable proposition, as a criterion or a hypothesis. In one sense, the requirement of social origins is redundant. For, as we have just seen, a social problem formally involves a discrepancy, judged intolerable, between social standards and social actuality. Another version of this is found in the observation that

> . . . *social groups create deviance by making the rules whose infraction constitutes deviance,* and by applying those rules to particular people and labeling them as outsiders. From this point of view, deviance is *not* a quality of the act the person commits, but rather a consequence of the application by others of rules and sanctions to an "offender." The deviant is one to whom that label has successfully been applied; deviant behavior is behavior that people so label.[7]

In this Pickwickian sense, all social problems have "social origins" inasmuch as they are not taken to be a problem until actual conditions are judged not to measure up sufficiently to social (that is, shared) standards.

But more than this is ordinarily meant by the proposal that only the problems that originate in social conditions or processes can usefully be regarded as social problems. It is being proposed that the substantive *causes* of social problems must themselves be social, not merely their formal attributes. According to this version of the idea, crime and suicide and family disorganization constitute social problems inasmuch as they result principally from identifiable social circumstances. On this view, socially disruptive events that are not society-made but nature-made would be excluded from consideration. Earthquakes, tornadoes, cyclones, hurricanes, eruptions of volcanoes, floods, perhaps famines and epidemics—these and all other nature-caused events that greatly affect the lives of men in society would be ruled out.

Like other investigators, sociologists are of course free to delimit the range of their inquiry. They are free to state the criteria of the phenomena that will be regarded as pertinent to systematic investigation. But in proposing particular criteria, sociologists, like other investigators, are required to show that these criteria are theoretically useful,* if the proposal is to be taken seriously by others. Freedom to define does not mean license to exclude. And until now, no satisfactory case has been made for confining the scope of social problems to only those problems that are in their origin social in the sense that the events precipitating them are initiated by people-in-society. Rather, it is proposed that, whatever the precipitating events, they enter into purview as part of a social problem whenever they give rise to significant discrepancies between social standards and social actuality. For whether the forces disrupting patterns of social life are nature-made or society-made, they will, in the end, confront members of the society with the task of responding to them, and the nature of that response is, in sociological principle, greatly affected by the structure of the society, by its institutions, and by its values.[8]

Perhaps later inquiry will find distinct patterns of social problems according to whether they are social both in precipitating origin and consequences or are precipitated by nonsocial events that have socially disruptive consequences. But this would only mean the working out of further discriminations. It would not mean scrapping the conception that social problems are defined by their consequences, whatever their origins.[9]

The Judges of Social Problems

We have noted the difficulties entailed in assessing the comparative scale of diverse social problems and the sense in which the unwanted discrepancy between social standards and social actuality makes for a social problem, irrespective of the character of the precipitating events that help create the discrepancy. A third ingredient entering into the diagnosis of social problems requires us to consider the people who judge that the discrepancy exists and that it matters. Sociologists often say that "many people" or a "functionally significant number of people" or even that "a majority of people" in a society

*Compare the section on the rationale of problem formulation in Chapter 2 of this volume—editors' note.

must regard a social circumstance as departing from their standards in order for this circumstance to qualify as a social problem. As a rough approximation, this formulation can serve for many cases. When social norms are a matter of overwhelming consensus, as with the norms proscribing murder or rape or kidnapping, a more exacting formulation is not required. But for many other kinds of social behavior and social conditions, this merely numerical criterion is no longer adequate. It becomes necessary to distinguish among "the many" who define certain recurrent events or a social condition as a problem.

Social definitions of social problems have this in common with other processes in society: those occupying strategic positions of authority and power of course carry more weight than others in deciding social policy and therefore, among other things, in identifying for the rest what are to be taken as significant departures from social standards. There is not a merely numerical democracy of judgment in which every appraisal is assigned the same voting power in defining a condition as a social problem. It is a mistaken, atomistic notion that each member of society sets about to define social problems for himself or herself, and that it is the aggregate of these independent judgments that decides the array of problems in the society and the comparative importance of each problem in the array. Even otherwise differing "schools of sociological thought" are agreed on the theoretical conception that all societies are differentiated into a variety of structurally connected social statuses. This is universally the case although societies vary, of course, in the degree of structural differentiation. Furthermore, people occupying different positions in the social structure tend to have distinctive interests and values (as well as sharing some interests and values with others). As a result, not all social standards are evenly distributed among diverse social positions. It follows logically and is found empirically that to the extent that these standards differ among social positions and groups within a society, the same circumstances will be variously evaluated as being at odds with the standards held by some and as consistent with standards held by others. Thus, one group's problem will be another group's asset.

Societies that are highly differentiated into a great variety of social statuses, with their characteristic interests and values, will tend to have correspondingly different, and often strongly conflicting, judgments of what in particular constitutes social problems. Scott Greer points out, for example, that traffic congestion may be defined as a problem by the drivers of automobiles but may be regarded as a distinct asset by the proprietors of stores along the routes of congestion. On the other hand, cheap and speedy transportation to the

downtown area of the city is scarcely defined as an asset by the sub-
urban merchant.[10] Or, to turn from structurally induced differences
of judgments based on calculations of material self-interest, consider
that in American society today, abortion is defined as a social problem
by many whose religiously based or otherwise legitimized values are
violated by it. Others define abortion as a means of preventing a
personal problem—having an unwanted child, whether legitimate or
illegitimate—which, aggregated for many cases, could become a serious social problem.[11] Or again, to take a stale and therefore at once
evident example, free and easy access to alcoholic drink was defined
by many Americans, two generations ago, as the source of an important social problem; therefore, for a time, such access was pro-
hibited by legislation. For a good many others—who also defined
alcohol*ism* as a problem—the would-be social cure was worse than the
ailment: prohibition was held to violate standards by entering the
private lives of Americans to regulate what they regarded as altogether personal decisions.

In short, full or substantial consensus in a complex, differentiated society exists for only a limited number of values, interests,
and derived standards for conduct. We must therefore be prepared
to find that the same social conditions and behaviors will be defined
by some as a social problem and by others as an agreeable and fitting
state of affairs. For the latter, indeed, the situation may begin to
become a problem only when the presumed remedy is introduced
by the former. What is loosely described as "socialized medicine," for
example, was defined as a social remedy by Walter Reuther and many
others in his constituency of the AFL-CIO just as it was defined as
a social problem by the successive presidents of the AMA and many
others in their constituency. In the eyes of some, unemployment
benefits help solve a problem by providing aid to people for their
work in the past and for willingness to work in the present; for others,
whose secure positions in society help them sustain the belief, these
benefits are at best a dole, morally suspect and socially undesirable.
For some, the widespread acceptance of things as they are registers
the social problem of public apathy; for others, the problem begins
with the appearance of organized social protest. Thus, as Kenneth
B. Clark observes:

> Continuing evidence of the pervasive moral apathy and political
> cynicism in the American mass culture is a significant negative
> in weighing the possibilities for social democracy. If constructive
> change were to depend on the chance of profound moral con-
> version, there might be cause for pessimism. Negroes must con-
> vince the majority, who are white, that continued oppression of
> the Negro minority hurts the white majority too. Nor is it sophis-

try to argue that this is indeed the case. If it were not the case, the Negro cause would be hopeless. Certainly the Negro cannot hope to argue his case primarily in terms of ethical concerns, for these historically have had only sentimental and verbal significance in themselves. They have never been the chief source of power for that social change which involves significant alteration of status between privileged versus unprivileged groups. Child labor legislation was not the direct result of a moral indignation against the exploitation of children in factories, mines, mills, but rather reflected a growing manpower shortage and the new rise of the labor unions. The value of ethical appeals is to be found only when they can be harnessed to more concrete appeals such as economic, political, or other power advantages to be derived from those with the power to facilitate or inhibit change. Ethical and moral appeal can be used to give theoretical support for a program of action, or in some cases to obscure and make the pragmatic aspects of that program more palatable to conscience. If moral force opposes economic or political ends, the goal of moral force may be postponed. The reverse may also be true. But where moral force and practical advantage are united, their momentum is hard to deny.[12]

What has been stated here concerning the situation of American Negroes as a social problem, and not merely as a problem of Negroes alone, holds for all manner of other discrepancies between widespread (though not unanimously held) social values and actual social situations. The gap between values and actuality is defined by those who perceive the gap as a problem confronting society. It must be closed by bringing social situations closer to social values, not by accommodating values to currently existing situations. But the judges of the problem who wield power and authority will succeed in inaugurating the change only to the degree that other forces in society work in the same direction as the moral mandate. When we speak of the times "being ripe for a designated social change" we are referring metaphorically to the convergence of moral and social system imperatives.

The fact that the conflicting values and interests of differentiated groups in a complex society result in disparate conceptions of the principal problems of society would at first seem to dissolve the concept of social problems in the acid of extreme relativism. But this is only apparently so; it is not an inevitable intellectual commitment. Sociologists need not and do not limit the scope of social problems to those expressly defined by the people they are studying and trying to understand. Fortunately, they have an alternative to the doctrine that "nothing is either a social problem or a social asset but thinking makes it so." They need not become separated from good sense by imprisoning themselves in the set of logically impregnable premises that only those situations constitute social problems which are so defined by the people involved in them. For social problems are not only subjective states of mind; they are also, and equally, objective states of affairs.

Manifest and Latent Social Problems

The sociologist investigating social problems assumes that they, along with other facets of human society, have both their subjective aspect, this appearing in the perceptions and evaluations of people in society who affirm or deny that something is a social problem, and their objective aspect, this appearing in the actual conditions that are being appraised.[13] For sociologists to confine themselves only to the conditions in society that a majority of people regard as undesirable would be to exclude study of all manner of other conditions that are in fact at odds with the declared values and purposes of those who accept or endorse these conditions. Such a limitation would require the sociologist to subscribe to an extreme subjectivism, under the self-deceiving guise of retaining the objectivity of the scientific observer. But it is possible to escape this heedless subjectivism that in effect abandons definition of the scope of sociological inquiry to the decisions of the people and groups under study. For not all conditions and processes of society inimical to designated values are recognized as such by those holding those values. It is the function of sociologists to discover and to report the human consequences of holding to certain values and practices just as it is their function to discover and to report the human consequences of departing from these values and practices.

Apart from *manifest* social problems—those objective social conditions identified by problem-definers as at odds with the values of the society—are *latent* social problems, conditions that are also at odds with values of the society but are not generally recognized as being so. Sociologists do not impose their values upon others when they undertake to supply knowledge about latent social problems. When the demographer Kingsley Davis, for example, identifies the social, economic, and cultural consequences of rapidly growing populations in diverse kinds of society, he in effect calls the advocates of alternative population policies to account for the results of one or another policy. They can no longer evade responsibility for the social consequences of policy by claiming these to be fundamentally unforeseeable. Or again, sociologists who demonstrate the "wastage of talent" that results from marked inequalities of opportunity for the training and exercise of socially prized talent bring to a focus what was experienced by many as only a personal problem rather than a problem of society. Or yet again, as our knowledge, still notoriously sparse, of the social, economic, and psychological consequences of racial segregation is enlarged—consequences for the dominant majority as well as for the subordinate minority—advocates of alternative policies will be brought increasingly to account for their distinctive positions. In this way, sociological knowledge eventually presses policy-makers to justify their social policies to their constituencies and the larger community.

Social Values and Sociological Analysis.   We should pause to take note of what is *not* involved in this analytical process of making latent social problems manifest; otherwise it will be easily mistaken for another version of an extreme and untenable sociological rationalism. It is not being said that the discovery and diffusion of knowledge about the consequences of adhering to current social beliefs and practices will automatically lead people to abandon the beliefs and practices that are shown to prevent them from realizing some of their own basic values. Men and women are not as strictly rational as all that. The sociological truth does not instantly make them free. It does not induce a sudden rupture with demonstrably dysfunctional arrangements in society. But by discovering more and more consequences of accepted practices and by making these known, the sociologist engaged in the study of social problems provides a basis for substantial reappraisals of these practices in the long run, if not necessarily at once. It might be asked, of course, why we should be interested in the long run since, as Maynard Keynes emphatically reminded us, in the long run we are all dead. The reply is as thoroughly evident as the question: because presumably, and contrary to our animal and egoistic faith, the world does not die with us.

In other words, there is a degree of rationalism in the sociological outlook, as there is in every other scientific outlook. But it is not rationalism run riot. New objective knowledge of the probable consequences of action need not lead people to act at once in the light of this knowledge. Sociology need not make us wise or even prudent. But, through its successive uncovering of latent social problems and through its clarification of manifest social problems, sociological inquiry does make us increasingly accountable for the outcome of our collective and institutionalized actions.

There is a further use of this distinction between manifest and latent social problems, between the social conditions currently judged by designated categories of people in society to be undesirable and the social conditions that would be so judged, were their multifarious consequences known. Among other things, the distinction helps sociologists themselves recognize how they can move beyond prevalent social beliefs, practices, and judgments without entering upon the misplaced career of trying to impose their own values upon others.[14] Through their work, sociologists do not remain aloof from social controversy, but in their capacity as sociologists—rather than as citizens—they take a distinctive and limited part in it. They introduce pertinent sociological truths so that the substantive morality and the social policy governing the issues at stake can take account of these truths. It does not follow, however, that these truths will shape morality and policy in their every aspect. As sociologists, emphatically not as citizens, students of social problems neither exhort nor denounce, neither advocate nor reject. It is enough that they uncover the great price people sometimes pay for their settled but insufficiently examined convictions and their established but inflexible practices.

Above all, this view of the sociologist's role avoids the opposite and equal errors of assuming that in any society, "whatever is, is right" or that "whatever is, is wrong." It discards the perspectives of both the "complacent old men" and the "angry young men." It repudiates the extravagant optimism that sees everything in society as bound to turn out all right in the end, just as it repudiates the extravagant pessimism that sees nothing but catastrophe ahead. Nor does it assume that the middle way is everywhere and always the right way: the disparaging connotations of the word *mediocrity*, the condition of being intermediate between extremes, should be enough to ward us off that bland and simple-minded assumption. Rather, this sociological outlook has us examine each set of social conditions in terms of its diverse and progressively discovered consequences for the human condition, including all those consequences that bear upon the values held in the particular society. In following this path, we avoid both forms of that insolent ignorance that would have us pretend to know that society is bound to move in the one direction of cumulative improvement or in the other of continuing decline. Not least, this sociological perspective has the scientifically extraneous but humanly solid merit of leaving a substantial place for people-making-their-future-history while avoiding the utopianism-that-beguiles by recognizing that the degrees of freedom people have in that task are variously and sometimes severely limited by the objective conditions set by nature, society, and culture.[15]

To some degree, then, the distinction between manifest and latent social problems crystallizes ideas governing the range of matters selected for sociological inquiry and the role of values in such inquiry. The distinction maintains that to confine the study of social problems to only those circumstances that are expressly defined as problems in the society is arbitrarily to discard a complement of conditions that are also dysfunctional to values held by people in that society. To adopt this course is to hamstring sociological analysis by setting unnecessary limits on the selection of problems for investigation. Under the philosophy intrinsic to the distinction between manifest and latent social problems, sociologists neither abdicate their intellectual and professional responsibilities nor usurp the position of sitting in moral judgment on others.

The Social Perception of Social Problems

Linked with the distinction between manifest and latent social problems is the variability in the degree of public attention accorded diverse manifest problems. We cannot take for granted a reasonably correct public imagery of social problems: of their scale, distribution, causation, consequences, and persistence or change. These public images are often egregiously mistaken, for reasons we are beginning to understand. Some, such as mental illness, are walled off and substantially denied for a time; others, such as "crime waves" and drug addiction, become a focus of popular attention to be regarded as of far greater magnitude and as far more consequential than investigation finds them to be.[16]

A familiar and comparatively simple kind of episode brings out the social-psychological processes that make for a disparity between the objective magnitude of events (even when this is gauged by the express values of those perceiving them) and the social perceptions of them. Many more people are killed each year in the United States by automobile accidents than by airplane accidents. The number of deaths occasioned by the two are of entirely different orders of magnitude: in 1979, for example, about 52,000 Americans were put to death by automobiles and 350 by planes. Yet the intensity of public attention accorded a dramatic airplane accident in newspapers, radio, and television far outruns that accorded the cumulatively greater number of deaths in automobile accidents. The dramatic collision of two planes in midair late in 1960, for instance, aroused nationwide interest—assuredly in the nation's press, radio, and television, with even the conservative *New York Times* devoting some ten pages to the event, and probably also in uncounted millions of conversations. Yet during the days that this then worst disaster in aviation history, with its toll of 137 killed, remained in the forefront of public attention, several hundred more had been killed by automobiles.

The particular instance of marked disparity between the objective magnitude of human tragedies and the popular perceptions of them only highlights the general point (the very familiarity of the case testifying to the generality of the pattern). Popular perceptions are no safe guide to the actual magnitude of a social problem. Ill-understood but partly known processes of social perception involve the patterned omitting, supplementing, and organizing of what is selectively perceived in the social reality.[17] In the case just under review, perception seems affected by what we are better able to describe than to explain: the dramatic quality of unitary events that evoke popular interest. The airplane disaster is perceived as a *single* event, although it is of course compounded of many occurrences that eventuated in the victims going to their death. In contrast, the hundreds of automobile accidents occurring on the same day, with their, say, 200 dead, comprise a compound event that can be detected only through the aggregation of cold and impersonal numbers.[18] The import of this kind of thing is clear. Pervasive social problems that seldom have dramatic and conspicuous manifestations are apt to arouse smaller public attention than problems, less serious even when judged by the beholder's own values, which erupt in the spotlight of public drama. This is another reason that the sociologist need not order the importance of social problems in the same way as the man-and-woman-in-the-street. For, as we have noted before, even when we take, as we do, the values of the people we are observing as one basis for assessing social problems—in the present case, the sanctity of life and the tragedy of premature death—the public's perception of these problems is often found to be badly distorted.

The perception of social problems is affected by the structure of social relations between people. Long ago, Pitirim Sorokin found experimentally that the greater the social distance between victims of catastrophe and the people made aware of it, the less are these people motivated to perceive it as a problem calling for effective action and sympathy.[19] Millions of victims of famine in India or China elicit less effective sympathy from Americans than do scores of victims of catastrophes within their own national borders. Further inquiry is needed to find out whether all kinds of social problems are apt to be perceived as less significant the greater the social distance between the observer and the people most directly and visibly affected by the problem.

Related to this fact is the apparently great disparity in people's concern with public and private troubles. This disparity has been depicted in a prototypal instance by the scientist, civil servant, and novelist C. P. Snow. In his novel, *The New Men,* he has his protagonist, Lewis Eliot, muse on the morning after the bomb has been dropped on Hiroshima:

> I went straight off to sleep, woke before four, and did not get

to sleep again. It was not a bad test of how public and private worries compare in depth, I thought, when I remembered the nights I had lain awake because of private trouble. Public trouble—how many such nights of insomnia had *that* given me? The answer was, just one. On the night after Munich, I had lain sleepless—and perhaps, as I went through the early hours of August 7th [1945], I could fairly count another half.[20]

What the novelist Snow observed of his emblematic and thinly fictionalized civil servant Eliot, the sociologist Stouffer found to be true for Americans generally.[21] Stouffer's study was conducted during the summer of 1954, better described as the time when the Army-McCarthy hearings were in full swing and were being avidly watched over television by millions of Americans. During this time of public troubles, less than 1 percent in each of two matched national samples of Americans reported that "they were worried either about the threat of Communists in the United States or about civil liberties." No more than 8 percent mentioned the danger of war or other forms of international conflict as a source of anxiety. Even when interviewers directed attention to public concerns by asking whether there are "other problems you worry about or are concerned about, especially political or world problems," as many as 52 percent had nothing to add to their previous account. The number referring to problems of civil liberties doubled, rising from the unimpressive total of 1 percent to the no more impressive total of 2 percent. When asked to report the kinds of problems they had discussed with friends during the preceding week or so, half of these representative Americans said they had talked about personal or family problems only. Evidently, there was something less than a burning preoccupation with some of the most demanding public troubles of the time. These seemed remote, crowded out by the personal problems in family and place of work that turn up and the day-by-day round of social life. This research, then, provides another indication that the judgments of individual members of the society afford anything but a secure guide to the objective saliency of social problems, even for themselves. The connections between public and private troubles are difficult to detect, and it cannot be assumed that they are perceived by most people as they live out their lives.

Chronic victims of collective suffering have on occasion sensed that their problems are invisible to many in the society and have taken dramatic steps to call public attention to their situation. Boycotts, picketing, sit-ins, teach-ins, and all manner of public demonstrations are designed to increase the visibility of problems that are otherwise largely ignored because, being chronic and widespread, they tend to be taken for granted. These expedients are rough functional equivalents for providing the high visibility that automatically comes, in this day of nearly instantaneous communication, from sudden mass disasters.[22] Whatever their other purposes and consequences, such demonstrations are aimed at, and sometimes succeed in, shaking people loose from the tacit conviction that whatever is, is inevitable, and so might as well be ignored.

Value Systems and Corrigibility of Social Problems

Functionally considered, unwanted discrepancies between social standards and social reality qualify as manifest social problems only when people believe that they can do something about them. The discrepancies must be perceived as corrigible. It must be thought possible to cope with the problem, to reduce its scale if not to eliminate it altogether. The social problems most completely manifest encompass those frustrations of human purpose on the large scale that are being subjected to active efforts at prevention or control.

From this it is evident that the value orientations in a society toward the preventability or controllability of unwanted social conditions will affect the perceptions of social problems. At one extreme are the societies—China of the fifth century B.C., for example, and early Islam—appreciably committed to fatalism, a system of beliefs that holds everything to have its appointed outcome, not to be avoided or modified by foreknowledge or by effort. Among those holding to such fatalistic beliefs, there will of course be little indigenous sense of social problems: rampant morbidities, high death rates, widespread poverty, and all the rest in the calendar of troubles are simply taken as inevitable. In such a society, the social problems are chiefly or altogether latent. Only the informed observer, exempt from this philosophy of resignation and quietism, sees the possibility of reducing or eliminating these frustrating conditions.

At the other extreme are societies largely committed to an activist philosophy of life that takes just about everything in society as being in principle subject to human control. Such a society, and this is only saying in so many words what has already been implied, that is in fact coping with many of its problems—actively reducing death rates, but still regarding them as "too high," curbing previously unchecked diseases, and doing away with acute poverty—such a society may have many manifest social problems though fewer problems altogether. The active, dissatisfied society will have the more manifest problems, for people in it not only focus on the discrepancies between what they want and what they have, but try to do something about these discrepancies. The fatalistic society, on the other hand, may have a greater complement of social problems altogether—both manifest and latent—because they are moved to do little about the disparity between what exists and what they would like to exist inasmuch as they come to identify what is with what is inevitable.

This relation between fatalism and social problems is not merely a matter of definition but, empirically, is one of mutual reinforcement. As many have noted, fatalism tends to develop among those living under conditions of extreme stress or rigorous arbitrary rule. Philosophy and conditions of life interact and reinforce one another: people are apt to think fatalistically under depressed conditions and they are apt to remain under these conditions because they think fatalistically. As this has been put by A. Eustace Haydon:

> For the social process the importance of fatalism lies in the ease with which it may serve as a way of escape from responsibility for social maladjustments. Conditions of unresolved wretchedness are fertile soil for the fatalistic attitude. In many cases the anaesthesia of fatalism combines with the rigidity of long established patterns of social behavior and the interests of privileged classes to produce the quietistic resignation which results in toleration of social wrongs and incapacity for experimental change.[23]

The contrast between fatalist and activist value systems and the societies in which they occur has been deliberately exaggerated in order to point up the theoretical idea. In concrete reality, few societies have maintained a wholly passive and fatalistic outlook on all their conditions of life, just as few societies have succeeded in maintaining a wholly active and voluntaristic outlook on all their unapproved conditions of life. Strands of active rebellion against fate are found in dominantly fatalistic societies just as strands of resignation and retreatism are found in dominantly activist societies. Yet if these extremes are seldom encountered in all their detailed contrast, they have nevertheless been approximated. As Max Weber and Karl Mannheim, among others, have pointed out, the ethic of fatalism has often been replaced by the ethic of responsibility, in which knowledge of the sources of social problems and efforts to control them become defined as a moral obligation.[24]

To the extent that the ethic of responsibility spreads in a society, social problems tend to become manifest rather than remaining latent. But even within such a society, largely oriented toward directed social change, countervailing processes make for the continued latency for a time of certain social problems. One of these processes has been described by the German jurist, Jellinek, as "the normative force of the actual."[25] By this phrase he refers to the tendency, of unknown scope and prevalence, for social practices, whatever their origins, to become converted into normatively prescribed practices.

Such legitimatizing of much that exists in society tends to militate against the perception of conditions that are in fact opposed to major values held by many in the society but are nevertheless regarded as normatively right.

Associated with this tendency to *legitimatize the existent* is another that makes for tacit acceptance of the existent, if not for its moral legitimacy. According to this attitude, unwanted conditions that are not deliberately intended but are by-products of other sought-for developments rank low in the scale of social problems. These unanticipated and undesired consequences of purposive action may become a focus of attention, but they are less apt to mobilize pressure for preventive or remedial measures than those problems that violate a prevailing morality.[26] Since the problem is unintended by those whose actions in the aggregate lead to it, moral sentiments are not activated by the unfortunate circumstance. Widespread states of anxiety in a population, the wastage of talent resulting from economic inequities of access to opportunity for the development of talent, the choking of transportation in tangled traffic—these are for a long time widely considered to be among the costs of a complex society even by many who pay these costs, partly because, undesirable as they are, they are not the result of deliberate intent. In contrast, the purposed behavior that is directly at odds with socially shared norms is at once defined as a problem of society. Crime is generally regarded as a social problem; widespread alienation from the job is not. In other words, people are less apt to experience social disorganization as a social problem than they are deviant behavior.

This observation on the contrasting public saliency of social disorganization and deviant behavior is of course only a first, loose approximation. It is scarcely true that popular concern with evidences of social disorganization is absent. After all, much organized effort is devoted to the replacing of slum housing by public housing; increasing effort is mounted to rescue talent; the city-planning movement aims to bring under control the unplanned sprawl and self-defeating traffic found in the great urban centers. But this enlarged concern with problems of social disorganization as distinct from problems of deviant behavior is itself a major social change. It is, in large part, the result of an accumulating social technology, just as other social changes are in large part the result of an accumulating physical technology. Whereas deviant behavior at once attracts the indignant notice of people whose norms and values have been violated by it, social disorganization tends not to (except as it eventuates in deviant behavior). Technical specialists, unattached intellectuals, and social critics play a central role in trying to alert greater numbers of people to what they take to be the greater immorality—living complacently under conditions of social disorganization that in principle can be brought under at least partial control. Under the progressive division of social labor it becomes the office of these specialists to try to cope with social disorganization. That the social change in this direction is far from complete can be inferred from the uniform complaints by these specialists about the public apathy toward the problems with which they deal.

Social problems have been identified as the substantial, unwanted discrepancies between what exists in a society and what a functionally significant collectivity within that society seriously (rather than in fantasy) wants to exist in it. The scale of these discrepancies is affected in either or both of two ways: by a raising of standards and by a deterioration of social conditions. There is no paradox, then, in finding that some complex, industrial societies, having a comparatively high plane of material life and rapid advancement of cultural values, may nevertheless be regarded by their members as more problem-ridden than other societies with substantially less material wealth and cultural achievement. Nor is there any longer a paradox in finding that as conditions improve in a society (as gauged by widespread values), popular satisfaction may nevertheless decline. Tocqueville noted this pattern more than a century ago:

> It was precisely in those parts of France [in the reign of Louis XIV] where there had been most improvements that popular discontent ran highest. . . . For it is not always when things are going from bad to worse that revolutions break out. On the contrary, it oftener happens that when a people which has put up with an oppressive rule over a long period without protest suddenly finds the government relaxing its pressure, it takes up arms against it. Thus the social order overthrown by a revolution is almost always better than the one immediately preceding it, and experience teaches us that, generally speaking, the most perilous moment for a bad government is one when it seeks to mend its ways. . . . For the mere fact that certain abuses have been remedied draws attention to others and they now appear more galling; people may suffer less, but their sensibility is exacerbated.[27]

In short, as the "rising tide of expectations" advances more than the achieving of shared objectives, there tends to develop a sense of collective "relative deprivation," a widespread feeling that people "are deprived of some desired state or thing, in comparison with some standard, or with the real or imagined condition of other people."[28] Thus, a study found that the urban racial disturbances of the 1960s were less a matter of responses to conditions in the local community than one of responses to "multiple deprivations and frustrations" suffered by blacks throughout the society.[29]

This observation reminds us once again of that major premise in sociology: *The discrepancies between social standards and actual social conditions that are defined as social problems have both subjective and objective components.**

"Value-free Sociology": Unmuddling a Muddle

The distinction we have drawn between manifest and latent social problems helps to clarify the question whether sociology is or is not "value-free," and the related question whether it is possible to achieve objective knowledge about social phenomena. Much of that debate has succeeded only in noisily obscuring the central theoretical issues formulated by Max Weber as early as the first decades of this century.[30]

Of course, Weber argued, scientists, like everyone else, have values. And, of course, those values influence their selection of problems for investigation. In that sense, science in general and sociology in particular are *not* value-free. Far from it; with or without intent, the choice of problems has "value-relevance" (*Wertbeziehung*). Their values may lead scientists to refuse to work on certain scientific problems—for example, research that will lead to still more catastrophic weapons systems—or may lead them to focus on certain other scientific problems—for example, research on the origins of cancer, or on the social mechanisms that perpetuate racial discrimination.

How do values enter into sociological inquiry? The question is important not merely for sociologists—an inconsiderable tribe, at best—but also for the considerable rest of society. Sociological research is increasingly employed as one basis for forming or justifying social policy. For example, the Coleman Report on Educational Opportunity has often been invoked to justify the practice of bussing pupils in order to decrease racial segregation in public schools and to improve the quality of education provided to children of the ethnic minorities.

The important question of how values affect sociological inquiry is often obscured, not clarified, by polemics. For that reason, it may be useful to look at a further example of how *moral issues inhere in the very formulation of problems for sociological research.*

A social scientist claiming to have no traffic with values may nonetheless have designed his or her research problems in such a way that the results will be useful to one group and not to another. For example, "value-free" sociologists investigating the use of prop-

*For an extended discussion of this premise, see "Social Knowledge and Public Policy," Chapter 9 in this volume—editors' note.

aganda for mass persuasion proceed with their study and state their findings: If certain techniques of persuasion are used, a given proportion of people will be induced to take the desired action. Investigators ostensibly do not take a stand; they merely report findings. But solution of a moral problem by abdicating moral responsibility is no solution at all. It overlooks the crux of the problem: the *first formulation* of the question was conditioned by implied values. Had they been influenced by democratic values like the dignity of the individual, they would have framed the problem in terms not only of the immediate result of propaganda but also of its more remote effects on the individual personality and the society. A society under a constant barrage of "effective" half-truths and exploitation of its mass anxieties may soon lose the mutual confidence and trust that a stable society needs. An investigation based in democratic values would be more likely than a "morally neutral" one to address such questions. Moreover, because of the way the investigation is formulated, the results they obtain are more likely to be of use to one group—the potential users of propaganda—than to others in the society at large.[31]

The interplay between values and sociological research moves beyond the formulation of problems. For once the investigation has begun, the modes of assessing the evidence for knowledge claims are again value-connected. The institution of science, like all other social institutions, has its values, specified in the form of norms. One of those norms, described as "organized skepticism," calls for critical surveillance of public claims to scientific knowledge by competent peers. The vigorous debates over the question of "value-free" science themselves exemplify organized skepticism in action, action carried out by some of the same scientists who deny that there are norms in science. But, of course, passionate criticism of others' work only exhibits in practice what the norm of organized skepticism calls for in principle.

It is no paradox, therefore, to say that values and norms can help to produce objectivity in scientific inquiry. Both tacit and explicit norms govern what kinds of evidence will be judged acceptable by the pertinent community of scientists, requiring individual scientists to approximate objectivity in their scientific work. Once again, as throughout this essay, we find that otherwise differing orientations in sociology share ideas, including this decisive one that science is more than a value-determined set of opinions. It is an idea central to structural and functional sociology, as we have seen, just as it is an idea central to symbolic interactionism, sometimes described as a conflicting orientation. Thus Howard Becker, a leading exponent of symbolic interactionism, writes:

> I take it that all social scientists agree that, given a question and
> a method of reaching an answer, any scientist, whatever his po-
> litical or other values, should arrive at much the same answer,
> an answer given by the world of recalcitrant fact that is "out
> there" whatever we think about it. Insofar as a Left Wing soci-
> ologist proposes to base political action on his own or others'
> research findings, he had better strive for this and hope that it
> can be done. Otherwise, his actions may fail because of what his
> values prevented him from seeing.[32]

It is misleading, then, to formulate the issue of a "value-free
sociology" in terms of the false alternatives of a science *entirely unrelated* to values and one *entirely determined* by values. From the early
work of Max Weber to the recent formulations by the scientist-phi-
losopher Michael Polanyi and the philosopher of science Karl Popper,
there has developed the understanding that objectivity in science is
in part possible because a framework of institutionalized values and
norms provides the basis for it.

To recapitulate the ways in which values and norms enter into
scientific work, including the sociological analysis of social problems,
without converting that work into collections of merely subjective
opinion:

1.   The values of scientists affect their selection and formulation
      of problems.
2.   Differently formulated problems have differing potentials
      of utility for differing sectors of the society.
3.   Moral choices are thus involved in the selection and for-
      mulation of problems.
4.   Science itself, as a social institution, has its own set of values
      and norms.
5.   That normative framework (for example, the norm of or-
      ganized skepticism) makes for objectivity in science.

To describe this array of ideas as expressing the view that science
in general and sociology in particular is "value-free" because it rejects
the notion of science as merely subjective sets of opinions would only
be to play fast and loose with language.

SOCIAL DISORGANIZATION

Social problems can be usefully thought of in two broad classes:
social disorganization and deviant behavior. Even without examining
the theoretical basis of these two concepts, we can be sure that they
focus not on totally different phenomena but on different aspects of
the same ones. We find in each kind of concrete social problem

evidence of both social disorganization and deviant behavior, though in differing compound. The distinction between matters of disorganization and matters of deviant behavior is useful if we note that the two interact and, under certain conditions, reinforce each other.

No single concept of social disorganization is employed by sociologists today, any more than yesterday. But there is much agreement. "Social disorganization" refers to inadequacies in a social system that keep people's collective and individual purposes from being as fully realized as they could be. Social disorganization is relative. It is not tied to any absolute standard, which would be Utopian, but to a standard of what, so far as we know, could be accomplished under attainable conditions. When we say that a group or organization or community or society is disorganized, we mean that its structure of statuses and roles is not working as effectively as it might to achieve valued purposes. Whatever the theoretical persuasion of the observer—functional sociologist, symbolic interactionist, or social critic— this type of statement amounts to a *technical judgment about the workings of social systems.*

Sources of Social Disorganization

We identify four major sources of social disorganization: conflicting interests and values, conflicting status and role obligations, faulty socialization, and faulty social communication. Put in general terms, the type of social problem involved in social disorganization arises not from people failing to live up to the requirements of their social statuses, as is the case with deviant behavior, but from the faulty organization of these statuses into a reasonably coherent social system.

Conflicting interests and values.   The potential for social disorganization comes partly from the basic structural fact that social groups and social strata have some interests and values in common and also some different, sometimes conflicting, interests and values. *People may work at cross-purposes precisely because they are living up to the norms of their respective positions in society.* When the social organization of an economy, for example, does not provide ways of settling clashes between workers, management, and stockholders, the result is an unstable condition in which interest groups cannot even estimate soundly what actions would be in their own interest. Such poorly regulated conflicts of interest, then, both reflect social disorganization and contribute to it.

Conflicting status and role obligations.   People inevitably occupy a set of statuses in society—say, as parent, Catholic, Democrat, carpenter, and labor-union member. The statuses in the status-set can pull in different directions by calling for opposed modes of behavior. When the social system fails to provide a widely shared set of priorities among these competing obligations, the individuals subject to them experience strains. Their behavior becomes unpredictable and socially disruptive, which may be judged "good" or "bad," but in either case remains disorganizing. Competition between obligations of home and work, of local mores and national law, of religion and state, of friendship and "the organization" makes for potential conflicts. When they do flare up and further disorganization results, the fault—not in a moral sense but in an objective, almost geological, one—lies in the inept structuring of the potential conflicts, not in the ineptitude of the people confronted with them.

Faulty socialization. Socialization is the acquisition of the attitudes, values, skills, and knowledge needed to fulfill social roles or to modify them effectively. Defects in this process are a prominent source of disorganization. For example, rapid social mobility for the individual or rapid social change in the social system often occurs without adequate resocialization of individuals involved in these processes. People simply do not know how to behave in their newly acquired statuses or in radically changed social situations. Not knowing the informal limits on his formally prescribed authority, the new boss may "throw his weight around," making demands on workers that, though well within the scope of formal authority, are far beyond the limits of the group's normative expectations. Or, not socialized to recognize significant changes in racial, ethnic, and gender roles, the boss or fellow workers continue to act in terms of obsolete images of what blacks or women "can do." The effectiveness of organized social effort declines in such cases, and problems of disorganization ensue.

Faulty social communication. Disorganization results also from structural inadequacies or partial breakdowns in channels of communication between people in a social system. The people in a purposive association, local community, or national society must be able to communicate since they depend on one another for doing what they are socially expected to do and what they individually want to do. Many studies have shown that faulty communication in an organization, even without strongly opposed interests and values, leads to disorganization.

Disorganization and Unorganization

Seen in time perspective, some social situations can be better thought of as cases of unorganization rather than of disorganization. In unorganization a system of social relations has not yet evolved, while in disorganization acute or chronic disruptions occur in a more or less established system of social relations. The difference is a little like the difference between an apartment about to be occupied by new tenants, with furniture still scattered almost at random, lacking structural arrangement and functional utility, and an apartment long lived in but now a shambles after a knock-down-drag-out fight. The first is a case of no array; the second, one of disarray. Corresponding social instances are a situation where the rules and the status structure are vague or still unevolved, as when people find themselves in a previously unexperienced kind of catastrophe, versus a situation where there is a complex of ill-assorted, incompatible, or badly linked statuses so that individual and collective purposes are frustrated.

DEVIANT BEHAVIOR

Deviant behavior on a sizable scale represents quite another kind of social problem. Whereas social disorganization refers to faults in the arrangement and working of social statuses and roles, deviant behavior refers to conduct that departs significantly from the norms set for people in their social statuses. The same behavior may be construed as deviant or conforming, depending upon the social statuses of the people exhibiting the behavior. This fact is simply a corollary of the sociological notion that each social status involves its own set of normative obligations (although many statuses may share some of the same obligations). When an adult acts "like a child" or a layman acts "like a physician," he or she engages in deviant behavior. But as these allusive phrases imply, the same behavior by children and by physicians would of course be in accord with normative expectations. That is why deviant behavior cannot be described in the abstract but must be related to the norms that are socially defined as technically appropriate and morally binding for people occupying various statuses.

As used by the sociologist, the term "deviant behavior" is thus a technical rather than a moralizing one. But as the term has entered into the vernacular, its morally neutral denotation has become overladen with the connotation of moral censure. The reasons for this are understandable and theoretically interesting. Moralistic responses to deviant behavior have one or another, or both, of two sources, depending upon the distance of people from that behavior. For associates who are in direct social interaction with a person, his or her sustained deviant behavior is apt to be disruptive. Failure to live up to socially defined expectations makes life difficult or miserable for others. They cannot safely count on that person, although in fact they must. Whatever the intent, deviant behavior interferes, at the least, with the measure of predictability required by social relations and thus results in a punishing experience for the associates of the deviating person. They in turn respond by a familiar and important kind of social control. Through spontaneous expression of their injured feelings or by more deliberate sanctioning behavior, role-partners act in such ways as to bring the deviating person back into line with their normative expectations, if only so that they can go about their usual business. This, then, is one source of response to deviant behavior.

Much the same type of response to observed deviant behavior occurs among members of a social system even when they are not *directly* engaged in immediate social relations with the deviating person. In such cases, their hostile responses can be described as disinterested. They themselves have little or nothing to lose by the deviating person's departures from norms; their own situation is not damaged by that behavior. Nevertheless, they too respond with hostility. For, having internalized the moral content of the norms that are being violated, they experience the deviant behavior as threatening or repudiating the social validity of norms that they hold to be right and important. Reprisals of various kinds can be described as stemming from moral indignation,[33] a disinterested attack on people who depart from norms of the group, even when the deviation does not interfere with the performance of one's own roles since one is not socially connected with the persons engaging in the deviant act. The pattern of moral indignation was exemplified in the 1960s by attacks of American construction workers ("hardhats") on radical students or on those who resembled these students in mere outward appearance.

Deviant Behavior and Social Response

When we say that deviant behavior departs from norms set for given statuses, we do not wish to imply that social responses to such deviation occur uniformly and without respect of person (or to use the sociologist Max Weber's favored phrase, *sine ira et studio*—"without anger or partiality"). On the contrary. We have noted throughout

Contemporary Social Problems, and especially in the chapter on crime and juvenile delinquency, that social sanctions are not evenly applied to all those who have violated social rules, with the race, ethnicity, class, sex, and age of violators being only among the more conspicuous bases for differentials.

If it were not already evident to most sociologists, the existence of such differentials in imposing sanctions would alert them to the necessity of having the theory of deviant behavior handle two distinct though related problems: (1) how to account for varying rates of rule-violating behavior in various groups, social strata and other social systems; and (2) how to account for differences in the societal reactions to such behavior, depending in part on the social characteristics of those exhibiting that behavior and of those judging it.

Nonconforming and Aberrant Behavior

As a first approximation, all substantial departures of behavior from social norms can be caught up in the single concept and associated term, deviant behavior. But first approximations are useful to the degree that they are recognized for what they are: rough discriminations to be progressively replaced by more exacting ones. And so it is with the concept of deviant behavior. Since departures from established norms differ greatly in both character and social consequences, they should not be indiscriminately grouped together.

Two major varieties of deviant behavior can be usefully distinguished on the basis of their structure and their consequences for social systems. The first may be called "nonconforming behavior"; the second, "aberrant behavior." Both types retain the technical conception of deviant behavior in sociological analysis; the distinction does not smuggle in moral judgments through the back door of connotative language. It only helps us to identify systematic differences in kinds of deviant behavior that are alike only in that they move away from what is prescribed by specifiable social norms.

These types of nonconforming behavior and aberrant behavior differ in several conjoint respects. *First,* nonconformers announce their dissent publicly; they do not try to hide their departures from social norms. Political or religious dissenters insist on making their dissent known to as many as will look or listen; aberrant criminals seek to avoid the limelight of public scrutiny. Contrast pacifists who burn their draft cards in public with draft dodgers who try to escape into obscurity.

This patterned attitude toward visibility links up with a *second* basic difference between the two kinds of deviants. Nonconformers challenge the legitimacy of social norms they reject, or at least challenge their applicability to certain kinds of situations. Organized "sit-in" campaigns designed to attack local norms of racial segregation in restaurants and schools afford familiar examples of this aspect of nonconforming behavior. Aberrants, in contrast, acknowledge the legitimacy of the norms they violate but consider such violation expedient or expressive of their state of mind. They may try to justify their own behavior, but they do not argue that theft is right and murder virtuous.

Third and correlatively, nonconformers aim to change the norms they are denying in practice. They want to replace what they believe to be morally suspect norms with ones having a sound moral basis. Aberrants, in contrast, try primarily to escape the sanctioning force of existing norms, without proposing substitutes for them. When subject to social sanction, nonconformers typically appeal to a higher morality; except as an instrumental device, aberrants do not; at most they appeal to extenuating circumstances.

Fourth, and possibly as a result of the preceding components of their behavior, nonconformers are acknowledged, however reluctantly, by conventional members of society to depart from prevailing norms for disinterested purposes and not for personal gain. Again in contrast, aberrants are generally assumed to be deviating from the norms in order to serve their own interests. Although the law of the land may not make the formal distinction between nonconformers and aberrants in this respect, many members of society do. Whatever the generic concept of deviant behavior might seem to pronounce to the contrary, the two types of social deviants are widely acknowledged as having far different social consequences. Those courageous highwaymen of seventeenth-century England, John Nevinson and his much advertised successor, Dick Turpin, were not of a sociological piece with that courageous nonconformist of their time, Oliver Cromwell. And in the event that one's political or religious sympathies, as well as the detachment made easy by historical distance, serve to make this observation self-evident, one should reexamine those judgments that once made Trotsky or Nehru little more than criminals heading up sizable gangs of followers.

Fifth, and for present purposes finally, nonconformers, with their appeal to an allegedly higher morality, can in historically propitious circumstances lay claim to legitimacy by drawing upon the ultimate values, rather than the particular norms, of the society. They are trying to make justice a social reality rather than an institutionalized fiction. They are for genuine freedom of speech rather than its everyday pretense. They would rearrange the social structure to provide actual equality of opportunity for all people to develop prized talents and not allow the social simulacra of equality to be mistaken for the real thing. In these ways, their nonconformity can appeal to the moral values that are in some measure being denied in social practice while being reaffirmed in ideological doctrine. Nonconformers can appeal to the tacit recognition by others of discrepancies between the prized values and the social reality.[34] They thus have at least the prospect of obtaining the assent of other, initially less critical and venturesome, members of society whose ambivalence toward the current social structure can be drawn upon for support. Nonconformity is not a private dereliction but a thrust toward a new morality or a promise to restore a morality held to have been put aside in social practice. In this respect again, nonconformers are far removed from aberrants, who have nothing new to propose and nothing old to restore, but seek only to satisfy their private interests or to express their private cravings.[35]

Future investigations into nonconformity will need to take care that they do not move from an unthinking orthodoxy to an equally unthinking heterodoxy by valuing nonconformity for its own sake. We must remember that what is nonconformity to the norms of one group is often conformity to the norms of another group. There is no merit in escaping the error of taking heterodoxy to be inevitably false or ugly or sinister only to be caught up in the opposite error of thinking heterodoxy to be inevitably true or beautiful or altogether excellent. Put in so many words, this is a commonplace. Yet people alienated from the world about them often do take heterodoxy as a good in itself, whatever its character. And others, perhaps in reaction to the cases, familiar in every age, of true merit being neglected or punished because it is unorthodox, are quick to value heterodoxy or countercyclicalism, all apart from its substance. In every time, apparently, shrewd men have recognized that an appropriate kind of seeming heterodoxy appeals greatly even to the more orthodox members of society. As British lecturers to American audiences have evidently known for a long period, and as "radical" American lecturers to civic clubs, literary societies, and businessmen's associations know now: there is no better way to win the hearts of their audiences than by attacking part of what they stand for while intimating that they are not beyond redemption. These and other expressions of specious nonconformity have long been recognized, particularly by some of the most notable nonconformers of their time. It has been said of Marx, for example, that "all his life [he] detested two phenomena with peculiar passion: disorderly life and histrionic display. It seemed to him that Bohemianism and deliberate flouting of conventions was but inverted Philistinism, emphasizing and paying homage to the very same false values by exaggerated protest against them, and exhibiting therefore the same fundamental vulgarity."[36]

Attributes of Social Norms and Deviant Behavior

Concepts such as conformity, nonconformity, and aberrant behavior must be kept under theoretical control if they are not to become misleading. To begin with, these concepts suggest that one can readily identify behavior that represents compliance with a norm or departure from it. But while such clarity can be achieved on the conceptual plane it is difficult to achieve in social practice. Law courts provide a vast abundance of examples testifying how difficult it is to find out whether a particular act was deviant by trying to match up the act with pertinent norms embodied in the law. It becomes even more difficult to compare acts with kinds of norms, such as folkways and mores, that are less carefully formulated than legal norms.

In terms of sociological theory, we identify several dimensions of social norms. *First,* norms vary in their location in the *spectrum of normative control.* This location can be roughly gauged by the "4 P's": Norms may *prescribe* behavior or *proscribe* it; they may only indicate what behavior is *preferred* or simply *permitted. Second,* norms differ in the *extent of agreement* they gain within the group or society. The range is from almost full consensus, as in most societies regarding the norm that proscribes the kidnapping of children, to limited agreement confined to a small sector, as, in some societies, with norms governing the payment of taxes upon income. *Third,* norms differ in the intensity of *affective or moral commitment to them.* They may engage deepseated values or only superficial support among those who subscribe to them. *Fourth,* norms differ in the *social structure of control* associated with them. These control structures range from agencies formally and specifically charged with responsibility for imposing social sanctions upon deviants to altogether diffuse, informal, and spontaneous sanctions resulting from the punitive responses of people who directly suffer from these deviations. *Fifth,* norms differ in the *kind of adherence* they require: only overt behavioral conformity, only inner assent, or both. *Sixth* and finally in this short listing, norms differ in the extent of their *elasticity,* sometimes requiring close adherence to a form of behavior or belief, sometimes allowing much leeway before behavior or belief is defined as significantly deviant.[37]

This last attribute of norms, their degree of elasticity, is particularly important in the study of deviant behavior. It reminds us that strict and continued compliance with rigorously defined norms is only a mental construct, at most only approximated for brief occasions in social life (as on highly ceremonial occasions). For the most part, social norms provide for a range of behavior that is judged admissible even though it departs from the strict letter of the norms. The extent of this range differs among norms and for the same norm under differing social conditions. For example, when it is widely felt that the group or society is in grave danger—as under conditions of war or after a great catastrophe—the range of permissiveness contracts, as exemplified by martial law. Much remains to be discovered about the social processes affecting the extent of patterned leeway for compliance with norms required by a group. Until this general knowledge of regularities grows considerably larger, variations in expected compliance must be empirically investigated in each case.

Institutionalized Evasions of Institutional Rules

Apart from the elasticity of norms that provides for degrees of socially acceptable conformity is another pattern that provides for systematic nonconformity to them. This has been described as the pattern of "institutionalized evasions of institutional rules."[38]

Evasions of institutional rules are themselves institutionalized when they are (1) patterned in fairly well-defined types; (2) adopted by substantial numbers of people rather than being scattered subterfuges independently and privately arrived at; (3) organized in the form of a fairly elaborate social machinery made up of tacitly cooperating participants, including those who are socially charged with implementing the rules; and (4) rarely punished and when they are, punished in largely symbolic forms that serve primarily to reaffirm the sanctity of the rules.[39]

These social patterns of evasion develop when practical exigencies confronting a collectivity require goal-oriented or adaptive behavior that is at odds with long-established norms or when newly formulated norms (most clearly in the form of new legislation) are at odds with long-established social practices and sentiments. Such evasions on the large scale are signs of malintegration between norms and widespread, socially induced needs.

When there is a gross discrepancy between newly instituted legal norms and local mores, all manner of procedures for evading the full force of the norms will be adopted: nullification, circumvention, subterfuge, connivance, and legal fictions. Even such crude qualitative knowledge (as distinct from precise quantitative knowledge) of the conditions making for institutionalized evasions can serve to forecast the occurrence of evasions on a substantial scale. Thus it was possible to anticipate, a half-dozen years before, the broad outlines of response to a decision such as that taken unanimously by the Supreme Court on May 17, 1954, which declared unconstitutional the separate-but-equal doctrine (*Plessy* v. *Ferguson*) that had enabled communities to exclude black children from public schools maintained for white children. One such forecast read as follows:

> In an unfavorable cultural climate—and this does not necessarily exclude the benign regions of the Far South—the immediate resort will probably have to be that of working through legal and administrative federal controls over extreme discrimination, with full recognition that, in all probability, these regulations will be systematically evaded for some time to come. In such cultural regions, we may expect nullification of the law as the common practice, perhaps as common as was the case in the nation at large with respect to the Eighteenth Amendment, often with the connivance of local officers of the law. The large gap between the new law and local mores will not *at once* produce significant change of prevailing practices: token punishments of violations will probably be more common than effective control. At best, one may assume that significant change will be fitful, and excruciatingly slow. But secular changes in the economy may in due course lend support to the new legal framework of control over discrimination. As the economic shoe pinches because the illiberals do not fully mobilize the resources of industrial manpower nor extend their local markets through equitable wage-payments, they may slowly abandon some discriminatory practices as they come to find that these do not always pay—even the discriminator.[40]

Another instance of the pattern of institutionalized evasions is provided by widespread social response to the law governing divorce in the state of New York. Here we see the law lagging behind the changing interests, values, and wants of a substantial part of the population. This lag has given rise to a social machinery built up of tacitly collaborating clients, lawyers, judges, trained connivers, and specialized inventors of make-believe evidence of adultery. A grand jury investigating the matter "confirmed what had long been suspected: fraud, perjury, collusion, and connivance pervade matrimonial actions of every type." They discovered "a wholesale system of fabricating evidence for a divorce, the service of a correspondent and witness being supplied for a fee." The institutionalized though ostensibly proscribed evasions are thoroughly known to officers of the court. As one lawyer summed it up: "Ninety percent of the undefended matrimonials are based on perjury. They are all arranged. The raids are made with the consent of the defendant. We all know this. The judges know it. It's embarrassing to go [to court]."[41]

We see in this particular case the dynamics of institutionalized evasions. A legal rule is experienced as excessively restrictive by a substantial number of people whose status in the community is otherwise "respectable" and conforming. This goes far toward subverting the legitimacy of the rule. A system of evasive practices develops to close the gap between the law and the socially legitimatized though illegal wants of many people. The law is maintained on the books, not as a result of "inertia" but in response to certain interested groups in the community that are sufficiently powerful to have their way. But they are not powerful enough to prevent the circumvention of the law by other "respectable" segments of the community who find it unduly cramping and who deny its legitimacy. During the interim of this social conflict, the social system evolves a pattern of institutionalized evasions in which the rules remain nominally intact while devices for neutralizing them evolve. Such institutionalized evasions give rise to institutional change—in this case, the change of the law governing divorce—when the balance of power between contending sectors of the "respectable" community shifts in favor of those who have made the evasions in the first place.[42]

Historical instances of institutionalized evasions that have run their full course bring out the connections between the pattern of regularized evasion and subsequent institutional change. A meticulously analyzed case is that of the eighteenth-century criminal law in England. The punishments for certain crimes then prescribed by law were so severe as to be at great variance with sentiments and values widely held in the society. As a result, the law was ridden with "absurd technicalities" that were designed to give "a criminal undue chances of escape from conviction by the practical revolt of jurymen against the immorality of penalties out of all proportion to moral guilt, and by the constant commutation of capital for some lighter punishment."[43] In due course, simple theft was no longer treated as a capital crime after generations in which "juries, judges, prosecutors, and complainants collaborated" to evade the full force of the extremely punitive law.[44] Once again we see that the social functionaries charged with administering the widely rejected norms are the best situated to evade their literal force and that they do precisely that. To some extent, all this was recognized by observers of human society long ago. From the time of the ancient Roman adage—*Quid leges sine moribus?* to what avail are laws without support of the mores?—down to the present, people have recognized that legal norms will be evaded on the large scale when they are substantially opposed to other norms or values or to what can be practically carried into effect.

The pattern of institutionalized evasions is not at all peculiar to complex literate societies. It has been amply identified in nonliterate societies by such anthropologists as Malinowski, Radcliffe-Brown, Firth, and others, the gist of their observations being admirably set forth by Alexander Macbeath, as when he notes that "even the most rigid rules, those which have a supernatural sanction, can be evaded or circumvented not only with the connivance but with the backing of public opinion and legalized usage, when the exceptions are in conformity with the people's sense of what is right."[45]

Since the persistence of institutionalized evasions tends to make for changes in the structure of social norms, actions that were at one time deviant behavior later become conforming behavior. This, then, reminds us of what we already know: Not only is deviant behavior relative to the norms of a designated group, so that it can simultaneously be described as deviation from one set of norms and conformance with another, but it is also relative to changing norms, so that what is regarded in one generation as deviation becomes in the next a self-evident kind of conformity.[46]

THEORIES OF DEVIANCE

No single theory of deviance is both exhaustive and exclusive. An exhaustive theory would explain every aspect of deviance. It would explain the formation of social rules and differing rates of rule-breaking in various groups, the processes leading people to enter upon careers as deviants, and the consequences of all this for different individuals and groups. An exclusive theory would have no rivals in accounting for the aspects of deviance it deals with. In place of one exhaustive and exclusive theory of deviance, there is, and will no doubt continue to be, a plurality of theories.

The principal theories of deviance—known as differential association, anomie-and-opportunity-structures, labeling, and social conflict theories—are merely introduced here in order to identify what they have in common; what distinguishes each from the rest; how they become extended or consolidated; how they become vulgarized as they are widely adopted for a time; and, most of all, how the focus on key questions in each theoretical orientation leaves largely untouched the questions central to the others.

Theories and Theoretical Orientations

To begin with, we must recognize that when sociologists speak of "theories" of deviance, they only adopt a convenient abbreviation. Strictly speaking, none is a theory in the exacting sense—a set of logically connected assumptions giving rise to a continuing flow of hypotheses that can be confirmed or falsified by empirical research. Rather, they are general theoretical orientations that indicate *kinds of sociological variables* to be taken into account in trying to understand deviance. They do not state definite relationships between sets of *specific variables*.[47] Thus, it has been noted that anomie theory identifies types of deviant behavior without specifying the conditions under which each will occur, and that "the labeling approach (with its lack of clear-cut definition, failure so far to produce a coherent set of interrelated propositions, testable hypotheses, and so on) ought not, at least at this stage, to be considered a theory in any formal sense." This critic rightly adds: "Formal theoretical status, however, should not be the major criterion in assessing its value."[48] These sets of ideas are therefore sometimes described not as theories but as theoretical perspectives, conceptual schemes, or paradigms. Nevertheless, we shall follow general practice by using the convenient abbreviation "theory" as we proceed to note its uses in raising significant questions about deviance and in proposing the forms which answers to those questions should take.

The existence of many theories need not mean that they are in conflict and that we must choose among them. Often they are complementary, not contradictory.[49] And so it is with sociological theories of deviance. Each has its own theoretical thrust. Each has its own key questions, focused on selected aspects of the complex social phenomena of deviance. Furthermore, each theory typically neglects other questions. For as the brilliant philosopher of literature, Kenneth Burke, once put it: "A way of seeing is also a way of not seeing—a focus upon object A involves a neglect of object B."[50]

The theory of *differential association,* set forth by the criminologist, E. H. Sutherland, states that individuals become deviants by associating with others, principally in face-to-face groups, who prefer and practice various forms of deviant behavior. This theory centers on the problem of the cultural transmission of deviant behavior. Its key question therefore inquires into the modes of socialization, the ways in which patterns of deviant behavior are learned from others. How does one learn to become a professional thief, for example, as compared with learning to become a professional lawyer or physician? With its focus on this key question, the theory has little to say about how those patterns of behavior developed in the first place.

The theory of *anomie-and-opportunity-structures,* set forth by Robert K. Merton, states that rates of various kinds of deviant behavior (not merely crime) are highest where people have little access to socially legitimate means for achieving culturally induced goals; for example, the culture affirms that all members of the society have a right to climb whatever is defined as the ladder of success, but many are excluded from acceptable means for doing so.[51] Since the key question directs us to the socially structured *sources* of deviant behavior, the theory has next to nothing to say about how such patterns of behavior are transmitted or how these initial departures from the rules sometimes crystallize into careers as deviants.

Labeling theory, or, as it is sometimes called, the societal reaction approach to deviance, was originally set forth by Edwin M. Lemert and Howard S. Becker and advanced by Kai T. Erikson, Aaron V. Cicourel, and John I. Kitsuse.[52] Becker states the theory crisply: "Social groups create deviance by making rules whose infraction constitutes deviance, and by applying those rules to particular people and labeling them as outsiders." The theory thus centers on the question: What are the processes through which people are assigned a social identity as deviants by others and enter upon ongoing careers as deviants? Lemert distinguishes between "primary" and "secondary" deviance. Primary deviance is the initial rule-breaking behavior that sometimes leads to the affixing of a stigmatizing label— like "delinquent," "criminal," or "psychotic"—to the rule breaker by such rule enforcers as the police and the courts. Secondary deviance refers to the responses stigmatized people make to such societal reactions to their deviance.

Labeling theory, with its focus on the key question of the formation of deviant careers, has little to say about the sources of primary deviance or of differing rates of deviant behavior in various groups, the very questions which are central to theories of differential association and anomie. As one of the founders of labeling theory perceptively notes, "when attention is turned to the rise and fall of moral ideas and the transformation of definitions of deviance, labeling theory and ethnomethodology do little to enlighten the process."[53]

It is precisely this sort of matter that *conflict theory* takes as its key question. The main thrust of this theory, as set forth in variant versions by Austin Turk and Richard Quinney, is that a more or less homogeneous power elite incorporates its interests in the making and imposing of legal rules.[54] It centers on the question: How do legal rules and other norms get formulated and administered? Focusing on this question means neglecting the other questions about deviant behavior that are central to the preceding theories we have touched upon. For that reason, the several theories have a *potential* for being complementary.

The various theoretical perspectives can be brought together in a more comprehensive theory, of course, only if they adopt mutually consistent assumptions and give rise to compatible hypotheses. This is far from the case. Exponents of one perspective often question the assumptions or empirical claims of others. To take only one example, the labeling theorist Lemert states, in opposition to the conflict theorists, that the empirical evidence now available makes it "doubtful that the emergence of new morality and procedures for defining deviance can be laid to the creations of any one group, class, or elite. Rather they are the products of the interaction of groups."[55]

Extensions and Fusions of Theory

Occasionally theories of deviance focusing on distinct key questions have been extended or consolidated. Richard Cloward and Lloyd Ohlin,[56] for example, consolidated Sutherland's differential association theory and Merton's theory of anomie-and-opportunity-structures. They did so by introducing the idea that some people have better access than others not only to the *legitimate* opportunity structure but also to the *illegitimate* one. For instance, in order to enter upon a sustained career of deviance in crime, drugs, and the like, one needs to learn the ropes from an accessible subculture. This theoretical development was extended further by Richard Jessor and his associates in an exacting field study of deviant behavior, especially the heavy use of alcohol, which combined the Merton and Cloward-and-Ohlin conceptions with the social learning theory of the psychologist Julian B. Rotter.[57] Another example is provided by the work of Albert K. Cohen, which fuses anomie and interactionist perspectives to arrive at a way of explaining collective responses to problems of adapting to anomic conditions.

Apart from explicit efforts to consolidate theories of deviance, sometimes the same particular ideas are used by theorists of differing perspectives. Labeling theorists, for example, have instructively adopted the concept of "the self-fulfilling prophecy." As we have seen, that concept refers to the process through which widespread beliefs about some people, even though false, create a social environment that so limits their range of options that their subsequent behavior seems to confirm those beliefs.* Becker, Erikson, and other labeling theorists have usefully applied the concept to the formation of deviant careers:

> Treating a person as though he were generally rather than specifically deviant produces a self-fulfilling prophecy. It sets in motion several mechanisms which conspire to shape the person in the image people have of him. One tends to be cut off, after

*The concept of the self-fulfilling prophecy is set forth in the concluding chapter of this book—editor's note.

being identified as deviant, from participation in more conventional groups. . . . When caught, one is treated in accordance with the popular diagnosis of why one is that way, and the treatment itself may likewise produce increasing deviance.[58]

Popular Distortions of Theories*

As sociological ideas spread into the society they undergo changes, and not always for the better. One such change is their oversimplification into proverbs, which invariably fail to state the conditions under which they presumably hold true. Thus differential-association theory can be vulgarized into the proverbial "evil companions corrupt"; anomie theory into the biblical statement that "many are called, but few are chosen"; labeling theory into the proverb "give a dog a bad name and hang him" as well as Hamlet's "there is nothing good or bad, but thinking makes it so"; and conflict theory into the proverbial "he who pays the piper calls the tune."

Along with simplifications of these theories are self-interested, made-to-order distortions of them, one of which has lately found its way into history. We can be reasonably confident that Richard Nixon was not given to reading treatises on the societal reaction perspective. But he invented a crude version of it by attacking the press and other mass media for *producing* the Watergate episode. For, in Nixon's opinion, it was not the *actions* of breaking into Democratic party headquarters, forging letters ascribed to opposing candidates for the presidency, pressuring corporations to contribute illegal funds to his election campaign, or repeatedly committing perjury that constituted the deviance. It was rather, he said, the pernicious societal labeling of the people engaged in these actions as thieves, forgers, bagmen, and liars-under-oath that created the deviance, with all of its personal and social consequences.

The defensive Nixon doctrine surely has no direct connection with any sociological theory. But it shows how readily the important, widely recognized element of truth in a theoretical orientation can be distorted in practice. Much more to the point, the Watergate episode exhibits the fallacy that arises when the labeling or societal-reaction theory is exaggerated into an exclusive explanation of repeated deviant behavior. Neither Nixon nor his powerful delinquent associates had been led into their career of continuing deviance by responding to stigmatizing labels applied to them. On the contrary,

---

*For observations on the fate of sociological terms as they enter into popular usage, see the following chapter, "Our Sociological Vernacular"— editors' note.

it could be said that being apprehended and labeled as criminal offenders by the courts and as unethical offenders by public opinion seems to have brought their deviant careers to a halt.

The Watergate episode also bears on the observation made by various sociologists about an assumption basic to labeling theory:

> If deviant behavior is defined only in terms of reactions to it, then Becker cannot speak properly of "secret deviance" [as he emphatically and usefully does]. . . . To be consistent, Becker, Kitsuse, and Erikson would have to insist that behavior which is contrary to a norm is not deviant unless it is discovered and there is a particular kind of reaction to it.[59]

Theory Shifts and Problem Shifts

Although they coexist, the four theories touched upon here were first formulated at different times: the differential-association and anomie theories in the late 1930s, labeling theory in the 1950s, and conflict theory in the 1960s. This does not mean that each theory has replaced the ones that emerged before. As we have seen, the theories all focus on distinctive questions, and to a degree complement rather than contradict one another.

One theory, then, does not simply replace another. Rather, shifts of attention occur in the focus of attention among workers in the sociological vineyard.[60] As a newly formulated theory elicits interest, the key questions in it are investigated and become somewhat better understood. But it will be remembered that a focus on A means a neglect of B. After a period of use, the new theory is subjected to intensive criticism.[61] New areas of ignorance are identified and new theoretical orientations develop to specify that ignorance. By contrast with aspects of the subject that have been long worked over, the neglected aspects take on even greater interest. A new focus of theory develops, and new research is done.* In this way, more often gradually than suddenly, some of the gaps in our understanding of deviance have been filled in.

Identified by sociologists of science since the 1930s and deeply analyzed in recent years by the historical philosopher of science, Imre Lakatos,[62] this process of shifts in foci of scientific attention is often misunderstood. It is especially apt to become obscured when enthusiastic exponents of a theoretical perspective come to regard it as both exhaustive and exclusive, even though it is equipped to deal

---

*See the observations in Chapter 2 of this book on problem shifts resulting from counter-emphases developing to redress imbalances in the foci of scientific attention—editors' note.

only with certain aspects of complex phenomena (such as deviance). There then ensue those noisy disagreements which, upon inspection, are found not to express contradictory ideas or conflicting empirical findings, but only to represent different interests and rival bids for support of work on different problems.[63]

SOCIAL PROBLEMS AND SOCIAL DYSFUNCTIONS

As has been noted many times before, the investigation of social problems holds a distinct intellectual interest altogether apart from its possible use in ultimately helping people to cope with the social troubles that confront them. One such major point of theoretical interest is that the study of social problems requires sociologists to attend to the dysfunctions of patterns of behavior, belief, and organization rather than focusing primarily or exclusively on their functions. It thus curbs any inadvertent or deliberate tendency in functional sociology to reinstitute the philosophy that everything in society works for "harmony" and "the good."[64]

The theoretical relation of social dysfunctions to social disorganization can be briefly stated. Social disorganization, it will be remembered, refers to the composite of faults in the operation of a social system that interferes with the fulfillment of its functional requirements. Social dysfunction refers to the particular inadequacies of a particular part of the system for a designated requirement.[65] Social disorganization can be thought of as the resultant of multiple social dysfunctions.

1. The first point essential to using the concept of social dysfunction for the analysis of social problems can stand repetitive emphasis if only because the point has so often been blunted in the course of usage. A social dysfunction refers to a *designated* set of consequences of a *designated* pattern of behavior, belief, or organization that interfere with a *designated* functional requirement of a *designated* social system. Otherwise, the term social dysfunction becomes little more than an epithet of disparagement or a largely vacuous expression of attitude. To say, for example, that a high rate of social mobility is "functional" or "dysfunctional," without indicating the particular consequences it has for particular attributes of a designated social system, is to say little. But it is quite another thing to say, as has been said, that a high rate of social mobility from the working class into the middle class is dysfunctional for effective attainment of its goals by a solidary working class, since mobility involves exporting talent from that class and a consequent depletion

of its potential leadership.[66] This type of statement is at the least and in principle a testable hypothesis about a dysfunction of social mobility, whatever the practical difficulties in putting it to decisive test. Easy imputations of social dysfunction in the abstract are no more defensible than easy imputations of social causation in the abstract. Like social causes, social dysfunctions must be discovered through inquiry. And it is no more to be expected that inquiry will promptly discover previously unknown dysfunctions of social patterns than it is that inquiry will promptly discover previously unknown causes of these same patterns.

2. It must be noted, secondly, that the same social pattern can be dysfunctional for some parts of a social system and functional for other parts. This arises from a characteristic of social structure that has been repeatedly emphasized in earlier work.[67] *Social patterns have multiple consequences, and, in a differentiated society, these consequences will tend to differ for individuals, groups, and social strata variously situated in the structure of the society.*

The continued persistence of a social pattern makes it improbable, not impossible, that it is uniformly dysfunctional for all groups. Thus relatively free access to higher education, irrespective of racial and other origin, is dysfunctional for maintaining a relatively fixed system of caste. Extended popular education militates against the fixing of caste position or resigned acceptance to it. But of course to the very same degree that higher education of the socially subordinate is dysfunctional for maintaining a caste system, it is functional for the enlarged attainment of culturally induced goals by those formerly excluded from higher education.

All this is something more than a paraphrase of Lucretius's adage that one man's meat is another man's poison. The general idea that serves as a beginning for the analysis of functions and dysfunctions of the same social pattern is, as we have noted, that various groups and strata in the structure of a society have *distinctive* interests and values and also *shared* interests and values. To the extent that this diversity, and sometimes this conflict, of values and interests is so distributed among statuses in the society, we should naturally be prepared to find social patterns serving the interests or values of some and interfering with the interests or values of other groups differently located in the society. This structural condition is one of the principal reasons why the periodically popular notion of a society in which everything works together for good is literally utopian, and describes an engaging utopia at that. But to forgo this image of a society entirely free of imperfections does not require us to assume that nothing can be done, through deliberate plan, to reduce the extent to which obsolescent institutions and disorganization work against the realization of values that men and women respect. Quite the contrary: it is precisely by discovering such dysfunctional social formations that functional analysis in sociology links up with critical morality as opposed to conventional morality.[68]

3. Not only is the same pattern sometimes functional for some groups and dysfunctional for others but it can also serve some and defeat other functional requirements of the *same* group. The reason for this is of the same general sort as the reason for cases in which the pattern is variously consequential for *different* groups. A group has diverse functional requirements: to take only one thoroughly investigated example, the group's need for enough social cohesion to provide a sense of group identity in contrast with the need to work toward group goals, to get a job done. It is not unusual, therefore, that activities functional for one of these requirements prove to be dysfunctional for the other. When this is true to a substantial degree, the group confronts an organizational problem.

This example of composite function-and-dysfunction for distinct properties of the same group can be profitably considered in a little more detail in order to bring out the general idea it exemplifies. In the main, sociologists have found that social cohesion facilitates the productivity of a group. This is what one might expect from everyday experience: In cohesive groups, people feel at one with each other and so are the better prepared to work together for joint ends. But this mutually reinforcing relation between social cohesion and productivity holds only under certain conditions. A functional imbalance can develop between the activity that serves chiefly to maintain cohesion and the activity that results chiefly in getting work done. Great social cohesion can restrict intragroup competition in performance;[69] members of a highly cohesive group may become reciprocally indulgent to the degree that they do not hold one another to exacting standards of performance: or a large part of the social interaction in the group may be devoted to expressing and reinforcing group cohesiveness at the expense of time and energy for getting the job done.[70] When such functional imbalances obtain, the problem confronting the group is one of establishing or of reestablishing a balance in the distribution of activities such that an optimal combination of the two properties of cohesion and goal attainment is approximated.[71]

It cannot be assumed, of course, that an optimal balance is one that maximizes both social cohesion and productivity. We do not yet know enough to say whether such simultaneous maxima are incompatible. The optimal balance depends upon the comparative value set upon social cohesion and productivity by members of the group, with their being prepared to reduce the one in order to enlarge the other. This is a prototype of the value decisions that must be made in social systems of all kinds. Morale and productivity, compassion and efficiency, personal ties and impersonal tasks—these are familiar enough pairs of values not simultaneously realizable to the fullest extent.[72] All this comprises a sociological near-equivalent to the economist's conception of opportunity costs, since it means, in effect, as Scott Greer has indicated, that under certain conditions one commitment reduces the opportunities to make other commitments. By recognizing the composite of function-and-dysfunction, we guard against that form of utopian thinking that neglects the social constraints upon pursuit of certain objectives that result from commitment to other, differing objectives. Neglect of these constraints leads to the false assumption that all values can be simultaneously maximized in society. But cost-free social action is only a sociological chimera.

4. It must be emphasized, above all, that the concept of social dysfunction does not harbor an implied moral judgment. Social dysfunction is not a term substituting for immorality, unethical practice, or the socially undesirable. It is an objective concept, not a morally evaluating one. Whether one judges a particular social dysfunction as good or bad, as desirable or regrettable, depends, not on the sociological analysis of the consequences for a particular social system, but upon the further and entirely independent judgment of the moral worth of that system. When we noted, for example, that enlarged opportunities for higher education are dysfunctional for the persistence of a caste system, we did not imply, let alone say, that the dysfunction was being judged as evil or undesirable. Or when it is observed that the extremely authoritarian character of the Nazi bureaucracy proved to be dysfunctional for the work of the bureaucracy by excessively restricting lines of communication among its several echelons, it is not to deplore that circumstance. Or when sociologists specify the functions of social conflict and, more specifically, the functions of racial conflict, they are engaged in sociological analysis, not in making moral judgments.[73] Sociological analyses of function and dysfunction are in a different universe of discourse from that of moral judgments; they are not merely different expressions for the same thing.[74]

All this need not be said were it not for the frequent assumption that nonconforming and other kinds of deviant behavior are necessarily dysfunctional to a social system and that social dysfunction, in turn, necessarily violates an ethical code. In the history of every society, one supposes, some of its culture heroes eventually come to be regarded as heroic in part because they are held to have had the courage and the vision to challenge the beliefs and routines of their

society. The rebel, revolutionary, nonconformist, heretic, or rene-
gade of an earlier day is often the culture hero of today. The distinction we have drawn between nonconforming and aberrant
behavior was in part designed to capture the basic differences in
forms of deviant behavior. As has been noted before:

> If sociology does not systematically develop the distinctions be-
> tween the social structure and functions of these diverse forms
> of deviant behavior, it will in effect . . . place a premium on the
> value to the group of conformity to its prevailing standards and
> imply that nonconformity is necessarily dysfunctional to the
> group. Yet, as has been emphasized at several places in this book,
> it is not infrequently the case that the nonconforming minority
> in a society represents the interests and ultimate values of the
> society more effectively than the conforming majority. This, it
> should be repeated, is not a moral but a functional judgment, not
> a statement in ethical theory but a statement in sociological the-
> ory.[75]

Moreover, the accumulation of dysfunctions in a social system is often
the prelude to concerted social change that may bring the system
closer to the values that enjoy the respect of members of the society.
For reasons of this kind, we end this section as we began it: The
concept of social dysfunction is not based on ethical premises for it
refers to how things work in society and not to their ethical worth.

The sociological art of drawing practical conclusions from theoretical premises and empirical investigation is of course still in the
making. But then, so are all the other arts and sciences, no matter
how advanced. At least, for the sake of their practitioners, one must
hope so. It would be a sad thing if any branch of knowledge and its
application had finished growing, with nothing left to be done. These
few pages may give some indication of how things stand with the
unfinished sociology of social problems.

NOTES

[1]As we shall see in the later section of this chapter devoted to social
values and sociological analysis, this sort of ambivalence has been conspicuous among sociologists of both the past and the present. For a general
formulation of the concept of sociological (as distinct from psychological)
ambivalence and of the various forms that this ambivalence takes, see Robert
K. Merton and Elinor Barber, "Sociological Ambivalence," in Edward A.
Tiryakian, ed., *Sociological Theory, Values, and Sociocultural Change: Essays
in Honor of Pitirim A. Sorokin* (New York: Free Press, 1963), pp. 91–120.
Reprinted in Robert K. Merton, *Sociological Ambivalence and Other Essays*
(New York: Free Press, 1976)—editors' note.

[2]To be found in almost all of the many editions of Macaulay's essays;

for example, Thomas Babington Macaulay, *Critical and Historical Essays* (London: Longmans, 1864), Vol. 1, pp. 346–414. Quotation is on p. 396.

[3]Claude C. Bowman has instructively examined these tendencies toward proposing mutually exclusive orientations as alone justifiable in "Polarities and the Impairment of Science," *American Sociological Review* 15(1950):580–589.

[4]Alfred North Whitehead, *The Aims of Education* (New York: New American Library, 1951), p. 107.

[5]Harry C. Bredemeier and Jackson Toby, *Social Problems in America* (New York: Wiley & Sons, 1960).

[6]"Currently" because it was not, of course, always so. What is now defined as petty larceny and subject to mild sanctions was in other times and places defined as a capital offense. In sixteenth- and seventeenth-century England, for example, thieves were savagely punished, with many of them included among the 72,000 estimated to have been executed during the reign of Henry VIII alone. See Jerome Hall, *Theft, Law, and Society* (Boston: Little, Brown, 1935), pp. 84–85.

[7]Howard S. Becker, *Outsiders: Studies in the Sociology of Deviance* (New York: Free Press, 1963), p. 9 (italics in original).

[8]This conception is developed and documented in the first edition of *Contemporary Social Problems*, in Charles Fritz's chapter dealing with disasters and catastrophes, pp. 682–694.

[9]Although they occasionally waver in their judgments of "physical problems—i.e., the usual array of nature-made catastrophes—as constituting social problems, Fuller and Myers conclude their excellent contribution to a sociological theory of social problems by setting forth much the same position adopted here. For example: "While the earthquake itself may involve no value-judgments, its consequences inevitably will call for moral judgments and decisions of policy. People will not agree on how much should be spent in reconstruction, how it should be spent, or how the funds should be raised." Richard C. Fuller and Richard R. Myers, "Some Aspects of a Theory of Social Problems," *American Sociologial Review* 6 (1941):27.

[10]See the discussion by Scott Greer in Chapter 13 of the first edition of *Contemporary Social Problems*.

[11]Edwin M. Schur, *Crimes Without Victims: Abortion, Homosexuality, and Drug Addiction* (Englewood Cliffs, N. J.: Prentice-Hall, 1965).

[12]Kenneth B. Clark, *Dark Ghetto: Dilemmas of Social Power* (New York: Harper, 1965), p. 204.

[13]This double aspect of social problems has been recognized for some time, as in the seminal paper by Fuller and Myers, "Some Aspects of a Theory of Social Problems." But often, recognition of the objective aspect of social problems has been blurred by a subjectivist conclusion as when Fuller and Myers say that "social problems are what people think they are." F. James Davis deliberately limits his purview to manifest social problems on the grounds that only problems identified by the public are defined by their values and beliefs rather than by those of the sociologist. F. James Davis, *Social Problems* (New York: Free Press, 1970).

[14]As the debate over the place of values in sociological inquiry becomes

ever more polarized, it invites increasingly extravagant statements of one's own position and stereotyped distortions of the other's position, as is generally the case when social conflict is substituted for intellectual disagreement. (On the process of conflict, see Robert K. Merton, "Social Conflict over Styles of Sociological Work," *Transactions* Fourth World Congress of Sociology, Vol. 3, 1959, pp. 21–44, especially p. 29 ff). For a muscular statement of the place of values in social science see Alvin W. Gouldner, *The Coming Crisis of Western Sociology* (New York: Basic Books, 1970). For a recent statement intellectually congenial to the position set forth here, see Robert Solow, "Science and Ideology in Economics," *The Public Interest* 21 (Fall 1970):94–107. Another position is set forth by Gunnar Myrdal in *Objectivity in Social Research* (New York: Pantheon, 1969). For still other shades of opinion, see Ralf Dahrendorf, *Essays in the Theory of Society* (Stanford: Stanford University Press, 1968), especially Chapters 1, 2, 10; and Gideon Sjoberg, ed., *Ethics, Politics and Social Research* (Cambridge, Mass.: Schenkman, 1967).

[15]This conception of deliberate social change being forced to operate within the limits set not only by nature (modified through technology) but also by the existing structure of society and culture is found in a variety of sociological theories of notably differing ideological origins. We have encountered it in Kenneth B. Clark's discussion of the Negro-white problem in the United States. It is central to functional analysis in sociology, principally in the form of the concept of structural context (or structural constraint). See, for example, Robert K. Merton, *Social Theory and Social Structure,* rev. ed. (New York: Free Press, 1957), pp. 52–53, 73–74, *passim.* It was also central to Marx's theories of social change (although not necessarily to the work of all those who profess to find the source of their ideas in Marx); see the summary in ibid., pp. 40–41. It is also basic to the theory of sociologists who see themselves as altogether at odds with Marxist theory; to take only one example, the penetrating paper by Willard Waller, "Social Problems and the Mores," *American Sociological Review* 1 (December 1936):922–933. In short, the conception of structural constraints on social change is one that transcends many, though not all, theoretical and ideological differences in sociology.

[16]For cases in point of public misperceptions of various social problems, see Gerald Gurin, Joseph Voroff, and Sheila Feld, *Americans View Their Mental Health* (New York: Basic Books, 1960); and Daniel Bell, "The Myth of Crime Waves," in his *The End of Ideology* (New York: Free Press, 1960), Chapter 8. An ingenious study of the reporting of crime news in four Colorado newspapers bears directly on this matter of the social perception of social problems. The amount of crime news varied independently of the amount of crime in the state. What is more, a public opinion survey found that the public perception of violent crimes and theft reflected trends in the amount of crime *news* rather than actual crime *rates.* F. James Davis, "Crime News in Colorado Newspapers," *American Journal of Sociology* 57 (1952):325–330.

[17]For a comprehensive overview of the subject, see Henry Tajfel, "Social and Cultural Factors in Perception," in *The Handbook of Social Psychology.* 2nd. ed., Vol. 3, Gardner Lindzey and Elliot Aronson, eds. (Reading, Mass.: Addison-Wesley, 1969), Chapter 22.

[18]For a psychological theory of what makes things seem to belong together and so to comprise an event or unit, see Fritz Heider, "Social Perception and Phenomenal Causality," *Psychological Review* 51 (1954):358–374; also F. Heider, *The Psychology of Interpersonal Relations* (New York: Wiley & Sons, 1958), pp. 60–64.

[19]Pitirim A. Sorokin et al., "An Experimental Study of Efficiency of Work under Various Conditions," *American Journal of Sociology* 35 (May 1930):765–782.

[20]London: Macmillan, 1954, p. 188.

[21]Samuel A. Stouffer, *Communism, Conformity, and Civil Liberties* (New York: Doubleday, 1955), pp. 59–74, reports the findings summarized here.

[22]For an instructive analysis of the differences in social response to large-scale chronic suffering and to sudden and acute episodes of collective stress, see Allen Barton, *Communities in Disaster: A Sociological Analysis of Collective Stress Situations* (New York: Doubleday, 1969), pp. 208, 232–238. For a general formulation of how visibility and observability enter into social processes, see Robert K. Merton, *Social Theory and Social Structure* (New York: The Free Press, 1968), pp. 373–376, 390–411. On the functions of violence and mass demonstrations in focusing public attention on otherwise chronic suffering, see Lewis Coser, *Continuities in the Study of Social Conflict* (New York: Free Press, 1967), Chapter 4. For an historical analysis of the changing functions of collective violence, see Charles Tilly, "Collective Violence in European Perspective," in *Violence in America*, Hugh D. Graham and Ted R. Gurr, eds. (New York: New American Library, 1969), pp. 4–42.

[23]A. Eustace Haydon, "Fatalism," *Encyclopedia of the Social Sciences* (New York: Macmillan, 1931), Vol. 6, p. 147.

[24]Max Weber, *Essays in Sociology*, trans. and ed. by H. H. Gerth and C. W. Mills (New York: Oxford University Press, 1946), pp. 120–125. Karl Mannheim, *Ideology and Utopia*, trans. by Louis Wirth and E. A. Shils (New York: Harcourt, Brace & World, 1936), pp. 170–171.

[25]Georg Jellinek, *Das Recht des modernen Staates* (Berlin: Häring, 1900). William G. Sumner made substantially the same observation, in his classic work, *Folkways* (Boston: Ginn, 1906), when he noted that "the notion of right is in the folkways." In much the same vein, Robert S. Lynd observes that ". . . man's inveterate need to feel pride and rightness in his achievements has prompted him to honor the accidents of his past after the fact by describing them as 'ordained by God' or as arising from the 'inner genius' of his race, culture or nation." *Knowledge For What?* (Princeton, N. J.: Princeton University Press, 1939), p. 64. And finally, N. S. Timasheff has incorporated the notion of the normative force of the actual in his *Introduction to the Sociology of Law* (Cambridge, Mass.: Harvard University Committee on Research in the Social Sciences, 1939).

[26]For the context of this statement, see Robert K. Merton, "The Unanticipated Consequences of Purposive Social Action," *American Sociological Review* 1 (December 1936):894–904.

[27]Alexis de Tocqueville, *The Old Régime and the French Revolution*, trans. by Stuart Gilbert, from the French ed. of 1858 (Garden City, N. J.: Doubleday, 1955), pp. 176–177.

[28]The concept of rising expectations implied by Tocqueville is the dynamic counterpart to the concept of relative deprivation introduced by Samuel Stouffer and incorporated into the theory of reference group behavior by Merton and Rossi. See Tocqueville, *Democracy in America*, Vol. II, (New York: Knopf, 1945, based on the Henry Reeve text of 1840), especially Book I, Chapter 8, "How Equality Suggests to the Americans the Idea of the Indefinite Perfectability of Man," and Book II, Chapter 13, "Why the Americans Are So Restless in the Midst of Their Prosperity." For a deep

analysis of Tocqueville's ideas, see Robert A. Nisbet, *The Sociological Tradition* (New York: Basic Books, 1966). On relative deprivation, see Samuel A. Stouffer et al., *The American Soldier* (Princeton, N. J.: Princeton University Press, 1949), Vol. I, *passim;* Herbert H. Hyman and Eleanor Singer, eds., *Readings in Reference Group Theory and Research* (New York: The Free Press, 1968); Robert K. Merton and Alice S. Rossi, "Contributions to the Theory of Reference Group Behavior," in Merton's *Social Theory and Social Structure,* pp. 279–334, especially pp. 281–290; Thomas J. Crawford and Murray Naditch, "Relative Deprivation, Powerlessness, and Militancy: The Psychology of Social Protest," *Psychiatry,* 33 (May 1970):208–223.

[29]Seymour Spilerman, "The Causes of Racial Disturbances: A Comparison of Alternative Explanations," *American Sociological Review* 35 (1970):627–640.

[30]No student of the subject should fail to read the classical essays of Max Weber on the subjects of "ethical neutrality" and "objectivity in social science" rather than rely upon second-hand, often distorted versions of them. Written in the first two decades of the century, they appear in English translation in Max Weber, *On the Methodology of the Social Sciences,* trans. by E. A. Shils and H. A. Finch (New York: Free Press, 1949), pp. 1–112. For more on Weber's notion of value-relevance, see Lewis A. Coser, *Masters of Sociological Thought* (New York: Harcourt Brace Jovanovich, 1977), pp. 219–222.

[31]This paragraph is drawn from a fuller statement first published in Robert K. Merton, *Mass Persuasion* (New York: Harper & Row, 1946), and reprinted in Robert K. Merton, *The Sociology of Science* (Chicago: University of Chicago Press, 1973), pp. 86–87.

[32]Howard S. Becker, *Outsiders,* rev. ed. (New York: The Free Press, 1973), p. 198.

[33]The *locus classicus* of the theory of moral indignation is in Svend Ranulf, *Moral Indignation and Middle Class Psychology* (Copenhagen: Levin & Munksgaard, 1938). As Ranulf emphasizes, his work develops the fundamental theory set out by Émile Durkheim. The earlier monograph on the subject by Ranulf can also be profitably consulted: *The Jealousy of the Gods and Criminal Law at Athens: A Contribution to the Sociology of Moral Indignation* (London: Williams & Norgate, 1933).

[34]Talcott Parsons long ago noted the important point that patterns of social deviation differ significantly according to whether or not they lay claim to legitimation. See *The Social System* (New York: The Free Press, 1951), pp. 291–297.

[35]The foregoing account of nonconforming behavior develops somewhat the pattern of behavior identified as "rebellion" in the typology set forth in "Social Structure and Anomie." In that same typology, innovation, ritualism, and retreatism would comprise forms of aberrant behavior. And, as has been indicated in the text, nonconforming and aberrant behavior together compose deviant behavior. See Merton, *Social Theory and Social Structure* (New York: The Free Press, 1968) p. 194.

[36]Isaiah Berlin, *Karl Marx* (London: Oxford University Press, 1960), p. 79.

[37]For an application of this list of attributes of social norms, see Aaron Rosenblatt, "The Application of Role Concepts to the Intake Process," *Social Casework* 43 (January 1961):8–14. On the elasticity of norms, see Lewis A.

Coser, "Some Functions of Deviant Behavior and Normative Flexibility," *American Journal of Sociology* 68 (September 1962):172–181. See also Richard T. Morris, "A Typology of Norms," *American Sociological Review* 21 (October 1956):610–613.

The interest of ethnomethodology in discovering the tacit norms in social interaction—the "logic-in-use" in contrast to "reconstructed logic"—apparently concerns the attribute of elasticity or flexibility in norms. In effect, ethnomethodologists try to track down the implicit rules involved in particular social interactions; see Aaron V. Cicourel, *The Social Organization of Juvenile Justice* (New York: Wiley, 1968).

[38]The analysis of institutionalized evasions was developed in lectures at Harvard in the late 1930s, with part of it first seeing print in Robert K. Merton, "Discrimination and the American Creed," in *Discrimination and National Welfare*, R. M. MacIver, ed. (New York: Harper, 1949), pp. 99–126, and in Merton, *Social Theory and Social Structure*, pp. 371–372, 397–400. For a variety of institutionalized evasions in various institutional spheres, see Wilbert E. Moore, *Industrial Relations and the Social Order*, rev. ed. (New York: Macmillan, 1951), p. 114; Kingsley Davis, *Human Society* (New York: Macmillan 1949), pp. 263–264; Robin M. Williams, Jr., *American Society* (New York: Knopf, 1951), Chapter 10; Charles P. and Zona K. Loomis, *Modern Social Theories* (Princeton, N. J.: Van Nostrand, 1961), pp. 156–157, 270–271, 529–530, 553–554, 615–616; Joseph R. Gusfield, *Symbolic Crusade* (Urbana, Ill.: University of Illinois Press, 1963), pp. 112–117; Rex Lucas, *Men in Crisis: A Study of a Mine Disaster* (New York: Basic Books, 1969), Chapter 5.

[39]Robert K. Merton in Hubert J. O'Gorman, *Lawyers and Matrimonial Cases: A Study of Informal Pressures in Private Professional Practice* (New York: The Free Press, 1963), pp. ix–xi; Robin M. Williams, Jr., *American Society*, p. 356.

[40]Robert K. Merton, "Discrimination and the American Creed," op cit. See also Lyle G. Warner and Rutledge M. Dennis, "Prejudice versus Discrimination: An Empirical Example and Theoretical Extension," *Social Forces* 48 (June 1970):473–484.

[41]O'Gorman, *Lawyers and Matrimonial Cases*, pp. 23, 33.

[42]For an analysis of the interaction between law and morality within a context of social stratification, see Troy Duster, *The Legislation of Morality* (New York: Free Press, 1970). Reiss suggests that it is theoretically useful to distinguish patterned evasions in which individuals deviate with a measure of social support from evasions which implicate an entire organizational system. Albert Reiss, "The Study of Deviant Behavior," *Ohio Valley Sociologist* 32 (Autumn 1966):1–12, reprinted in Mark Lefton et al., *Approaches to Deviance* (New York: Appleton-Century-Crofts, 1968), pp. 55–66.

[43]A. V. Dicey, *Lectures on the Relation Between Law and Public Opinion in England During the Nineteenth Century* (London: Macmillan, 1905), pp. 79–80. This classic is chock-full of historical materials bearing on the emergence of institutionalized evasions of institutional rules. Another classic, published just about a century ago, Henry Sumner Maine's *Ancient Law*, 5th ed. (New York: Holt, 1887), also sets forth apposite materials in the second chapter.

[44]Jerome Hall, *Theft, Law, and Society* (Boston: Little, Brown, 1935), p. 87. Hall has given us a remarkably analytical account of the process through which the evasion of institutional rules has led to a new body of rules,

especially in his Chapter 3, significantly entitled "The Function of Technicality and Discretion in Criminal Law Administration," pp. 68–121.

Oliver Wendell Holmes, like Roscoe Pound and Benjamin Cardozo after him, has argued that law is inevitably subject to social and cultural lag. He writes: "It cannot be helped, it is as it should be, that the law is behind the times. . . . As law embodies beliefs that have triumphed in the battle of ideas and then have translated themselves into action, while there still is doubt, while opposite convictions still keep a battle front against each other, the time for law has not yet come; the notion destined to prevail is not yet entitled to the field." What we note here is that institutionalized evasions emerge to take up the slack during this interim of changing social interests and lagging legal norms. Holmes, *Collected Legal Papers* (Boston: Little, Brown, 1920), pp. 290, 294.

[45]Alexander Macbeath, *Experiments in Living* (London: Macmillan, 1952), pp. 144–147. For some of the factual bases of this summary statement, see B. Malinowski, *Crime and Custom in Savage Society* (New York: Harcourt Brace Jovanovich, 1931), pp. 80–81; A. R. Radcliffe-Brown, "The Social Organization of Australian Tribes," *Oceania* 1, nos. 1–4 (1930–1931):34–63; 206–246, 322–341, 426–456; Raymond Firth, *We, the Tikopia* (London: Allen & Unwin, 1936), p. 129; Edward Norbeck, "African Rituals of Conflict," *American Anthropologist* 65 (December 1963):1254–1279.

[46]As has been noted by Joseph R. Gusfield: "What is attacked as criminal today may be seen as sick next year and fought over as possibly legitimate by the next generation." "Moral Passage: The Symbolic Process in Public Designations of Deviance," *Social Problems* 15 (Fall 1967):175–188.

[47]On the differences between theory and general theoretical orientations, see Merton, *Social Theory and Social Structure*, pp. 141–155. Erich Goode incisively examines such differences in the case of one approach to deviant behavior: "On Behalf of Labeling Theory," *Social Problems* 22 (1975):570–583.

[48]Edwin M. Schur, *Labeling Deviant Behavior* (New York: Random House, 1971), p. 35.

[49]On the complementary relations in a plurality of paradigms, see Robert K. Merton, "Structural Analysis in Sociology," in *Approaches to the Study of Social Structure*, Peter M. Blau, ed. (New York: The Free Press, 1975), pp. 47–52.

[50]Kenneth Burke, *Permanence and Change* (New York: New Republic, 1935), pp. 50ff.

[51]For a brief comparative application of this theoretical orientation to American and Soviet societies, see the concluding section, "Pressures toward Deviation," in the chapter on inequality by Seymour Martin Lipset in *Contemporary Social Problems* (1976).

[52]Edwin M. Lemert, *Social Pathology* (New York: McGraw-Hill, 1951); *Human Deviance, Social Problems and Social Control* (Englewood Cliffs, N.J.: Prentice-Hall, 1972); "Beyond Mead: The Societal Reaction to Deviance," *Social Problems* 21 (1973):457–468; Howard S. Becker, *Outsiders*, rev. ed. (New York: The Free Press, 1973); Howard S. Becker, ed., *The Other Side: Perspectives on Deviance* (New York: The Free Press, 1964) which includes the seminal paper by Kai T. Erikson, "Notes on the Sociology of Deviance," pp. 9–21, and another by John I. Kitsuse, "Societal Reaction to Deviant Behavior," pp. 87–102; John I. Kitsuse and Aaron V. Cicourel, "A

Note on the Uses of Official Statistics," *Social Problems* 11 (1963):131–139; Cicourel, *The Social Organization of Juvenile Justice.*

[53]Lemert, "Beyond Mead," p. 462.

[54]Austin Turk, *Criminality and the Legal Order* (Chicago: Rand McNally, 1969); Richard Quinney, *The Social Reality of Crime* (Boston: Little, Brown, 1970).

[55]Lemert, "Beyond Mead," p. 462.

[56]See Richard A. Cloward and Lloyd E. Ohlin, *Delinquency and Opportunity* (New York: The Free Press, 1960); Richard A. Cloward, "Illegitimate Means, Anomie, and Deviant Behavior," *American Sociological Review* 24 (1959):164–176; Robert K. Merton, "Social Conformity, Deviation and Opportunity Structures," *American Sociological Review* 24 (1959):177–189; E. H. Mizruchi, *Success and Opportunity: Class Values and Anomie in American Life* (New York: The Free Press, 1964).

[57]Richard Jessor et al., *Society, Personality, and Deviant Behavior* (New York: Holt, 1968); Julian B. Rotter, *Social Learning and Clinical Psychology* (Englewood Cliffs, N.J.: Prentice-Hall, 1954). See also the important paper by Lucien Laforest, "Force et Faiblesse de la Théorie de l'Anomie comme Source Explicative de la Déviance Alcoolique," *Toxicomanies* 8 (1975):219–238.

[58]Becker, *Outsiders*, p. 34. See also Kai T. Erikson, *Wayward Puritans: A Study in the Sociology of Deviance* (New York: Wiley, 1966), p. 17ff.; Erikson, "Notes on the Sociology of Deviance," p. 17; William D. Payne, "Negative Labels: Passageways and Prisons," *Crime and Delinquency* (1973):39–40.

[59]Jack P. Gibbs, "Conceptions of Deviant Behavior: The Old and the New," *Pacific Sociological Review* 9 (1966):13. Other pointed formulations indicate that a theory of deviance must deal with *both* the sources of deviant acts and societal responses to them: Milton Mankoff, "Societal Reaction and Career Deviance," *The Sociological Quarterly* 12 (1971):204–218; Ronald L. Akers, "Problems in the Sociology of Deviance: Social Definitions and Behavior," *Social Forces* 46 (1968):455–465. Charles R. Tittle, "Deterrents or Labeling?" *Social Forces* 53 (1975):399–410, examines the research evidence and concludes that deterrence as well as secondary deviance results from the use of sanctions, with the actual outcome depending upon some known and some unknown specifiable conditions.

[60]For a detailed analysis of such shifts, see Stephen Cole, "The Growth of Scientific Knowledge: Theories of Deviance as a Case Study," in *The Idea of Social Structure*, Lewis Coser, ed., pp. 175–220.

[61]The older theories of differential association and anomie-and-opportunity-structures have long been subject to intensive criticism, in accord with the norm of science described as "organized skepticism." In due course, this is now the case for labeling theory. Note the observation by Goode (op. cit., p. 570): "by the early 1970s the antilabeling stance became almost as fashionable as labeling had been a decade earlier." See also J. W. Rogers and M. D. Buffalo, "Fighting Back: Nine Modes of Adaptation to a Deviant Label," *Social Problems* 22 (1974):101.

[62]Imre Lakatos's formulation of problem-shifts and "scientific research programmes" contributes greatly to our understanding of how scientific thought develops. See his "History of Science and Its Rational Reconstruction," *Boston Studies in the Philosophy of Science* 8 (1971):91–136, 174–182, and his "Falsification and the Methodology of Scientific Research Pro-

grammes," in *Criticism and the Growth of Knowledge,* Imre Lakatos and Alan Musgrave, eds. (Cambridge: Cambridge University Press, 1970), pp. 91–195.

[63]Since the theoretical perspectives are not altogether mutually exclusive, they do sometimes lead to conflicting hypotheses or predictions (for example, on the question of whether sanctions for deviant behavior deter from renewed deviance or only help bring it about).

[64]Without considering the question of the extent to which current functional sociology has exhibited this tendency—a question that would take us far afield—we might note the claim that such a tendency has been expressed in physiology, especially in that part of physiology heavily influenced by Walter B. Cannon's notion of *homeostasis* (the maintenance of steady states in the organism). For Cannon's ideas were also influential in the resurgence of a functional outlook in sociology. The criticism is set forth, in sufficiently nontechnical fashion that even those without a thorough grounding in physiology may learn as they read, by the physician and physiologist, Dickinson W. Richards (who was later to become a Nobel laureate for his work on catheterization of the heart). See his account of "The Stupidity of the Body," designed as a complement to rather than a substitute for Cannon's *The Wisdom of the Body* (New York: W. W. Norton, [1932] 1967), in his paper, "Homeostasis Versus Hyperexis," *The Scientific Monthly* 77 (December 1953):289–294, reprinted in his *Medical Priesthoods and Other Essays* (Connecticut Printers, 1970), pp. 46–57.

[65]A more exact formal statement is provided by Ernest Nagel, "A Formalization of Functionalism," in his *Logic Without Metaphysics* (New York: The Free Press, 1956), especially p. 269.

[66]This hypothesis was in effect adopted not long ago by a branch of the Labour Party in Birmingham; that is, by people who were, of course, ideologically and in the abstract, staunch supporters of enlarging opportunity for social mobility. Nevertheless, they officially stated that "from Labour's point of view, the objection to the grammar school system was that it had the effect of taking the brightest children of the working class and in effect de-classing them by separation from children in the modern [essentially vocational] schools. Eventually, they get white-collar jobs and upon marriage go to live in the outer suburbs and vote Tory." Substantially, the same hypothesis about the dysfunctions of rapid and large-scale mobility for maintaining the solidarity and effective goal attainment of a working class was set forth by such ideologically opposed theorists as Karl Marx and Vilfredo Pareto. See Marx, *Capital* (Chicago: Kerr, [1867–79] 1906), pp. 648–649; Pareto, *The Mind and Society* (New York: Harcourt Brace Jovanovich, 1935), Vol. 3, pp. 1419–1432; Vol. 4, pp. 1836–1846. For an analysis of this pattern of "cognitive agreement and value disagreement," see Merton, "Social Conflict over Styles of Sociological Work," *Transactions,* pp. 21–46, especially pp. 39–40. Most recently, the same ambivalence toward social mobility among a disadvantaged population is found among "the masses of lower-class Negroes [who] regard this movement up the ladder with mixed feelings, both proud and resentful of the success of 'one of their own.' " (Kenneth B. Clark, *Dark Ghetto: Dilemmas of Social Power,* pp. 57–58.) In the same ambivalent fashion, the collective efforts to have many more black scholars appointed to the faculties of major universities and colleges is now being described as "the black brain drain to white colleges"; *New York Times,* February 6, 1969, p. 34.

[67]Merton, *Social Theory and Social Structure, passim.*

[68]Ralph Ross, *Obligation: A Social Theory* (Ann Arbor: University of

Michigan Press, 1970), especially Chapter 5, "Critical Morality," and Chapters 8, 9.

[69]Indeed, this conception that activities directed toward instrumental and system-maintenance functions are antithetical is basic to the functional analysis of social problems. This is one of the several respects in which, contrary to much superficial opinion, the assumption of structural and functional *conflict* is inherent in functional sociology. Considerable observational and experimental work bears on this example of composite function-and-dysfunction; for a summary of this one finding, see James G. March and Herbert A. Simon, *Organizations* (New York: Wiley, 1958), pp. 60–61.

[70]For a few of the many studies to this effect, see A. B. Horsfall and C. M. Arensberg, "Teamwork and Productivity in a Shoe Factory," *Human Organization* 8 (1949):13–25; J. G. Darley, Neal Gross, and W. E. Martin, "Studies of Group Behavior: Factors Associated with the Productivity of Groups," *Journal of Applied Psychology* 36 (1952):396–403; N. Babchuk and W. J. Goode, "Work Incentives in a Self-Determined Group," *American Sociological Review* 16 (1951):679–687.

[71]On the conception of the net balance of an aggregate of social consequences, see Merton, *Social Theory and Social Structure*, pp. 105–108; Ralph M. Stogdill, *Individual Behavior and Group Achievement* (New York: Oxford University Press, 1959), pp. 222 ff. Melvin Tumin has indicated that the difficult problem of measuring this net balance has not yet been solved. That is the case. But it should also be noted that this problem, which has been identified in functional sociology as a focus of inquiry and analysis, is of course implicit in other sociological analyses of social disorganization and deviant behavior. In short, the same analytical difficulty is there, whether recognized or implicit. See Melvin Tumin, "The Functionalist Approach to Social Problems," *Social Problems* 12 (Spring 1965):379–388.

[72]Cf. Robert K. Merton and Elinor Barber, "Sociological Ambivalence," in R. K. Merton, *Sociological Ambivalence* (New York: The Free Press, 1976), pp. 3–31. A rough analogy with the dysfunctional associates of functional genes does not of course supply evidence for the sociological parallel but does provide a sense that this combination is not confined to the plane of human society. Note, for example, the observation by the biochemist and geneticist, Caryl P. Haskins: ". . . the genes . . . do not assort completely independently in inheritance, but are associated into linkage groups. . . . These linked genes are inherited together, though each group as a whole assorts independently of other groups. This means that genetic characteristics which are disadvantageous or are of neutral value to the organism may be firmly linked to other characteristics which are of predominant survival value. Thus shielded by them in evolution, as it were, they may persist for very long periods merely by virtue of the fact that, under normal circumstances, they are inseparable from the benefactor genes and the damage which they cause the organism is much less serious than the evolutionary advantages conferred by the partners." *Of Societies and Men* (New York: Norton, 1951), pp. 113–114.

[73]Dorothy Emmet, *Function, Purpose, and Powers* (London: Macmillan, 1958), pp. 78–82.

[74]Lewis A. Coser, *The Functions of Social Conflict* (New York: The Free Press, 1956); Joseph S. Himes, "The Functions of Racial Conflict," *Social Forces* 45 (September 1966):1–10; Robert A. Dentler and Kai T. Erikson, "The Functions of Deviance in Groups," *Social Problems* 7 (1959):98–107.

See also the implications of theories affirming the value of lower-class social life as these are drawn by Lewis A. Coser, "Unanticipated Conservative Consequences of Liberal Theorizing," *Social Problems* 16 (Winter 1969):263–272.

[75]Merton, *Social Theory and Social Structure,* pp. 107, 428; and Alvin Boskoff, "Social Indecision: A Dysfunctional Focus of Transitional Society," *Social Forces* 37 (1959):305–311.

CHAPTER 4

Our Sociological Vernacular*

A man coynes not a new word without some perill, and less fruit; for if it happen to be received, the praise is but moderate; if refus'd, the scorne is assur'd. Yet wee must adventure, for things, at first hard and rough, are by use made tender and gentle.

BEN JONSON
TIMBER: OR, DISCOVERIES, 1641

Virgil's counsels to the vicious neologist, who debases the purity of English diction by affecting new words or phrases, may too frequently be applied.

ISAAC DISRAELI
THE CALAMITIES AND QUARRELS
OF AUTHORS, [1814] 1859

When Richard Nixon was still president, he made the surprising public confession that he was a Keynesian, an admission that was probably not vetted by Milton Friedman. Misplaced as it may have been, Nixon's confession irresistibly brought to mind Keynes's well-known remark that "practical men, who believe themselves to be quite exempt from any intellectual influences, are usually the slaves of

*Reprinted by permission of the publisher, *Columbia*, November 1981, 42–44. Copyright by the Trustees of Columbia University.

some defunct economist." What Keynes had to say about the relation between "practical men" and "defunct economists" can be para- phrased to hold for men and women of every condition in relation to sociologists, both living and defunct. For like it or not, and many of us do not like it at all, ours has become an age pervaded by sociology.

Not that sociologists have successfully imposed themselves and their thoughts upon the rest of us. They are as much the objects of popular ambivalence as they ever were and perhaps all the more so, as they have become increasingly visible and audible. It is not that the sociologists have achieved their pertinence for our times; it is, rather, that the course of contemporary history has made them per- tinent. For much of what preoccupies us collectively—for example, the cleavages and conflicts between social groups and strata of every kind (ethnic, gender, generational, and socioeconomic)—is perva- sively sociological. As that hard-bitten observer of our society, the late Richard Rovere, once put it: "Those of us who have been educated in the twentieth century habitually think in sociological terms, whether or not we have had any training in sociology."

We "habitually think in sociological terms" partly because a great variety of sociological terms have drifted into our everyday language. In some cases, the diffusion of those words occurred so long ago that we are wholly unaware of their sociological origins. Take the word "altruism," for instance. Who now knows, or cares, that that much- needed word was coined about 150 years ago by one of the several fathers of sociology, the French philosopher of history and secular prophet, Auguste Comte? This is the same Comte, of course, who created the domain-term "sociology," thus seeing to it that the field of inquiry would be in disrepute from the start, since that barbarous hybrid rooted in both Latin and Greek was bound to offend the etymological sensibilities of classicists everywhere. (Just as the clas- sicists of the day were offended by that other indispensable hybrid, "scientist," coined a bare two years later by the confirmed neologist and philosopher-historian of science, William Whewell.)

Many other sociological words are deeply enough embedded in our language as to have their origins forgotten while they continue to affect our perceptions of the social world in which we live. "Folk- ways" and "mores" have become part of the vernacular since they were introduced soon after the turn of the century in the classic book, *Folkways,* by the Yale sociologist, William Graham Sumner. The notion of folkways was designed to remind us that many ways of behavior are retained only because they were once experienced as effective, just as the notion of mores was designed to remind us that certain customs, held to be imbued with moral significance, are not easily changed even under greatly changed conditions.

Sumner, sometimes described as the Karl Marx of the Middle Classes, coined a good many other sociological words which have entered the language to affect our perceptions of the world around us and our evaluations of what we perceive. Another of his prime coinages is "ethnocentrism." The very existence of the word alerts us to the propensity of social groups and societies to think of themselves as the center of the social universe and the center of all things good and valuable. Sumner also gave us the words-cum-associated-ideas of "in-group" and "out-group," words lately taken up in undiscriminating excess by all manner of people innocently unaware of their sociological origins.

Much better known in its origins and, I believe, vastly consequential in shaping the social perceptions of large numbers of us, is the sociological metaphor, "stereotype," introduced, of course, some sixty years ago by that perdurable sociologist-*malgré-lui*, Walter Lippmann, in his book *Public Opinion* (a book, incidentally, which all of us would do well to re-read every other year or so—at least, its first, vastly instructive half).

Along with these older sociological terms which are now part of the language are many newer ones, each of them having its distinctive cues to ways of construing the society in which we live. Some of these terms were in a degree prognostic, as when the Harvard sociologist, Talcott Parsons, alerted us almost two generations ago, to the existence of a "youth culture," and the criminological sage of Indiana, E.H. Sutherland, forced us to recognize through his term "white-collar crime" that criminal behavior was not really the exclusive province of the poor since each of the various social strata had its own readily accessible varieties of crime.

Prognostic also was the term "minority groups," which has led such a conspicuously active existence in recent years. The term was coined in 1932 by the then University of Pennsylvania sociologist, Donald Young, in his compendious textbook, *American Minority Peoples*. National minorities had of course been singled out for attention long before. But with his distinctly sociological orientation, Young wanted to tag a more widespread and more differentiated array of social phenomena. He wanted to get away from the shortsighted assumption tucked away in the usage of "minorities" to refer only to national or ethnic minorities as though these alone were subject to systematic discriminatory treatment. He was concerned also to avoid the readily accessible racist implications of the then widely current notion of "race" as involving biologically determined and therefore inevitable inferiorities and superiorities of various ethnic collectivities. And so it is that today, when blacks, women, Hispanics and Italians, lesbians and homosexuals, among others, declare their liberation and examine their condition as "minority groups," whether they know it or not, they are adopting a mode of collective self-scrutiny that is heavily indebted to the defunct but still consequential sociologist Donald Young and many another since.

THE SELF-FULFILLING PROPHECY

Other sociological terms of more recent vintage have found their way into everyday language. With fatherly interest and no little angst, I have been monitoring the fate of the term "the self-fulfilling prophecy" ever since my article by that title appeared in *The Antioch Review* precisely a third of a century ago.* The self-fulfilling prophecy refers to a pattern of individual or collective behavior found in every department of social life. In that pattern, an initially false but widely shared prediction, expectation, or belief is fulfilled in practice not because it was at the outset true, but because enough people took it to be true and, by acting accordingly, produced the outcome that would otherwise not have occurred. So it was that back in the days before federal deposit insurance was instituted, rumors of insolvency could produce runs on banks through which the rumors brought about their own fulfillment. The specious validity of the self-fulfilling prophecy perpetuates a reign of error since the prophet(s) will cite the actual course of events as proof of having been right from the start.

Hundreds of papers in sociology, social psychology, psychology, economics, philosophy, political science, anthropology, educational research, and public administration have made use of the concept of the self-fulfilling prophecy (and its counterpart, the self-defeating prophecy). It has also made its way, often with uncritical ease, into everyday discourse with its tacitly sociological thinking. Most conspicuously, it has become diffused through all the media of mass communication, principally newspapers and magazines but radio and television as well. *The New York Times,* as a prime example, has made frequent use of the concept (not merely the phrase) in editorials, letters to the editor, and the Op-Ed page, as well as in the columns on economic developments—nowadays with growing frequency, what with the rediscovery of the notion of inflationary expectations. For that matter, it has appeared from time to time on the sports page

*Reprinted as Chapter 10 in this volume—editors' note.

of *The New York Times,* as one or another of its perceptive columnists takes note of the self-fulfilling prophecy at work in that competitive arena.

Not least the concept has been put to use in the halls of congress and in presidential documents. Again, not always with discriminating judgment. I recall the mixed feelings with which I read in President Nixon's budget message of 1971, issued soon after that casual confession about his having been converted to Keynesian doctrines, that he counted on his optimistic forecast becoming—the language is his— "a self-fulfilling prophecy." Like many another, I cherished the promised outcome but was minded to inform the President that prophecies become self-fulfilling only when the prophet has acquired wide credibility.

VOGUE WORDS

All of which is perhaps enough to serve notice that as these words pass into the vernacular, they suffer distinct fates. Some, like ethnocentrism, retain much of their original meaning and serve as an aid to social analysis and thought. Others are avidly picked up by one group or another and are soon done to death as vogue words. "Anomie," that sixteenth-century theological term transformed by the French master sociologist, Émile Durkheim, in the 1890s to refer to the breakdown of social norms virtually to a condition of normlessness, is now suffering the fate of excess indiscriminate popularity. One newsweekly has even attempted to spread the vogue word by means of folksy sibilance: " 'Boy, that's what I call acute anomie,' whistled Bleecker Totten"—a sociological whistle which one somehow doubts ever got whistled.

Or consider the even more brutal fate of "charisma," that ancient term of theology meaning a God-given gift of grace, which was adapted by the classical German sociologist, Max Weber, early in the century to designate extraordinary, even superhuman qualities attributed to the rare individual who can then claim absolute loyalty as a leader. Charisma now plainly belongs to that class of words, including those with excellently precise meanings, which have been worn out by frequent undiscriminating use, not least by the Madison Avenue agents who buy access to newspapers and television for their masters. For them, charisma has become little more than a chant or a grunt, emptied of any precise meaning. Even the august advertising columns of the *Times* have carried a scarehead which reads in its entirety so: "Charisma! Charisma! Charisma! Charisma! Camden

County's got it . . . and you can share it!" Merging the sacred and the profane, the review of an "exciting movie" announces that "the charisma is money in the bank." And almost after the fashion of Aldous Huxley's quasi-palindrome which has the sacred "god" transformed in the profane "dog," Manhattan now boasts a shop known as "Canine Charisma." Through heedless reiteration, the marketplace has proceeded to thoroughly demean this once reasonably exact and graceful word into a mindless catchword. Witness only an abbreviated catalog of recent usage which begins, properly enough, with

Charisma Communication Ltd.,
continues with

Charisma Records,
Charisma Furs, Inc.,
Charisma Jewelry, Inc.,
Charisma Legal Supplies, Inc.,
Charisma Business Supplies Company,
and presumably reaches bottom with

Charisma Carpet Corporation.

So it is that in an age increasingly aware of its social problems, many sociological words become modish, boringly reiterated with successive diminution of meaning. We sociologists cannot really claim all the discredit for these popular abuses. After all, we have had enough troubles with our own use of language not to require borrowing additional troubles. And having introduced *that* subject, I must say that the endemic pasting of sociologists for their clumsy language is often misplaced. Sociologists are said by Malcolm Cowley and Russell Kirk, for example, to be addicted to the use of many-syllabled, high-sounding words. No doubt. But, as it can be shown, no more so than the members of other arts, crafts, or sciences. After all, as I have told, sociologists have their monosyllabic or bisyllabic moments as well; consider anew in-group and out-group, folkways and mores, caste and class, peer groups, and the like. Another charge leveled against this guild is that its practitioners are overly given to the use of nouns as modifiers rather than as the free-standing words they syntactically are. This is no canard. Like other twentieth-century Americans, American sociologists often do use pairs of nouns, with the first serving to modify the second. So it is that they have introduced such terms as opinion leaders, role models, youth culture, peer groups, opportunity structures, power elites, and power structures (all of them fated to enter into the vernacular subject to the hazards attending such diffusion). Yet this is not altogether a liability. Kept under reasonable restraint, the grouping of nouns is a tolerable and sometimes useful practice. That restraint sees to it that the nouns do not proliferate and expand into long successions of nouns, with each forced to modify the ones that come after in the fashion known to high-minded users of the language as "freight-train constructions" (a triplet of nouns that beautifully exemplifies in practice what it ostensibly rejects in principle).

In spite of such periodic attacks on the sometimes innocent guild, sociological ideas have plainly been infused into public thinking through the widespread adoption of sociological words. It is consoling to find that these words-cum-ideas need not always be distorted and that they need not be the legacy of *defunct* sociologists. And so I shall continue to watch, with keen egotistic interest, the fate of such sociological terms as the self-fulfilling prophecy, manifest and latent functions, the displacement of goals, retreatism (a social phenomenon become widely known a generation later as 'opting out'), opportunity structure, role-sets and status-sets, local and cosmopolitan influentials, the Matthew effect, accumulation of advantage, theories of the middle range, homophily (friendships between people of the same kind, *not* as more recently proposed, a synonym for homosexuality) and heterophily, strategic research site, obliteration by incorporation, potentials of relevance, and the acronym OTSOG (standing for the title of a book of mine, *On The Shoulders of Giants,* which explores the behavior of scholars and the ways in which science and learning develop).

With luck, a few of these terms may escape the distortions experienced by many another sociological word which has captured some significant aspect of the social world in which we live.

PART II

Sociology of the Practicing Professions

CHAPTER 5

Institutionalized Altruism: The Case of the Professions*

(with Thomas F. Gieryn)

Catching murderers isn't a soft job, or a sheltered job. It takes a lot of time and energy, and you might easily get injured or killed. I dare say he does it for fun, but at any rate, he does do it. Scores of people must have as much reason to thank him as I have. You can't call that nothing.

I absolutely agree," said the Dean. "I think one ought to be very grateful to people who do dirty jobs for nothing, whatever their reason is.

Dorothy R. Sayers
GAUDY NIGHT, 1936

*Reprinted with permission from T. Lynn Smith and Man Singh Das, (eds.) *Sociocultural Change Since 1950:* A Festschrift for Carle C. Zimmerman (New Delhi: Vikas Publishing House, 1978) pp. 309–344. The editors chose to omit the first part of this essay, a review of the diverse literature on studies of altruism, in light of Thomas F. Gieryn's substantial revisions in his forthcoming paper, "The Sociology of Altruism," *Annual Review of Sociology* (1982). The writing of this paper was supported by a grant from the National Science Foundation to the Program in the Sociology of Science, Columbia University. The decidedly senior author is indebted to Gardner Lindzey and the staff of the Center for Advanced Study in the Behavioral Sciences for a superb milieu in which to work. Complete bibliographic information will be found in the list of references at the end of the chapter— editors' note.

It is symbolically apt that the word *altruism* should have been coined by one of the several fathers of sociology, Auguste Comte (1890–1895, Vol. II, Chapter 2). The injunction *"Vive pour autrui"* was central to Comte's positivist religion, and was directed toward counteracting the assumption of egoism believed central tothe emerging classical economics, an assumption he never found congenial. From Comte's day to the present, a systematic sociological study of altruism has been hampered by difficulties surrounding the definition of the basic concept of altruism. Of necessity, our paper begins with an attempt to distinguish among diverse types of apparently altruistic behavior, with a focus on the type identified as "institutionalized altruism."

We define altruism generically as behavior which benefits others at the expense of the benefactor. By expense, we mean only that the yield to the benefactors is less in the short run than if they had not engaged in altruistic behavior. Of course, we are not limiting the term reward to material gain: the benefits for both beneficiary and benefactor may be in terms of whatever is socially defined and personally experienced as a reward: prestige and esteem, upward mobility, money, power.

Institutionalized altruism is the special form of altruism in which structural arrangements, notably the distribution of rewards and penalties, promote behavior that is beneficial to others. Institutionalized altruism focuses attention on alternatives of action that are weighted by social structures to increase the rate at which individuals choose altruistic actions beyond what it would otherwise be (if based wholly upon human nature, prior socialization, or other dispositional tendencies).

To understand the nature and social patterning of altruistic behavior, we must take note of the motivations of the benefactor, the consequences of the behavior for the "beneficiary," and the consequences for the benefactor. The following typology is a start toward comprehending the range of outwardly altruistic behavior:

Motivation of Benefactor	Consequences for Beneficiary	Consequences for Benefactor	Type
Altruistic	Reward	Reward	Reciprocated altruism
Altruistic	Reward	No reward	Pure altruism
Altruistic	No reward	Reward	Unwitting exploitation (pseudo-altruism)

Altruistic	No reward	No reward	Trivial altruism
Egoistic	Reward	Reward	Enlightened self-interest
Egoistic	Reward	No reward	Unwitting altruism
Egoistic	No reward	Reward	Pure selfishness
Egoistic	No reward	No reward	Ineffectual behavior

The typology of behavior does not take into account normative prescriptions and preferences that channel behavior into one of the eight categories in patterned ways. Where altruism has been institutionalized, we expect an increase in the kinds of behavior benefiting others, whether the benefactor's motives are altruistic or egoistic. In such arrangements, the failure to provide rewards for beneficiaries tends to make for loss by the individual institutionally defined as a benefactor. This is the limiting case of what has long been described as "enlightened self-interest." The pure altruism exhibited in the paradigmatic case of the good Samaritan represents ideal norms seldom expected to be put into consistent practice as a matter of course.[1] In contrast, institutionalized altruism in the form of doing more for the beneficiary than is strictly required (for example, by common law or other prescription) does occur with some frequency if only because the reward-system yields *some* return to the benefactor.

An important feature of institutionalized altruism is the mechanism through which rewards are returned to the initial benefactor.* When altruism is institutionalized, it operates beyond the bounds of friendship, and dyads generally. Unlike the cases of altruism, where the rewards (if any) pass back from the original beneficiary to the benefactor, in the institutionalized arrangement, the benefactor's rewards are more likely to come from other individuals in the social system of which they are a part. To jump ahead to the special example discussed in this paper, it is the professional's peers, in the first instance, who determine whether their behavior is in accordance with preferred and not merely with prescribed patterns, and indirectly it is they who determine the rewards the professional is to receive by way of standing in the field.

The typology also fails to convey a second pattern in institutionalized altruism. Rewards received by the initial benefactor are typically delayed, especially if the reward is an intangible benefit such as the esteem of peers or upward mobility. This suggests that behavior considered altruistic in the short run may over the long run

*For an important elaboration and specification of such social processes, see Kadushin (1981).

become a case of enlightened self-interest. Institutional altruists are informed by the recognition that even when not motivated by a primary regard for others, they will be prudent in the long run by acting as if they had the interests of others in mind if not in heart. However, the notion of enlightened self-interest, with its focus on *individual behavior,* differs significantly from institutionalized altruism, which directs attention chiefly to the structural context within which individuals must make patterned choices. It emphasizes such institutional arrangements as the reward-system that determine what will be in one's self-interest, and that channel interested motives into behavior benefiting others beyond the limits of what is strictly prescribed.

Examples of structural arrangements that transform a variety of motives and practical reasons into behavior benefiting others are not hard to come by. The tax law that encourages philanthropy provides a familiar example in which indirect benefits accruing to the donor enlarge the extent of altruistic behavior beyond that which would occur in the absence of such an arrangement. Titmuss's (1971) agencies for *voluntary* and quasi-anonymous donations of blood exhibit, under the lens of his analysis, comparable indirect benefits and, in some measure, these are replicated in organizations that provide for the literal donation of parts of oneself (for example, eye banks).

In the rest of this chapter we focus on the set of social arrangements that make for the institutionalizing of altruistic behavior in one sector of the society: the professions. By way of emphatic reminder, this is not to say that professional men and women largely engage in such behavior; it is only to say that it occurs more frequently than would be the case in the absence of the designated institutional arrangements.

THE CASE OF THE PROFESSIONS[2]

Public Appraisals

The business of trying to define the essentials of a profession has been going on for some time—for at least four centuries in the Western world — and seems to have greatly accelerated in our own time. Why this perduring effort—that varies chiefly in focus upon attributive, structural, functional, or depictive accounts of these occupations—to distill the essence of that subset of occupations commonly designated as professions? A clue is afforded by the fairly constant features of these attempts at definition, whether by Flexner (1915), Brandeis (1925), Carr-Saunders and Wilson (1933), Greenwood (1957), Hall (1968), or Goode (1973).[3] Either in so many words or by implication they all treat the professions as somehow "superior" to other occupations. In this aspect, their appraisals are of a piece with those prevailing in the population at large.

To be parochial by confining our attention to the United States, we note much evidence testifying that the professions hold the esteem of Americans beyond all other classes of occupations. With some differences in detail among them, the professions of medicine, law, university teaching, the ministry, and architecture rank near the top in the occupational hierarchy of prestige.[4] The professions are out-ranked by the highest posts in government—justices of the Supreme Court, for example—but these are topmost positions within a profession rather than professions in themselves.

Much of the same picture emerges when Americans are asked to recommend a preferred occupation for youth. Fully half of all Americans repeatedly prefer the professions to all the rest, counter-ing even the generic tendency for fathers to want their sons to follow in their own footsteps, if not of mothers wanting their daughters to follow in theirs. Here again, medicine ranks foremost, with the law not far behind. Beyond all other occupations, many more feel them-selves called to the professions than are, or currently can be, chosen.

This selective process has a major consequence for people in the professions. For they, more than any others in our world, are in occupations they want to be in rather than in ones they happen to be in. With slight variations over a period of decades, it has been found that some nine in every ten Americans in one of the core professions had elected it as their first occupational choice. That proportion dips to a third for those in clerical or sales jobs, and drops to only one in ten for semiskilled jobs. Despite all the grumbling, when the chips are down in the pragmatic sense of William James, professionals generally want to remain professionals.

In a variety of respects, then, the professions are marked off from other classes of occupations. They rank high in public esteem, have been the first choice of most practitioners in them, and are least often occasion for regret when actual experience is compared with expectation. Judging from the available evidence, which covers an array of investigations extending over the past four decades, the professions come as close to affording a satisfying kind of work as our society now provides. How this was in other times is a matter for intensive historical inquiry, but comparative sociological study finds strong evidence that the pattern of evaluation is today much the same in industrialized countries of every political and ideological persua-sion.[5]

The uniform finding that the professions outrank all other

broad classes of occupations has somewhat deflected the attention of
sociologists from the sources and consequences of hostility that has
also been directed toward the professions over the years. As the
professionals understandably note for themselves, their fields are, to
varying extent, the objects of ambivalence: of praise, often extravagant praise, and of sharp, sometimes immoderate, censure. They are,
in short, the object of all manner of positive feelings and all manner
of negative ones. Looking ahead, we shall see that hostility toward
the professions largely results from manifest failures to meet minimum standards of practice as gauged by laymen and peers, as well
as from sociological ambivalence inhering in the structure of relations
between practitioner and client. Hostility is also generated by the
institutionalized expectation of altruistic behavior that leads clients
to look for help greater than what practitioners can actually provide.
In this connection, Everett Hughes has observed that the increasing
public concern with the professions relates to a historical shift in
social values. It arises in part, he suggests,

> from the growing belief that everyone has a right to education,
> health, and to those other kinds of increase of life which [Herbert]
> Spencer had said it was the function of professions to provide
> . . . [As a result,] more and more philanthropic and public
> agencies have become more and more involved in the distribu-
> tion of professional services; more and more of the cost is paid
> by various risk- and cost-spreading agencies other than the
> professional practitioner himself. (Hughes 1971:366)

Since the core professions are generally esteemed beyond all other
classes of occupations, they are at the focus of widespread attention.
Along with the intellectual interest of scholars in the subject, there
is a popular curiosity in discovering what it is about the professions
that enables them to enjoy the esteem generally accorded them.

Triad of Values in the Professions

The professions can be thought of as rooted in a triad of human
values. These are, first, the value assigned to systematic knowledge
and specialized intellect: *knowing*. Almost every definition of a profession makes reference to its distinctive body of theoretically and empirically derived knowledge that is not widely distributed among the
population at large. A profession not grounded in expanding systematically arranged knowledge becomes, in Whitehead's description,
"a welter of bygone flashes of intelligence relapsing into customary
procedures" (Whitehead 1933:60).[6]

Second, the professions assign high value to trained capacity and technical skill: *doing.* Professionals are expected to apply their theoretically derived knowledge to the solution of paramount problems in life: disease, injustice, sin, and violation of human rights. To find ways of coping with the major troubles generally takes precedence over the routine demands of everyday life. Professional expertise is called in at points of crisis where stakes and uncertainties are great.

And third, at the focus of attention here, is the value embedded in the professional role of getting this conjoint knowledge and skill to work in the disciplined service of others: *helping.* The professions are repeatedly distinguished from other occupations by their commitment to an "ideal of service" (Goode 1957), their "collectivity-orientation" (Parsons 1951), and their "service to the public" (Tawney [1922] 1946:96). Professional relations are to be guided by a principle of equity which has the practitioners becoming in effect the fiduciary trustee of the clients' interests (Carr-Saunders and Wilson 1933:422).

Occupations have their distinctive "affectively toned complex of values and norms . . . [which] are expressed in the form of prescriptions, proscriptions, preferences, and permissions. They are legitimatized in terms of institutional values" (Merton [1942] 1968:605). The value of "helping," specified in the norm of altruism, along with the values of "knowing" and "doing," is part of the ethos of the professions. In what sense, then, is a physician or lawyer normatively expected to be altruistic—that is, in apparent paradox, *to do more* for the client *than is expressly required?*

The Norm of Altruism

Although the norm of altruism has both prescriptive and proscriptive elements, it is primarily directed toward *preferred* behavior. It prescribes that professionals should do everything they can for a client, to a degree even at the expense of maximizing their own distinct interests. Correlatively, the norm proscribes professionals acting in ways that will result to their advantage, and not only monetary advantage, when this is at the expense of clients. Thus, the norm calls for professionals to do more for clients than is legally required of them. As normatively *preferred* rather than *required,* altruism involves a voluntary element in which the professional does more than is required. In a word, altruism is supererogatory.

Perhaps professionals are expected to put their personal interest second to client needs because the opportunities for self-interested exploitation of others are greater than in other occupations. Since professional practice often draws upon specialized knowledge and esoteric technical skills, clients cannot readily understand or assess what is being done to them. The use of professional patois does not do much to help. Clients are vulnerable in other ways. Often, they must reveal private information that is ordinarily kept wholly to themselves or made known only to closest associates. The functional requirement of revealing these dark secrets—which has given rise to the doctrine of privileged communications—can place the client in a possibly compromising situation.

The potential for exploitation is greater because associations with professionals are not routine events; they typically occur at critical intervals rather than being everyday interactions. This greatly limits the accumulation of pertinent information about the practices of this or that professional and makes it difficult for clients to compare services received from several practitioners. New social mechanisms are emerging to handle this problem. Consumer-advocate groups that publish listings evaluating professional services in designated regions constitute one structural response to clients' simultaneous "need to know" and their institutionalized inability to find out.

Like the role of the professional, the role of the client is being redefined. Bernard Barber has contrasted the "old" and "new" models of the patient in his recent study of medical experimentation. The old model has patients in a passive relationship to physicians, unquestioningly accepting commands from the doctor. The new model has patients becoming more involved in decisions made on their behalf, and in a manner of speaking, becoming the physician's colleague in a joint venture (Barber 1976). The new model calls for patients to learn more about what is being done to them, and thus reduces the potential for professional exploitation. But there are manifest limits on how "collegial" professionals and clients can become: expanding professional knowledge and specialized techniques increase the cognitive disparity even as client-education programs seek to decrease it. So long as professional-client relationships remain one-to-one relationships, the potential for exploitation remains.

The potential for exploitation is not limited to dyadic relations between practitioner and client. To the extent that knowledge is power, in the Baconian phrase, and to the extent that professionals monopolize certain forms of knowledge, the professions constitute a powerful occupational sector. There are, of course, other routes to professional power than the monopoly of useful knowledge. The professions have often been able to extend their power and influence beyond their sphere of special expertise. As Max Weber observed, for example, the operations of the modern state have been disproportionately in the hands of lawyers, not simply because of their expertise, but because of their structurally patterned availability to assume governmental responsibilities (Weber [1919] 1946:84). Perhaps that is the sort of thing that had the rebel Jack Cade in Part II of *Henry VI* taking kindly to the suggestion that "The first thing we do, let's kill all the lawyers."

As compared with other occupations, the professions are accorded a high degree of autonomy. Correlatively, they are required to exercise social control over the practices of their members, including the violation of more or less established standards of ethics that are more demanding than legally imposed requirements. In exchange for this measure of autonomy, professionals are expected to place severe limits upon self-interested behavior in their relationships with clients. As we have noted, the expertise and privileged position of professionals confer authority, power, and prestige that can readily be utilized in their own interest rather than their clients' interest. Normative constraints are designed as a counterpoise to such structurally induced temptations for the exploitation of clients. In short, *noblesse oblige,* not *caveat emptor,* is the rule, though far from being the behavioral fact. (It is the Adam Smith of *The Theory of Moral Sentiments* rather than the Adam Smith of *The Wealth of Nations* that is most in point here.)

In practice, the strain toward cooperation extends neither to all phases of professional service nor to all types of practitioners. Social arrangements can curb rather than aid cooperation in the clients' interest. Among lawyers, for example, Jerome Carlin finds that those specializing in personal injury, local taxes, or collections ordinarily have their clients referred to them by brokers or business suppliers. In such situations, lawyers feel their primary obligation is to the broker, the source of their clientele; the client is, in Carlin's word, "expendable" unless seen as a potential source of new business. Competition for professional work can make for deviation from the norm of altruism. One of Carlin's responding lawyers observed, "It's too bad the general practice doesn't adhere more closely to the Canons [Code of Ethics]. It's because of competition in the profession. They must do unscrupulous acts" (Carlin 1962:192).

The norm of altruism incidentally helps absolve the conscientious and competent practitioner from liability or guilt in situations of failure. Everett C. Hughes reminds us that "all patients are lost in the long run [and] half of all cases contested are lost. . . ." (Hughes 1971:361).[7] Costs of failure in professional services are typically quite high. The patterned norm that everything feasible is to be done for the client serves to dampen hostility toward the concerned, competent practitioner, just as the normative expectation can shield the deviant practitioner from penalties for self-interested or incompetent behavior.

In sum, restraints upon self-interested practices exert controls directed toward practices primarily in the interest of others. Although not uniformly effective, structural arrangements make for the institutionalization of altruism.

Institutionalizing Altruism in Professional Practice

These observations about altruism in the professions must have the hollow sound of piety masquerading as reality. It invites each of us to remember the last occasion on which a physician, lawyer, or clergyman proved how far behavior can depart from normative expectations. One potent source of ambivalence toward the professions involves respect for what the profession professes and contempt for what members of the profession sometimes do. Especially when technical expertise is employed without coordinate regard for the purposes to which it is put, there develops that kind of imbalance which often makes professionalism a term of abuse.

As long as we attend to the sociological concept of a profession in terms of normative structure and social organization and thus ignore the distribution of actual behavior by professionals, what we say will have the sound of mere sentimentality. To avoid even the appearance of professional piety in the face of well-known facts to the contrary, we make two observations.

First, it is not being said that professional men and women uniformly live up to professional commitments.[8] Sociologists are not given to confusing norms with actual practice. They hold only that practice would be different if norms did not exist. Applying the general idea to the specific case, we are suggesting only that the norm of altruism *and* associated structural arrangements lead professionals to put the interests of their clients foremost more often than they would in the absence of the norm and structure. There is reason to suppose that altruistic acts are not as rare in the professions as Mark Twain authoritatively informs us the Recording Angel found them to be in another occupation:

> To: Abner Scofield
>   Coal Dealer
>   Buffalo, New York
> I have the honor as per command, to inform you that your recent act of benevolence and self-sacrifice has been recorded upon a page of the Book called *Golden Deeds of Men;* a distinction, I am permitted to remark, which is not merely extraordinary, it is unique.

In the professions, the extraordinary becomes the expected, although it is not the case that every professional uniformly achieves that distinction.

Second and even more emphatically, it is not being said—as professionals themselves sometimes intimate—that professionals have a nature-given inclination for altruism, a principled, primary concern for the interests of the other. Our point is that the professions do not require practitioners to *feel* altruistic; in fact, in some professions, that is suspect.[9] They only require practitioners to *act* altruistically, at least to some degree. From the perspective of structural analysis, it need not be the case that individual members of a profession are uniformly motivated by altruistic sentiments, although such motivation makes it easier for them to live up to the role expectation of altruism.

The essential point is that, to a greater extent than other occupations, the core professions have managed to institutionalize altruism. *By means of a reward system in which moral obligation and self-interest often coincide and fuse, the institutional arrangements of the professions tend to make it a matter of self-interest for individual practitioners to act altruistically.* When these arrangements work effectively—and the reason for their often failing to do so is both a basic social and sociological problem—various forms of reward (prestige, esteem, income, authority) are distributed according to the extent that professionals live up to normative expectations associated with the role. The collective effort is to devise arrangements such that, in the long run, the exploitation of clients is counter-productive for attaining self-interested ends.[10] As we have noted, this aims to institutionalize the principle of *noblesse oblige*, rather than that of *caveat emptor*.

All this does not, of course, hold only in the case of the professions. Structural changes can induce comparable changes in behavior in domains ideologically committed to self-interest. New institutional arrangements can make it a matter of self-interest for practitioners in business (whose practices are often taken as contrast to the professional's concern for clients) to behave altruistically. In the long run, it may be profitable for industrial corporations to undertake programs which clean up the physical or social environment at substantial cost in the short run. Baumol has observed that such behavior reflects not a change toward more altruistic motives, but a change in the rules of the game:

> The firm is not expected to do anything as a pure act of benevolence. Rather it is faced with a new set of conditions under which it and its competitors must operate, and they must adapt themselves as effectively as they can. The two most important characteristics of such changes in the rules . . . are that there is

nothing voluntary about following them, and that it applies equally to all competitors. (Baumol 1975:51)

The general thesis recalls Marx's observation that capitalists exploit not because they are *by nature* evil, but because the social and economic system of capitalism forces them to behave in this way in order to survive as a class.

Returning to the case of the professions, we should note that they are, on the average, though not at the outermost limits, the best paid of all classes of occupations. In the United States, the median annual income of self-employed physicians in 1973 was $42,140; for incorporated physicians, $67,500. There are, of course, great variations of income both within and among the professions: for every surgeon driving a new Mercedes-Benz, there is a clergyman practically as poor as a churchmouse. In such cases, psychic income seems to be partial compensation for material income.

Since the professions as a class yield relatively high psychic and material returns, it may seem bizarre to suggest that they are oriented to the norm of altruism. But sociologists need not be reminded of the differences between motives and outcomes of human behavior or the differences between culturally defined ends and institutionally prescribed means. In the professions, a major criterion used by peers to evaluate the quality of role performance is the competent exercise of expertise in the client's interest. (In some professions, most visibly in the law, this need not be in the societal interest as well.) Whatever the complex motives of this or that practitioner, substantial rewards, psychic and material, accrue from conforming to the professional role expectations linked with the composite values of "knowing, doing, and helping." Under such circumstances, there is no zero-sum relationship between altruism and reward: putting clients' interests first becomes the institutionally prescribed means for moving toward practitioners' own ends, beyond altruism itself. Professionals are expected to suspend their egoistic short-range interests, with the often-enough validated assumption that long-range benefits will accrue from conforming to the norm of altruism.

Historically, as we have noted in passing, the professions have attained substantial autonomy, principally in the form of self-regulation and control. External controls have typically been general and unexacting. Throughout most of the twentieth century, the professional communities have been largely responsible for certifying practitioners, developing the range and forms of professional services, loosely defining fee schedules, and evaluating professional services.

Autonomy has included the privilege of *de facto* and in some cases *de jure* monopoly over the dispensing of designated services. Monopolies result *de facto* from legitimatized rights to control professional education, and so to determine the diffusion of specialized knowledge and techniques that make up the foundation of their practice. Exclusivity over services is frequently reinforced by government legislation which restricts professional services to people possessing designated qualifications.[11]

We are now better able to understand how professionals have institutionalized a reward-system that makes for altruism and self-interest becoming mutually reinforcing. Professional privileges—their autonomy and monopoly over services—are granted by the society in exchange for the guarantee that practitioners will not use these privileges to exploit clients. Eliot Freidson has observed that "the profession's service orientation is a public imputation it has successfully won in a process by which its leaders have persuaded society to grant and support its autonomy" (Freidson 1970:82). The exchange of privileges for safeguards enters into the institutionalization of altruism: it is one of the institutional processes through which it generally becomes a matter of long-range self-interest for professions to act altruistically because of the advantageous opportunities granted by society in return for such behavior.[12] To the extent that the control system decays and the laity comes to perceive a decline in the altruism of professionals, this places a strain on the system and curbs or undermines the continuation of these privileges. If only as a matter of collective self-interest, the professional community is periodically required to attempt the social control of widespread deviance from the norm of altruism. Whether professional practice and the structural arrangements have deteriorated, and have done so irreversibly in some times and places, remains a basic theoretical and empirical question calling for intensive systematic investigation.

PROFESSIONAL SOCIALIZATION AND SOCIAL CONTROL

As in any social system, action oriented to norms in the professions is more or less maintained through processes of socialization and social control. Little need be said here of professional socialization. Insofar as practitioners are socialized to internalize normative orientations to clients, they are of course less likely to experience conflict in meeting professional role expectations.

The Columbia studies of student-physicians (Merton, Reader, and Kendall 1957) and the Chicago studies of boys-in-white (Becker et al. 1961), differing as they do in several respects, nevertheless agree in describing the difficulties encountered in sensitizing students to conflicting norms associated with the professional role. The Columbia studies found, for example, that medical students learn to temper concern for the patient with a degree of detachment that allows for the objectivity required to perform instrumental tasks effectively. There evolves a composite behavioral norm of "detached concern."[13] The evolution of the norm is further testimony to the general sociological rule that, with social norms as with any unrestricted belief in absolutes, there can be too much of a good thing. Total commitment becomes self-defeating. Professional compassion without detachment is ineffectual; professional detachment without compassion, cruel.

Other norms prescribed for the professional role often conflict with the norm of altruism. These competing normative expectations account for some ambivalent behavior of professionals, often perceived by laymen as a retreat from the ideal of service.

First, the extent of help provided by a professional is limited by a norm of functional specificity.[14] Practitioners are expected to offer services only within the limited range of their expertise.

Second, professionals are expected to be universalistic in accepting clients and dispensing services. This can confront them with a dilemma: doing everything possible for one client can keep them from providing similar services for another. In a study of medical liability, Allan H. McCoid found that courts often expected physicians to offer assistance whenever confronted with situations where their expertise could be put to beneficial use. While courts are taking this position with greater frequency, McCoid (1959:18) observes that the trend has not yet reached a point where there are "unlimited demands upon a doctor's time and energy that would be likely to result in inadequate care for all."

Third, the dependence of the professions upon an evolving body of theoretical and technical knowledge requires that some professionals view their clients not only as presenting "problems to be solved" but as providing "solutions to theoretical problems." Those engaged in medical research, for example, often experience ambivalence as they feel obliged to do everything they can for a patient while also wanting to use the "case" to advance knowledge (and their own research career) in the field. The behavior of researchers in relation to human subjects in scientific and professional experiments is being systematically investigated (Katz 1972, Barber et al. 1973). From the first American legal suit involving medical experimentation in 1767 (won, incidentally, by a patient who claimed that experimental techniques had failed to straighten his leg), courts have generally allowed medical innovation so long as the experiment was judged to be in the best interest of the patient. Such judgments are not easy to come by.

Structural Constraints upon Social Control

Historically, the locus of social control in the established professions has come to reside chiefly within the professional community. The effectiveness of that control is limited by several structural constraints which work against the professions going to great pains to identify and penalize deviations from the norm of altruism.[15]

To begin with, the criteria for evaluating professional services are often ambiguous. The norm of altruism is directed toward moral obligations, not technical procedures. Compared with the question of technically appropriate treatment for a client's problem, which can itself become extraordinarily complex, the question of a practitioner's moral obligations to the client is often difficult and diffuse.

A second constraint upon effective social control by the profession derives from a basic attribute of the social organization of professional practice: the comparatively low degree of "observability" of role performance.[16] Much of what professionals do, especially the professionals at work within the confines of their own offices (whether in the private practice, so-called, of physicians in the United States or in the National Health Service of England), is ordinarily not open to observation by professional peers or superiors qualified to assess faults in what is being proposed or being done. And, we remind ourselves, clients themselves are for the most part not qualified to judge. This structural constraint of little observability greatly limits the potentiality of internal social control. When it occurs at all, it is apt to be initiated primarily in cases of extreme malpractice, as gauged by technical standards of performance rather than by the more diffuse and imperfectly specified norm of altruism. Awareness of the comparative invisibility of much medical practice has given rise to the idea and, to a still limited extent, the institutional arrangement of "peer review." Provision for regular assessments of the quality of practice by fellow physicians is an institutional analogue to the long-established procedure of peer review in scientific research, where fellow scientists serving as referees appraise the quality of proposals for research funding or of manuscripts for publication in scientific journals.

A third constraint is imposed by the existence of professional solidarity on the large scale and by interpersonal relations between immediate professional colleagues on the small scale. Both of these are often at odds with the effective exercise of internal social control. Solidarity helps maintain the comfortable presumption that, by and large, professional practitioners do far more for their clients than, say, business practitioners do for their customers. Moreover, professionals know that the outcome of a professionally problematic situation is not *prima facie* evidence of professional incompetence, let alone evidence of negligent or self-interested violation of altruistic standards. Once again, therefore, only the most glaring cases of deviant behavior will lead solitary professionals to put in question the structurally induced presumption that even when things go badly for the client, all that should have been done probably has been done. Or at least that, "considering the circumstances," it was a better kind of role performance than would ordinarily be found in other occupations.

Fourth and on this accounting finally, the structure of professional practice also provides occasion for self-interested motivation among professionals not to report the behavior of fellow practitioners which they perceive as violating the norm of altruism. To question the practices of this or that practitioner publicly means running the risk of alienating other professional colleagues; not alone the one accused but others in the local system of practitioners who come to see themselves as potential objects of uncomfortably close surveillance and evaluation. To "inform" is to violate the code of professional solidarity; it is to become isolated as a pariah "informer" rather than integrated as a conscientious "informant." Public disclosure from within threatens professional *esprit de corps* and generates a degree of mutual mistrust. Rather than being identified as an agent of legitimate formal control, the informer becomes the object of informal social control, and is subjected to a range of sanctions. At the least, the informer risks losing referrals from alienated colleagues and, far beyond that, may suffer something akin to professional ostracism.

Most professionals and many laymen are thoroughly aware of these structural constraints. That awareness encourages the often-voiced, not necessarily cynical, belief that far more self-interested, unethical, and incompetent practitioners are at work in the professions than are publicly identified or subjected to professional sanctions.

The Dilemma of Social Control

The professions, as physically dispersed but occupationally cohesive communities, find themselves particularly subject to a basic dilemma of social control: to publicize or not to publicize deviant behavior. Groups, organizations, and communities differ in the extent of the socially patterned leeway for deviation from the rules which will be tolerated.[17] From the standpoint of the solidary members of the professions, every publicly identified case of departure from the norm of altruism serves to undermine public confidence in the professional community as a whole. It could give rise to a widespread misperception about the actual extent of deviant behavior in the given professional community. Having long been beneficiaries of a community halo effect, many professionals fear being encircled by a tarnished halo as a member of a profession that (to descend a bit) conscientiously insists on washing its dirty linen in public. Contributing to the dilemma of social control is the apparent fact that public perceptions derive principally from variations in the extent of publicity accorded deviant behavior. As we have noted, for example, public estimates of the amount of violent crime and theft reflected trends in the perception of crime *news* in print rather than in recorded crime rates.[18] All this makes for a collective preference to avoid the costs of fully reporting identifiable violations of the code—the phenomenon of the collective cover-up, for example, as indelibly portrayed in Ibsen's *An Enemy of the People*.

But as is generally the case with dilemmas, the other horn of the dilemma of social control has substantial costs as well. To retain an inefficient system for detecting and publicizing deviant behavior becomes dysfunctional to the professional community concerned to retain social esteem and relative autonomy. The public correction of deviance has important boundary-maintaining functions for the professional community: by imposing sanctions on violators of norms, the profession reinforces standards of conduct for its members and confidence in its integrity among members of the larger society. Continued and visible failure to control deviant practices jeopardizes the implicit exchange of professional privileges (including relative autonomy) for practical altruism. As recent social change testifies, the society will not continue indefinitely to grant the professions autonomy when self-regulation proves conspicuously ineffectual.

There is of course nothing new about the indicated structural constraints and dilemma of social control facing the professional community. The constraints and the dilemma probably contribute to the long-standing ambivalence of attitudes directed toward the professions: professionals are esteemed for their institutional commitment to altruism in principle, but when, not unlike the rest of us in other institutional domains, they remain a little lower than the angels in practice, public disenchantment with them becomes all the greater precisely because of the high standards they profess. Moreover, changes in the larger society introduce new contexts for old problems. Among these changes, two in particular make for decreasing public acceptance of autonomous self-regulation by the professions and increasing demands for their public regulation.

The first of these contextual changes is the great rise in the average level of formal education in modern industrialized societies.

The evidence indicates that education need not make people wise or prudent. But it does deepen their confidence in asserting their own legitimatized wants and appraising the extent to which they are being met. Along with this structural change is the growing belief, noted by Everett Hughes ([1960] 1971:365) that people have an inextinguishable moral right to education, to health, and to other kinds of increase in all the good things of life. With education and a consequent sense of self-competence becoming more widespread, demands upon the professions become more insistent and clients more exacting in assessing the role performance of professionals. Putting these developments together, one would expect a secular trend toward advocating public control of the professions, to complement control from within the professional community.

THE PERCEIVED RETREAT FROM ALTRUISM

No one really knows the extent of negligence, delinquency, crime, and other forms of misbehavior in the professions. The evidence available on this is even more defective than the notoriously inadequate crime statistics in general. As we have seen, much professional practice is unobservable by qualified judges, and it must be assumed that some, perhaps much, deviant behavior is never discovered since, unlike the case of most crimes, the victims do not even know that they have been victimized. Other deviations from the norm that are observable by colleagues are never reported, for reasons we have touched upon. The residual cases which are reported—some of them ending in the mounting number of suits for malpractice—are not routinely compiled. Even then, they would remain inadequate as indicators of actual rates of deviance, registering only the product of variations in deviant behavior and in local systems of social control. As a result of all this, the growing stock of social indicators continues to have a conspicuous gap when it comes to time-series indicating changes in the rates of deviant behavior in the professions. In turn, the absence of such systematic data leaves ample space for individual and social constructions of "what must actually be going on" in the professions, based largely upon motivated perceptions of personal experience and secondary accounts of like kind.

In this field like others since the invention of the sample survey, systematic data are more readily available on the subjective than on the objective aspects of social phenomena. Thus, the Gallup and Harris polls in the United States have reported for some years the extent of confidence expressed in various institutions, occupations, and public figures. These time-series uniformly exhibit a recent decline of public trust in most institutions and occupations, including all the designated professions. The Harris Survey reports that the percentage of respondents having a great deal of confidence in medicine (as an occupation) fell from 73 percent in 1966 to 37 percent in 1981; for organized religion, the proportion dropped from 41 percent to 22 percent for the same period; with predictable trend, those expressing great confidence in the U.S. Congress dropped from 42 percent of those polled in 1966 to 16 percent. Along with this decline in public trust is an inferred growth of what is perceived as less than altruistic behavior by professionals.

As we have noted, it would come as no surprise to learn that increasing violations of the altruistic norm, fully reported, would erode public confidence in the professions. The professional monopoly of pertinent knowledge and information provides a ready basis for various forms of exploitation of clients who know neither the potential price of the service given them nor the quality of service required. There would seem nothing analytically problematic about declining trust in the professions if these opportunities for exploitation (in the strict sense) were increasingly being taken up in such deviant or marginal practices as charging exorbitant fees, avoiding or rejecting clients unable to pay these fees, experimenting with human subjects at a risk they cannot assess, or cutting corners in order to handle large numbers of fee-paying clients.

Increasing public distrust of the professions can have less direct sources than actual malpractice. Paradoxically, certain kinds of changes in modes of professional practice may actually improve health care (here, we limit ourselves to the profession of medicine) and yet be experienced as departures from clients' expectations of altruism. To many patients, the bureaucratization of medical care in hospitals or local clinics may seem a retreat from the family physician, that accomplished friend routinely willing to make house calls. Although with each generation this becomes more myth than memory, the idea of excellent health care at home remains an engaging vision.* As a general practitioner, that vision holds, the family doctor was able to handle just about every health problem that came along. The growth of specialization has of course converted the general practitioner into a rare bird indeed; in 1906, about 66 percent of all physicians in the United States were GPs; by 1950, about 36 percent; as

---

*For an informed, perceptive account of the family physician as historical fact and as myth, see the forthcoming memoir by Lewis Thomas, *The Youngest Science: Notes of a Medicine-Watcher* (New York: Harper & Row, 1982).

late as 1965, about 22 percent; and in 1973, a mere 13 percent. The fragmentation and frequent bureaucratization of medical services may be another contextual source of the decline of personal ties with physicians and the perceived retreat from the norm of altruism.[19]

Comparable changes in the structure of legal practice may have contributed to a comparable result. Professional specialization limits the range of clientele and this, in turn, can affect professional perspectives. A growing proportion of lawyers in the United States are employed by business corporations. Officer of the court or no, the lawyer is defined as having a primary obligation to this client, whether individual or corporate. But commitment to the large corporation as client is often identified as opposed to the public interest. As the jurist Harlan Fiske Stone once observed:

> The vast expansion of business has steadily drawn some of the best skill and capacity of the legal profession into the exacting and specialized service of business and finance. At its best, this has brought to the command of the business world a superb proficiency and technical skill. At its worst, it has made the learned profession . . . the obsequious servant of business, and painted it with the morals and manners of the marketplace in its most antisocial manifestations.

Adolph Berle made much the same point, noting that far too many practitioners in the law have become so specialized as to run the danger of becoming "intellectual jobbers and contractors," advancing the interests of their clients at the expense of the larger public interest. In short, primary commitment to a client can become defined as conflicting with larger social commitments.

In seeming Tocquevillian paradox, a growing capability for providing professional service can lead to growing doubt that historically improved service is being provided. As Robin Williams (1975:358–359) observed in his comprehensive analysis of the pattern of relative deprivation:

> . . . prior to 1930 doctors could do very little to cure disease, but expectations and the physicians' performance were congruent. But with vastly improved capacity to actually cure, medical care is subject to expectations that outrun performance; hopes outrun expectations; and disappointment often is tinged with moral outrage concerning inequities in availability of help. Once more, in this sense, we see that "nothing fails like success."

And we might add within the present context, actual rates of departures from the norm of altruism may be magnified by changes in the social contexts of professional work which displace traditional indicators of personal concern with the client.

Such disaffection with technically competent but impersonal

professional service can lead to a search for others who may have less expertise but more concern. Impatient patients, filled with doubt about receiving altruistic care from hospital-based physicians, become willing to trade technical skill for guaranteed concern by seeking help from non-professionals with whom they share a personal relationship.* More than two decades ago, Talcott Parsons (1951:423–433) predicted that as medical care became increasingly bureaucratized, people would turn to lay sources of help in the form of compassionate care. That prediction has become social fact in the form of numerous medical self-help programs. Arguments for the decentralization of professional services, designed to recapture professional expertise, have been put forward most emphatically by Ivan Illich in his *Medical Nemesis* (1976). But much goodwill and compassion coupled with only a modicum of technical competence simply will not do for certain kinds of problems. Open-heart surgery, for example, not only requires great surgical skill but a specialized infrastructure ordinarily found only in a modern hospital.

Other structural changes are being proposed or introduced to offset what is being defined as a decline, and may in fact be a decline, in the effective working of institutionalized altruism. One of these changes provides for enlarged lay participation in the planning and evaluation of professional services. Government mandated peer-review and control boards for community health care represent other changes. Sociologically, these developments represent a shift in the nature of status-judges from insiders to outsiders, with the traditional quasi-autonomy of the professions becoming successively circumscribed.

CONCLUSION

This essay has examined the workings of institutionalized altruism in the case of the professions. Since that discussion lends itself easily to misunderstanding in terms of imputed stereotyped ideas, we reiterate two basic points. First, we do not at all suggest that professionals are uniformly and primarily motivated by an altruistic concern for their clients; the changing extent to which this is so remains an empirical question. What we do suggest is that, again in changing fashion, the reward structure in the professional community reinforces self-interest in a concern for clients' welfare beyond that

*Lewis Thomas is particularly instructive on this in his forthcoming *The Youngest Science, ibid.*

legally or contractually defined as part of the professional's role. Second, we recognize that professionals, like others, do not uniformly act in accord with the norm that defines altruistic behavior as professionally preferred. We argue only that the frequency of exploitative behavior by professionals is less than it would be if the institutionalized norm of altruism were not operative.

The idea of institutionalized altruism draws attention to similar patterns of behavior in substantively different sectors of social life. A similar kind of underlying social structure encourages both the donation of blood and the offering of professional services, the recycling of an eye and the creation of a philanthropic foundation. In every case, an institutional arrangement fuses self-interest and a concern for others in ways that promote altruistic behavior despite a diverse range of concrete motives.

REFERENCES

Barber, Bernard. 1976. "The Social Control of the Professions: Toward a Solution of an Ethical Crisis," *Columbia University Seminar Reports* 3:128–133.

Barber, Bernard et al. 1973. *Research on Human Subjects*. New York: Russell Sage.

Baumol, William J. 1975. "Business Responsibility and Economic Behavior," in *Altruism, Morality, and Economic Theory*, Edmund S. Phelps, ed. New York: Russell Sage. Pp. 45–56.

Becker, Howard S. et al. 1961. *Boys in White: Student Culture in Medical School*. Chicago: University of Chicago Press.

Ben-David, Joseph. 1958. "The Professional Role of the Physician in Bureaucratic Medicine: A Study in Role-Conflict," *Human Relations* 11:255–274.

Bennion, F.A.R. 1966. *Professional Ethics: The Consultant Professions and Their Code*. London: Charles Knight & Co.

Blauner, Robert. 1966. "Work, Satisfaction, and Industrial Trends in Modern Society." in *Class, Status and Power*. 2nd ed. R. Bendix and S.M. Lipset, eds. New York: The Free Press. Pp. 473–487.

Brandeis, Louis D. 1925. *Business—A Profession*. Boston: Small, Maynard.

Carlin, Jerome E. 1962. *Lawyers on Their Own*. New Brunswick, N.J.: Rutgers University Press.

———. 1966. *Lawyer's Ethics: A Survey of the New York City Bar*. New York: Russell Sage.

Carr-Saunders, A.M., and Wilson, P.A. 1933. *The Professions*. Oxford: The Clarendon Press.

Comte, August. 1890–1895. *Système de politique positive*. 3rd edition, 4 vols. Paris.

Coombs, R.H., and Goldman, L.J. 1973. "Maintenance and Discontinuity of Coping Mechanisms in the Intensive Care Unit," *Social Problems* 20:342–343.

Davis, Arlene K. 1973. "How Free Should Professions Be?", in *The Professions and Their Prospects,* Eliot Freidson, ed. Beverly Hills: Sage. Pp. 39–57.

Davis, F. James. 1952. "Crime Waves in Colorado Newspapers," *American Journal of Sociology* 57:325–330.

Durkheim, Emile. [1925] 1961. *Moral Education.* New York: The Free Press.

Flexner, Abraham. 1915. "Is Social Work a Profession?", *Proceedings of the National Conference of Charities and Corrections.* Chicago. Pp. 576–590.

Fox, Renée. 1959. *Experiment Perilous.* New York: The Free Press.

Freidson, Eliot. 1970. *Profession of Medicine: A Study of the Sociology of Applied Knowledge.* New York: Dodd, Mead and Company.

Goode, William J. 1957. "Community Within a Community: The Professions." *American Sociological Review* 22:194–200.

———. 1967. "The Protection of the Inept," *American Sociological Review* 32:5–19.

———. 1973. *Explorations in Social Theory.* New York: Oxford University Press.

Goss, Mary E.W. [1959]. 1980. *Physicians in Bureaucracy: A Case Study of Professional Pressures on Organizational Roles.* New York: Arno Press.

———. 1961. "Influence and Authority Among Physicians in an Out-Patient Clinic," *American Sociological Review* 26:39–50.

Greenwood, Ernest. 1957. "Attributes of a Profession," *Social Work* 2:44–55.

Hall, Richard H. 1968. "Professionalization and Bureaucratization," *American Sociological Review* 33:92–104.

Hodge, Robert W., Siegel, Paul M., and Rossi, Peter H. 1964. "Occupational Prestige in the United States: 1925–1963," *American Journal of Sociology* 70:286–302.

Hughes, Everett C. 1971. *The Sociological Eye: Selected Papers.* Chicago: Aldine, Atherton.

Ichheiser, Gustav. 1970. *Appearance and Realities: Misunderstanding in Human Relations.* San Francisco: Jossey-Bass.

Illich, Ivan. 1976. *Medical Nemesis.* New York: Pantheon.

Kadushin, Charles. 1981. "Notes on Expectations of Reward in N-Person Networks," in *Continuities in Structural Inquiry,* P.M. Blau and R.K. Merton, eds. London and Beverly Hills: Sage. Pp. 235–254.

Katz, Jay. 1972. *Experimentation with Human Beings.* New York: Russell Sage.

Lewis, Howard R., and Lewis, Martha E. 1970. *The Medical Offenders.* New York: Simon and Schuster.

Lieberman, Jethro K. 1970. *The Tyranny of the Experts.* New York: Walker and Company.

Lief, H.I., and Fox, Renée C. 1963. "The Medical Student's Training for 'Detached Concern'," in *The Psychological Basis of Medical Practice,* H.I. Lief, V. Lief, and N.R. Lief, eds. New York: Harper and Row. Pp. 12–35.

McCoid, Allan H. 1960. "The Care Required of Medical Practitioners," in *Professional Negligence*, T.G. Roady and W.R. Anderson, eds. Nashville: Vanderbilt University Press.

Mills, C. Wright. 1951. *White Collar*. New York: Oxford University Press.

Merton, Robert K. 1938. "Social Structure and Anomie," *American Sociological Review* 3. Pp. 672–82.

———. [1942] 1973. "The Normative Structure of Science," in Robert K. Merton, *The Sociology of Science*, Norman W. Storer, ed. Chicago: University of Chicago Press; Chapter 1 of this volume.

———. 1959. "Notes on Problem-finding in Sociology," in *Sociology Today*, Robert K. Merton, Leonard Broom, and Leonard S. Cottrell, Jr., eds. New York: Basic Books. Pp. ix–xxxiv. Reprinted as Chapter 2 of this volume—editors' note.

———. 1960. "Some Thoughts on the Professions in American Society," *Brown University Papers* 37:1–17.

———. 1960. "The Ambivalences of LeBon's *The Crowd*" (Introduction to the Compass Edition of Gustave LeBon, *The Crowd*). New York: Viking Press. Pp. v–xxxix.

———. 1963. "Foreword" in Hubert J. O'Gorman, *Lawyers and Matrimonial Cases: A Study of Informal Pressures in Private Professional Practices*. New York: The Free Press.

———. [1963] 1969. "Introduction" to Allen Barton, *Communities in Disaster: A Sociological Analysis of Collective Stress Situations*. Garden City, N.Y.: Doubleday & Co. Pp. vii–xxxvii.

———. 1968. *Social Theory and Social Structure*. Enlarged Edition. New York: The Free Press.

———. 1975. "The Uses of Institutionalized Altruism," *Columbia University Seminar Reports* 3, No. 6:105–113.

———. 1976. *Sociological Ambivalence and Other Essays*. New York: The Free Press.

———. 1976. "The Sociology of Social Problems," in *Contemporary Social Problems*, Robert K. Merton and Robert A. Nisbet, eds. 4th ed. New York: Harcourt Brace Jovanovich.

Merton, Robert K., and Barber, Elinor. [1963] 1976. "Sociological Ambivalence," reprinted in Merton, *Sociological Ambivalence and Other Essays*. Pp. 3–31.

Merton, Robert K. et al. 1957. *The Student-Physician: Introductory Studies in the Sociology of Medical Education*. Cambridge, Mass.: Harvard University Press.

Parsons, Talcott. [1939] 1949. "The Professions and Social Structure," in *Essays in Sociological Theory*. New York: The Free Press.

———. 1951. *The Social System*. New York: The Free Press.

Scott, W. Richard. 1966. "Professionals in Bureaucracies—Areas of Conflict," in *Professionalization*, H.M. Vollmer and D.L. Mills, eds. Englewood Cliffs, N.J.: Prentice-Hall. Pp. 265–275.

Tawney, R.H. [1922] 1946. *The Acquisitive Society*. New York: Harvest Books.

Terkel, Studs. 1972. *Working*. New York: Pantheon.

Thomas, Lewis, forthcoming 1982. *The Youngest Science:* Notes of a Medicine-Watcher. New York: Harper & Row.

Titmuss, Richard M. 1971. *The Gift Relationship: From Human Blood to Social Policy.* New York: Random House-Pantheon.

Treiman, Donald J., and Terrell, Kermit. 1975a. "Sex and the Process of Status Attainment: A Comparison of Working Women and Men," *American Sociological Review* 40:174–200.

————. 1975b. "The Process of Status Attainment in the United States and Great Britain," *American Journal of Sociology* 81:563–583.

Weber, Max. 1946. *From Max Weber: Essays in Sociology,* Hans Gerth and C. Wright Mills, eds. New York: Oxford University Press.

Whitehead, Alfred North. [1933] 1961. *Adventures of Ideas.* New York: The Free Press.

Wilensky, Harold L., and Lebeaux, Charles N. 1958. *Industrial Society and Social Welfare.* New York: Russell Sage.

Williams, Robin. 1975. "Relative Deprivation," in *The Idea of Social Structure,* Lewis Coser, ed. New York: Harcourt Brace Jovanovich. Pp. 355–378.

NOTES

[1] In *Moral Education,* Durkheim made the Simmel-like observation that "egoism and altruism are two abstractions that do not exist in a pure state; one always implies the other at least to some degree, although in a given concrete situation, they are never developed in the same degree" ([1925] 1961:217).

[2] This section derives substantially from Merton (1975).

[3] We shall spare the reader still another learned definition of a profession. Our analysis is concerned mainly with medicine and law, but applies as well to the two other core professions of the ministry and university teaching.

[4] On the relatively stable occupational prestige hierarchy in the United States, see Hodge, Siegel, and Rossi (1964). On worker satisfaction, see Blauner (1966).

[5] For comparative studies, see Treiman and Terrell (1975a, 1975b).

[6] For an example of this criterion, the National Labor Relations Board ruled in 1976 that newspaper journalists were not professionals. The decision of the board hinged on the legal definition of a professional as "any employee engaged in work requiring knowledge of an advanced type in a field of science or learning customarily acquired by a prolonged course of specialized instruction."

[7] The decades-long studies of the professions by Everett C. Hughes are in large measure consistent with the principal themes of this paper. See especially "Professions" (1965) and "The Professions in Society" (1960), both reprinted in Hughes, *The Sociological Eye: Collected Papers* (1971).

[8] From the large library of works on the various types and distribution of unethical medical practice, consult, for examples, Lewis and Lewis (1970).

[9]Motivated altruism is sometimes seen as deviance from institutionally prescribed attitudes. Studs Terkel, interviewing a "poor people's lawyer," elicited the following response: "I don't consider myself a real lawyer. I'm not a lawyer in the sense that the better job I do, the more money I get from my client. I'm just trying to help." (Terkel 1972:539) The classic discussion of the differences between institutional and motivational analysis is Talcott Parsons (1951: Chapter 10).

[10]This basic claim has long been advanced by Talcott Parsons (1951), Goode (1957), and others.

[11]On the autonomy and monopoly of services in the professions, see Lieberman (1970) and Davis (1973).

[12]C. Wright Mills observes in *White Collar* that the code of professional ethics was an "obsolete mythology" (1951:120). Nevertheless, he points out that because of the guild-like institutional structure governing the distribution of professional rewards, many professionals conform to what we have called the norm of altruism "so as best to promote [their] long-run self interest" (1951:138).

[13]The concept of detached concern is discussed in Merton, Reader, and Kendall (1957), Fox (1959), Lief and Fox (1963), Merton and Barber ([1963]1976), and Coombs and Goldman (1973).

[14]See Parsons's library of works on the subject of functional specificity, especially *The Social System* (1951).

[15]We say nothing here about professional codes of ethics or of the mechanics involved in handling deviations from the norm of altruism. Two informative works on this subject are Bennion (1969) and Carlin (1966).

[16]On structural variations in the "observability" of role performance and the consequences of such variations for processes of social control, see Merton (1968:373–376, 395–400, 428–43) and Chapter 6 of this volume.

[17]On this and the related pattern of "the institutionalized evasion of institutional rules," see Merton (1968:371–372); Merton, "Foreword," in O'Gorman (1963:xii–xiv); also Chapter 3 of this volume.

[18]See the early pointed investigation by F. James Davis (1952). On the general subject of misperception in social life, see Gustav Ichheiser (1970); on misperceptions of rates of deviant behavior, see Chapter 3.

[19]The literature on professionals in bureaucracies is large and growing. For a useful introduction, see Scott (1966). Ben-David (1958) has examined the special case of bureaucratized medicine, and Mary E. W. Goss ([1959]1980, 1961) has analyzed the interaction of administrative and professional hierarchies in hospitals.

CHAPTER 6

Preliminaries to a Sociology of Medical Education*

Every human society has its healers charged with responsibility for the care and cure of the sick. As Dr. Dana Atchley, himself a notable clinician, observed, even without training in scientific medicine "the genuinely talented healer [who] can understand the personality and environment of his patient . . . may be of such value that the patient's life is happily altered while nature is curing the ailment that led him to seek help." Particularly if they are aware of the great extent of their ignorance, so that they do not mistake it for sound knowledge, healers can do good, even in the absence of scientific knowledge. In this large sense, the practice of healing and of medicine is institutionally provided for in all societies.

THE INSTITUTIONAL SETTING

Although some socially patterned provision for the practice of healing and medicine is universal, it is only in fairly recent times that

*Reprinted by permission of the publishers from *The Student-Physician,* edited by Robert K. Merton, George G. Reader, and Patricia L. Kendall, Cambridge, Mass.: Harvard University Press, copyright ©1957 by The Commonwealth Fund.

the empirical craft and art of the healer have been greatly supplemented by the sciences which, in composite, make up the science of human biology. In this vastly enlarged form, the arts and sciences of medicine and health care have become the core of one of the major social institutions of our time. An inventory of the major institutions of American society—for example, the family; the economy; political, religious, military, scientific, communications, and recreational institutions—must include the institution of medicine and health care.

This institution can be sociologically regarded as uniting large numbers of people in the performance of numerous and diversified tasks all aimed at the same central purposes: the prevention of illness, the care and cure of the sick, and ultimately the active mobilization of personal resources by those in a state of comparative health and well-being. From the sociological standpoint, also, the organization of medical and associated personnel has as its major and pervasive *social function* (whether or not this be the *intent* of individual practitioners) the provision of means for coping with a major internal threat to the effective operation of the economy and the society. The most immediate personal impact of illness is, of course, upon the sick and upon those intimately linked with them in close-knit primary groups of family and friends. But the more general social impact is upon wider social systems, as familiar statistics amply attest. A crude measure of the magnitude of the task is provided by the fact that some 7 million Americans are disabled by illness and infirmity on an average day. The failure of these millions to perform their ordinary social roles affects the work and lives of many millions more. To consider the direct economic consequences alone, illness and disability annually reduce the labor force available to the country by 6 to 8 percent. But the disturbances to the social system occasioned by illness and disability are, of course, not fully registered in these figures; the consequences of illness for many other kinds of groups find no direct reflection in statistics.

Other well-known figures testify to the large scope of medicine as one of the major institutions of our society. In the late 1970s about 10 percent of consumer expenditures by Americans were devoted to medical care and associated services, this amounting to some $120 billion annually. In 1976 about three-quarters of Americans were enrolled in voluntary health insurance programs. Altogether, the organizations directly concerned with the prevention of illness, the care of the sick, and the maintenance of health now form a vast institutional complex, bringing together into one interdependent whole a great variety of personnel, organizations, and facilities—patients and physicians; nurses and social workers, dentists and pharmacists; proliferating numbers and varieties of health technicians;

diversified and specialized hospitals; many kinds of centers devoted to medical research; agencies designed to protect the public health; philanthropic organizations aiding research, practice, and education in medicine; large, growing, and highly competitive drug houses; associations to provide health insurance; and professional schools, in and out of universities, to educate health personnel. This great complex confronts the society with the formidable task of finding means for coordinating and consolidating these components into an effective whole.

At the heart of this large, sprawling institutional complex is the medical school and teaching hospital, a center of advances in the scientific knowledge upon which much of medicine is based, a center of would-be advances in ways of practicing medicine, and, of course, a center concerned with the preparation of those who are to be physicians. As part of this larger institutional system, the medical school cannot help being affected by events taking place elsewhere within the system. More distantly, the medical school is continuously subject to changing social demands and expectations.

To say that medical schools are interdependent with other parts of the institutional complex is to say that they must take these into account. The schools do not merely adapt themselves to the rest of the institutional system. Like other social institutions, but particularly the institutions centered on the various professions, medical schools have a measure of autonomy; they have their own definitions of objectives and procedures, which are sometimes at odds with the expectations and demands of particular groups in society. A professional school without substantial autonomy becomes a tenuous association of men and women uncertain of their way.

Free societies continue to grant relative autonomy to their component institutions as long as these more or less effectively discharge their functions. This implies unending change in medical schools, as in other social institutions. A society in the course of change, a body of knowledge continuously growing in scope and content, the changing composition of the major health problems of the society in part brought about by the antecedent accomplishments of medicine itself—all these press for changes within medical education as well. Like other institutions, also, medical schools develop vested sentiments and interests, continue with established ways of doing things not only when they are still optimum ways but also, on occasion, when they are no longer appropriate to the announced purposes of the institution. So it is that the mores of medicine require continued scrutiny in the light of changing needs and opportunities.

Oddly enough, the capacity for functionally appropriate changes in medicine and medical education can be reinforced by a strong emphasis upon the *traditions* of medicine. We ordinarily think of tradition as that cultural component which resists change, persisting for a time even when it is out of tune with newly emerging requirements of the society. But this is a wholly formal view, not a substantive one. The social function of tradition depends upon its content. Great traditions in medicine are typically associated with celebrated physicians of the past, with those who have shown a capacity to move forward when most of their colleagues were satisfied to let things remain as they were. They involve commitment to the search for improved, and therefore changing, ways of coping with the problems of the sick. In this sense respect for medical tradition is an enduring part of the culture of medical education. Frequent ceremonies are designed to keep alive a sense of the core values of medicine as these are exemplified in the achievements of those who have gone before. In this sense, also, outstanding physicians are in some degree historians of medicine, taking pride and finding precedent in the values and accomplishments of the great physicians of the past. Medical schools become the guardians of values basic to the practice of medicine.

It is the function of medical schools to transmit and advance the culture of medicine. It is their goal to shape novices into effective practitioners of medicine, to give them available knowledge and skills, and to provide them with a professional identity so that they come to think, act, and feel like a physician. It is their problem to enable physicians to live up to the expectations of the professional role long after they have left the sustaining value-environment provided by the school. This is the context within which psychological and sociological inquiry into medical schools can identify the extent to which and the ways in which all this comes about.

But before examining the character of such inquiries, we should consider problems of medical education in historical perspective.

HISTORICAL PERSPECTIVES: MORGAN'S *DISCOURSE*

It requires an active effort of mind to see the contemporary scene in its historical context. Moreover, that effort is hemmed in by lack of access to that wisdom of hindsight which is one of the principal assets of historians. This is as true of medical education as of other social institutions. *Ex post* wisdom is easy to come by; *ex ante* wisdom, difficult. It is not easy to identify current developments which will have cumulative consequences for the future and to discriminate these from passing enthusiasms, best forgotten before they have run their course. It is difficult to distinguish the resistance to change which aims to maintain intact the core values of medical education from the resistance which is merely a product of professional folkways, sentiment, self-interests, and the uncritical wish to let thoroughly alone what superficially seems to be well enough. To detect the rudiments of basic institutional change is perhaps more difficult than to detect the persistence of practices grown anachronistic. As the medical historian, John F. Fulton, has remarked, ". . . important history is often being made in our midst, passing largely unrecognized. . . ."

There is no need here to outline the long, checkered history of medical education.[1] But we may gain needed perspective by examining one early development in the history of American medical education in a little detail and touching on some later climactic episodes. For, as we shall see, the first proposal in this country for new forms of social organization designed to transmit the culture of medicine—its knowledge and skills, values and attitudes—adopted what was, in effect, a distinctly sociological orientation toward medical education.

Dr. John Morgan, the first American professor of the theory and practice of medicine, delivered his justly celebrated *Discourse upon the Institution of Medical Schools in America* in 1765.[2] The *Discourse* has long been recognized as a prescient and eloquent statement of a philosophy of medical education. It is that, of course, but it is something more. In its methodical regard for the kinds of social arrangements which, in Morgan's judgment, were required to educate physicians, it exhibits a remarkable sociological sense of what this entailed. A short analytical résumé of the principal ideas in the *Discourse* will serve to identify those problems and to underscore the continued pertinence of some of them.

Morgan in effect adopted a sociological perspective on medical education, directed toward developing an effective social organization for learning, rather than adopting a psychological perspective, directed toward identifying the attributes of individuals that qualify them to become physicians. Not, of course, that Morgan neglected these personal attributes; only that he saw with singular clarity the respects in which even the ablest persons might be less than able physicians if the organized arrangements for their education and training were defective. Morgan thus affords an object lesson easily overlooked, as we shall see, in present-day research on medical education. The process of education, he says in effect, can be instructively examined not only in terms of the *psychology* of learning, focused on the processes by which organisms undergo those functional changes classified as learning, but also in terms of the *sociology* of learning, focused on the social and cultural environments which facilitate or hamper learning.

The Division of Medical Practice

Morgan starts from the premise that the education of the physician must take due account of what he regarded as the effective organization of medical practice. In making his case for the division of labor (specialization) in medicine, Morgan importantly anticipated Adam Smith, whose *Wealth of Nations* was to appear only a decade later. The parallel between the two extends even to the detail of drawing upon the then-popular analogy with experience gained in the manufacture of pins, in which, Morgan reminds his readers:

> . . . a variety of hands, no less commonly than five, six or seven different artists unite their industry. By this means they finish more work in a limited time, and can afford to sell it at a cheaper rate, than they could, if every individual was employed in all the separate branches. But each having a particular province assigned to himself, while all conspire in one uniform plan, they become more skillful and dextrous in their respective parts, and all more usefully subservient to one end. Are the good qualities of accuracy, dispatch, and cheapness, not to speak of the greater perfection of the work, no recommendation to the manner of doing it? (p. xv)

In drawing this prudent analogy between social arrangements for the lowly manufacture of pins and the lofty practice of medicine, Morgan was well aware that he was departing from the long-established tradition which would not allow that the prestigious scientist or scholar can learn anything from the experience of the artisan.

All apart from his assumptions of specialized capacities for particular skills, Morgan is quick to see some of the problems of education to which specialization in the medical arts gives rise. An extreme of specialized knowledge will produce the narrow man untutored except in his own specialty. It will produce only limited competence and special biases, with little basis for a consensus of values among those engaged in their distinct spheres of activity. But this, he points out, need occur only if the formal training of the physician is confined to a specialty. Such an extreme he rules out; a liberal education should precede medical studies. Along with this general education in the arts and sciences, there must be general education in medicine.

Morgan thought in terms of new arrangements designed to meet the health requirements of the society and linked these up with his proposals for medical education. Much the same philosophy underlies current efforts to revamp medical education as some critical educators become aware of its enlarged role in society.

The Division of Labor in Medical Instruction

In Morgan's view, the same principles of division of labor hold for both medical practice and the effective organization of medical education. The then-prevailing pattern of medical apprenticeship meant that the novice learned principally from a single busy practitioner, who was neither omnicompetent nor readily accessible. Fresh from his years of study in Europe, Morgan was prepared to advocate a radically different organization of medical instruction which called for the "united efforts" of diversely accomplished physicians.

And then, with an organizational foresight not translated into institutional reality for more than a century, Morgan virtually states the case for fulltime teachers of medicine. What is more to the present point, in doing so he proceeds on the sociological premise, only worked out in detail since his day, that motivations are characteristically translated into corresponding behavior only when the social context provides for this. The same motives in different institutional settings take different expression: the same conscientious devotion to duty leads soldiers to destroy life and physicians to save it. Correlatively, differing motives in the same institutional setting may take approximately the same expression: egoistic motives for self-advancement, like altruistic motives, can be harnessed to professionally competent work.* New and functionally appropriate social arrangements are needed to make it readily possible for physicians to achieve professional objectives.

In short, the goodwill of good men, indispensable as it is for the purpose in hand, is not enough to get the job done. A basic reorganization of the modes of medical instruction is required if able men are to achieve their otherwise frustrated objectives. By direct implication, this focuses attention not only upon the important matter of selecting men of great capacity both for teaching and for practice, but also upon the equally important matter of developing organizational arrangements in which these capacities are given optimum occasion for development. Morgan observes that the activities of talented men have quite different consequences, depending on whether they are carried out severally or through "united efforts" (p. 28). If organization is not all, as it evidently is not, neither is unorganized talent enough.

*See Chapter 5, "Institutionalized Altruism: The Case of the Professions—editors' note."

Patterned Sequences in the Medical Curriculum

From matters of organization, Morgan turns to matters of curriculum. The particular ordering of curriculum content which he advocated is of course only of historical interest. He would begin with anatomy, followed by "The Materia Medica and Botany," chemistry, the theory of medicine, and would conclude with the study of practice. But what has more enduring significance is his view that it is not alone the substance of what is taught that matters, but, as well, the sequence in which it is taught.

Again, almost a century intervened before a graded sequence of instruction was regularly introduced into American medical schools. In more immediate point, the problem is, by general assent, even now far from solved. Current experiments in medical education aim almost as much at discovering an optimum sequence of instruction as they do at identifying its most effective content. Although he may have thought the solution more nearly at hand than it proved to be, Morgan sensed the strategic problem of discovering what it is best for students to learn contemporaneously, and what sequentially.

Sources of Resistance to Institutional Change

Morgan was thoroughly aware that his proposals would meet with objections founded not only on defects of his ideas but, beyond these, upon the commitments of his colleagues to competing ways of doing things. Institutional procedures, once functional for their time and place, engage the loyalties of the people involved in them. These colleagues, able to point to the undoubted accomplishments of the past and confident that their motives are above suspicion, find proposed new arrangements unsettling and excessively unsure. When the relative merits of competing alternatives are difficult to demonstrate, as they commonly are in establishing or modifying social institutions, the resistance to change is all the more intense. Morgan suggests that institutional change, however uncomfortable it may be, is in the order of things.

Among those who see merit in the proposal to try a new kind of medical education, says Morgan, some will hold that the society is not ready to sustain the experiment. Not all proposals for institutional change are necessarily sound or, if sound in principle, necessarily suited to the social circumstances of the time. Yet, it should be considered that "the longer we follow any faulty system, the more difficult we find the task to break through the shackles of it, even when it enslaves us to our greatest detriment" (p. 40).

As we know, Morgan won his case, at least in part, though he was far from having envisaged what was to follow, if not as a direct consequence, at least as an aftermath. He was appointed to a chair of the theory and practice of medicine in what was eventually to become the School of Medicine of the University of Pennsylvania. But as is often the case with planned institutional change, the essentials of the plan, as these have been reviewed, were far from being fully incorporated into schools of medicine for generations to come.

Instead, there followed the great nineteenth-century decline in which the outer appearance of a medical school was taken for the reality. As Flexner and others have noted, the decisive importance of the affiliation of the medical school with the university, which Morgan had emphasized, was lost to view. Medical colleges multiplied as private enterprises. There were, of course, such developments as the reforms which Eliot imposed on Harvard, and a little later, the requirement for a three-year medical course at Pennsylvania. But even so, the gap between the standards which such medical educators as Pepper and Osler felt should obtain, and the operating reality, became a source of malaise, if not of despair. When Osler, for example, said in 1889 that "the American 'system' of medical education [had become] a byword amongst the nations," he was only saying in public what many others were saying in private. Yet the perceptive eye of an Osler could detect a "revolution" in the teaching of medicine, even before the delayed opening of the Johns Hopkins medical school, and could bear authoritative witness to the changes that were required.

FIRST OSLER, THEN FLEXNER

Like Morgan, Osler had a distinct sense that the profession of medicine must set its house in order, or the environing society would insist on having it done. Like Morgan, also, he had an acute sense of the basic role of organization, as well as of curriculum and personnel, in bringing this silent revolution to pass. With virtual prescience of the Flexner report which was not to come for almost two decades, he could envisage the requirements that there be an "organic union" of the schools of medicine with university seats of learning, a bringing together of student and patient into close contact "not through the cloudy knowledge of the amphitheatre, but by means of the accurate, critical knowledge of the wards," and an adequate recognition of the teacher of science in the medical schools.

What Osler proclaimed to audiences of physicians, whenever

the occasion presented itself or could be contrived, was in a sense generally "known." But there was still little in the way of a concerted social force to lessen or close the gap between what was privately known, or known within the profession, and what was imposed upon the attention of the public at large. It was the celebrated Flexner report which served this historic function.

Following upon the conferences and reports in 1906–07 of the Council on Medical Education of the then recently reorganized American Medical Association—intramural reports which largely identified the substandard condition of many medical schools—Flexner put diplomacy to one side and dramatically publicized the parlous condition of most of the 155 institutions ostensibly providing medical education in the United States and Canada.[3] The distinctive function of the famous Bulletin Number Four was that of bringing into the public eye the extreme departures from generally acknowledged standards of medical education which obtained in the medical schools of the time. There is something to be learned in this connection from Malinowski's observations among the Trobriand Islanders. There, Malinowski reports, organized social action is not taken on behavior which departs widely from a social norm unless there is *public* announcement and demonstration of the deviation. This is not merely a matter of acquainting individuals in the group with the facts of the case. Many of these *individuals* have already had private knowledge of at least the broad outlines of the facts. But they do not press for concerted action until the deviations from norms are made public simultaneously for all. Only then are tensions set in train between the "privately tolerated" and the "publicly acknowledgeable."

The social and psychological mechanisms making for the great impact of the Flexner report would seem to have operated along the same lines. After all, exacting standards and norms prove distinctly inconvenient for at least some individuals in the society. They militate against the satisfaction of certain wants and interests. When many find these standards excessively burdensome, there is some measure of leniency in applying them, both to themselves and to others. Departures from these standards develop, and the departures are privately tolerated, though not approved.* But this continues only so long as individuals can avoid taking a public stand on the issues.

Publicity, such as that provided by the Flexner report, enforces public recognition of the deviations. It requires individuals to take a stand. They must either range themselves with the deviants, thus repudiating the generally accepted standards and asserting that they too are outside the framework of norms, or, whatever their private

*See Chapter 3 on "institutionalized evasions of institutional rules" editors' note.

predilections, they must fall into line and support these standards. The publicity afforded by the Flexner report largely closed the gap between private knowledge of departures from accepted standards and public insistence upon the standards. It exerted pressure for an overriding set of high standards for medical education by preventing continued public evasion of the issue. It called forth public reaffirmation of the norms and, in increasing degree, greater conformity to these norms.[4]

From the outset, the sociological study of medical education should be distinguished in purpose, character, and functions from such technical appraisals of medical education as that represented by the celebrated Flexner report. For Flexner's purposes, it was enough to engage in what he later described as a "swift tour of medical schools." As everyone knows, that swift tour early in the century enabled Flexner to discover numerous chambers of educational horrors, principally in the proprietary schools but in university-affiliated schools as well. Lucrative professional "chairs" were being sold to the highest bidders, eager to lay their hands on the rich fees accruing to lecturers. Requirements for admission to medical study were negligible. At times, they came to little more than the ability to pay tuition fees. Examinations were often farcical. Some schools lacked laboratories altogether or included make-believe laboratories with little or no apparatus. Members of faculties were ineptly trained and clinical facilities were meagre or altogether absent.

Since these faults were so gross and lay so near the surface, Flexner soon concluded (and history has borne him out) that "in the course of a few hours a reliable estimate could be made respecting the possibilities of teaching modern medicine in almost any of the 155 schools I visited. . . ."[5] It scarcely required prolonged and detailed inquiry to conclude that a physiological laboratory which consisted in its entirety of one small sphygmograph was less than adequately equipped or that schools without access to dispensaries were hardly prepared to provide suitable clinical training. Quick, incisive inventories of glaring deficiencies were enough for the purpose; more detailed and extended study of the educational environments provided by these schools would have been wasteful and pointless.

Partly as a result of the Flexner report and of the marked advancement of medical knowledge, that condition of the medical schools soon changed. Proprietary schools eventually disappeared; sectarian schools dwindled in number and improved in character; a growing proportion of medical schools became affiliated with universities. All in all, the last half-century of medical education can be set down as one of the more remarkable periods of institutional change in the history of modern education. Morgan, Osler, and Welch planted, Flexner watered; but generations of physicians, scientists, and medical educators gave the increase.*

A new wave of change is in the making. Witness the current, fairly widespread efforts by the faculties of a good many medical schools to reexamine, reassess, and reconstitute the organization and content of medical education. What was the revolution of preceding generations has become the accepted pattern for the next. But it seems that these changes do not occur at a uniform tempo. Great forward strides in one direction—for example, systematic incorporation of the basic sciences into medical education—elicit, after a time, not so much a counter movement as a correlative movement to bring other advances in medicine, still more or less unconsolidated in education, abreast of the developments which have moved forward most rapidly. It is as though medical educators, successively aware of the uneven development, try to straighten out the lines of advance. Research in the laboratories and clinics has steadily advanced, changing the nature of medical knowledge and, in some degree, the nature of medical practice. Not, of course, that all changes in medical practice have uniformly been for the better.

Many medical educators have come to believe that these advances call for correlative and continuing experimentation in the form and substance of medical education. But recognizing that change need not mean improvement, the educators engaged in reorganizing the educational environment constituted by the medical school want to have examined, in as methodical and detached a fashion as can now be done, some of the consequences of these changes for the development of the medical student. It is in this historical context that sociological studies of medical education have begun.

CONVERGENCE TOWARD THE SOCIOLOGY OF MEDICAL EDUCATION

Richard Shryock is one among many to have noted that before the nineteenth century, physicians *observed* their patients; thereafter, they began to *examine* them.[6] In much the same sense, it can be said that medical educators have long been teaching students, but only since the middle of this century have they begun to examine their

*Prompted by an editor, I reluctantly cite the paraphrased source: 1 Corinthians III:6. "I have planted, Apollos watered; but God gave the increase."

teaching and the educational environment they create for students. This recently emerging interest in medical education as a social and psychological process appears to be the result of a convergence of distinct forces at work in medicine and in sociology.

Sources of Convergence in Medicine

Advancement of medical knowledge. The growth of science provides one important source of continuing and periodically intensified scrutiny of the current content and organization of medical education. Every considerable advance in medical knowledge, or in the sciences upon which medicine draws, brings in its wake the pressing question of how this new knowledge can be effectively taught.

Barry Wood points out, for example, that advances in psychosomatic medicine have "been based upon as clear scientific evidence as those of any other branch of clinical medicine." These advances at once raise the question of how this new knowledge can most effectively be incorporated into medical education: by training more psychiatrists, by establishing departments of psychosomatic medicine, or, as Dr. Wood advocates, by placing experts in this branch in departments of internal medicine, pediatrics, surgery, and obstetrics in order "to convince undergraduate students that this important field belongs in everyday clinical practice." Whatever the institutional answers to this question, and these will doubtless continue to vary for some time, these increments in clinical knowledge, like those coming from the laboratory sciences, press for reexamination of the methods, content, and organization of medical instruction. Such reexamination, as we shall soon see, has distinctively sociological aspects which are beginning to gain recognition.

Stresses on time-budget of the curriculum. The results of research in laboratories and clinics are not alone in exerting pressure upon medical educators for an unending series of institutional decisions about the nature of the education they are providing. The time-bound character of the curriculum also has this consequence. As everyone connected with it is acutely aware, the timetable of a medical school is fixed within fairly narrow limits.[7] The time set aside for instruction has been steadily increasing during the past half-century, but it is not indefinitely expansible.

This means, of course, that departments and faculty members of the medical school in effect compete for the scarce time of the student just as patients compete for the scarce time of the physician. Hours of instruction are carefully computed and parceled out. The introduction of new teaching materials and courses must often be at the expense of other materials and courses. All apart from the particular personalities and motivations of members of the various departments, the relatively fixed number of available hours means continued competition among departments for their share of time. In this sense, and without pejorative implication of the word, some degree of competition among faculty members for time in the curriculum is built into the structure of medical education, with its numerous branches of knowledge and application.

The prevailing organization of medical schools as a federation of departments contributes further to this form of competition. As with political states in federative union, so with departments federated in the medical school. Departmental loyalties take hold. It requires a strong sense of loyalty to the school as a whole and an appreciable consensus on the nature and purposes of medical education for departments to relinquish willingly, rather than under the duress of colleagues, long-established or newly emerging claims to a particular share of time in the curriculum. As with competition generally, rules of the game—agreed-upon norms or standards for judgment—develop to govern the process. These norms are then used to adjudicate competing claims to the limited time of the student, ideally in terms of the assumed functional significance of each kind of knowledge for the effective training of the physician. The curriculum is a public register of the provisional outcome of this process in the medical school, in about the same sense that prices, the comparative growth of firms, and profits compose a register of the provisional outcome of competition in the marketplace.

Apart from this similarity, there is, of course, a basic difference between the forms of competition in the medical school and in the marketplace. However much they may differ in their conception of how this is best to be achieved, the departments of a medical school are expected to be committed to the same shared values of providing optimum medical training for the student. Unlike the competition among business firms, self-aggrandizement is not institutionally legitimized. Nevertheless, the process of competition for time which is built into the structure of the curriculum, as well as the more intensely personal conflicts which sometimes develop among departments and among their members, does serve, whatever its other outcomes, to keep many medical educators alerted to new problems and potentialities of medical instruction. It becomes more difficult for them, were they so inclined, to rest comfortably on their oars.

The departmental form of organization and the resulting competition thus lead to a fairly continual, greater or less, pressure for examining the current curriculum and modes of instruction. This pressure need not actually result in substantial change. There some-times develops a balance of forces among departments loath to give up their established claims in the curriculum, with the result that all remains much as it was. This is the type of circumstance, presumably, which led the medical dean described by John F. Fulton to exclaim in despair, "It's easier to move a cemetery than to change the cur-riculum."

Occasionally, the pressures derived from advancing knowledge also produce the discomforts of change, leading some medical ed-ucators to maintain an alert and, under the stress of competition, a sometimes disproportionate concern with change—or lack of change. Individual departments cannot easily remain aloof from this process. There are few schools, it seems, in which the structure of authority is so centralized that change in the form and content of instruction can effectively originate by decree from the administration. Rather, the more typical pattern seems to be one of pulling and hauling among departments, each feudal-like domain persuaded of the im-portance and legitimacy of its own claims on the time of the student. All this places a great premium upon an appreciable consensus among the divisions of a medical school on the purposes, standards, and values of education as a basis for coping with periodic disturb-ances to the equilibrium of social relationships among them.[8]

Rediscovery of the patient as person. Contributing further to an emerging interest in the sociological study of medical education is the renewed emphasis, within medicine, upon the concept of "the patient as a whole person." The lineage of this idea is, of course, ancient. Medical chapter and verse can easily be cited to show that some physicians in every age have recognized that the patient must be seen as a whole, including, that is to say, the patient's interpersonal relations and social environment. Not to reach back to the time and practice of Hippocrates, we know that this was regarded as a com-monplace in the time of John Locke. Or, to move to the more recent past, the implications of this concept were epitomized by Francis Weld Peabody in his classic paper on "The Care of the Patient."

Although the conception of "the patient as a person" has been long recognized in medical circles, it is also said to be a conception more honored in the breach than the observance. Many physicians, it is said, continue to regard the patient as a case of sickness rather than as a person. This suggests that forces in the situation make it difficult for some physicians to live up to this conception. It is, there-fore, held essential that these forces be counteracted by methods of education designed for the purpose.

In an earlier day local physicians could have an intimate knowledge and understanding of their patients. The personal relations between physician and patient were often sustained and close—though not, perhaps, as often as we now like to suppose. To the extent that this was so, "the old-fashioned general practitioner intuitively recognized [the factors making up the patient's environment, factors] which can sometimes be discovered only through intimate acquaintance with the patient and familiarity with his environment, with his life day by day, and with his family history."[9] In short, the structure of the society and the organization of medical practice were such that many practitioners would intuitively and almost automatically take into account both the stresses and the potentials for therapeutic support which the environment afforded the patient.

With the growing complexity of the social environment, the increasing specialization of medical practice, and the often diminished association of physicians with their patients outside the sphere of health care, the problem of taking the social context of the patient into account has become greatly enlarged. Faced with such exigencies, physicians find themselves backsliding from what they acknowledge to be the appropriate conception of the patient. Patients, in turn, often confronting physicians whom they know only slightly or not at all, are more apt to become those "frightened people" described by Elton Mayo. They find it more difficult to communicate a sense of their daily lives—their relationships within the family and outside, the stresses of their work situations, their difficulties in coping with the demands of their multiple roles in society. The joint changes of the social structure and of the profession of medicine create new difficulties in treating the patient as a person.

These social changes have evidently induced a newly emphasized concern with the old problem of having the patient regarded as a whole person. The changes are, of course, not confined to the United States. It is symptomatic, for example, that the First World Conference on Medical Education in 1954 returned to this theme. Dr. S.M.K. Mallick, of the Dow Medical College at Karachi, maintained that "consideration of the patient as an individual with a peculiar environment and a particular psychic background is largely ignored."[10] Sir Geoffrey Jefferson, professor of neurosurgery at the University of Manchester, observed: "Patients are people. The student must find out who these people are, get a mental picture of their lives and of the ways they have lived them, discover how they have come to be sick. Call this psychosomatic medicine or sociology if you will; the things that are newest are their names."[11] Dr. A. Querido, professor of social medicine at the University of Amsterdam, set forth a particularly lucid conception of the contemporary role of sociology in relation to medicine, taking it as his task to consider these questions: "How can the social elements which have contributed to the syndrome of illness of a certain patient be integrated in the clinical teaching? And how can the social factors that may benefit the patient's recovery and rehabilitation be properly evaluated?"[12]

But even those physicians who see a distinct and growing place for a sociological orientation in medicine sometimes write as if the social environment affected only the socially disadvantaged patient: the poor, the uneducated, the decrepit. In suggesting that the sociological orientation should be included in the curriculum of the medical school, Sir Henry Cohen elected to put the case in just these illustrative terms:

> . . . the student must ever have it borne in on him that when a patient comes into hospital he leaves his environment, his occupation, his family, and his friends behind. Yet these might well have played a major part in the genesis and course of his illness. The patient in hospital—clean, well clad, tidy, lying in a comfortable bed and earning three good meals a day—is often a very different being in the squalor, anxieties, and discords of his home and job. The student today sees too little of the conditions in which disease thrives—the overcrowded, ill-ventilated, and unheated homes, the under-nutrition which results from poverty, the effects of chronic illness in the home, the moral cankers of unemployment, and the like. Our training must ensure that the doctor is not a man of confined vision.[13]

It is true, of course, that medical students often encounter patients, on the wards and in the outpatient department, who live in surroundings such as these. But this should not invite the fallacious inference that sociological considerations are pertinent only in such instances of gross defects of environment. Well-fed patients living in well-ventilated and well-heated houses may also be subject to less conspicuous but no less stressful conditions of environment, in their homes, at work, and in the other groups of which they are a part.

Some physicians apparently have another image of sociology, in which it is pictured as a means of equipping medical students with the indispensable professional qualities of sympathy and tact. In more invidious terms, this sometimes appears in the opinion that a sociological orientation toward the patient leads the student to replace a scientific point of view by gross sentimentality.

That these distorted images of sociology bear no resemblance to the reality is the gist of the following observations by Professor Querido:

> There is no reason why the social data should not be of the same scientific value as those from the laboratory or x-ray department. The time is gone when we had to content ourselves with infor-

mation on the composition of the family, number of rooms, rent, sleeping arrangements, and the questionable presence of a bath, when asking about the social conditions of our patient. We know now that in order to understand the patient we must learn about his family relations, ties, and tensions, his work, friends, aspirations, hopes, and frustrations, about his development, his attitude to his place in society, his habits, his compensating and escape mechanisms.[14]

Though far less frequent than it evidently once was, another image of sociology still occasionally intrudes itself among physicians. This is the conception that sociology advocates "the socialization of medicine." It is reported, for example, that an "inspiring address" before the House of Delegates of the American Medical Association concluded with the remark that: "Sociologists, economists and political scientists have made strenuous efforts to bring medicine under the domination of . . . [nonprofessional] groups through the mechanism of legislative enactment."[15] In this respect, sociology finds itself in much the same situation as "social medicine." As Dr. Hubbard has observed: "The average citizen—and many a physician too—doesn't really know what he means by socialized medicine, but he is sure it is bad. And social medicine doesn't sound very different."[16]

But such misconceptions of the nature of sociology are being dissipated by collaboration among physicians, medical educators, and sociologists. Indeed, it is being suggested that in *one* of its principal aspects, medicine can itself be usefully conceived as a social science. This was a frequent assertion by the middle of the nineteenth century,[17] but it was then more nearly a figure of speech than an analytical and descriptive account. By 1936, however, L. J. Henderson could write, in an exacting and responsible sense, of "The Practice of Medicine as Applied Sociology."[18] And by 1955, the dean of the Faculty of Medicine of Columbia University could state that medicine ". . . must be recognized as a social as well as a biological science. It is imperative today that medical instruction recognize and deal with the social, economic, emotional, and other environmental elements in illness, health, and incapacity because the concern of the present-day physician must be with society as well as with medicine, with human beings in their environment and with their multitude of anxieties and emotions as well as with their pathology."[19]

The emergence of new perspectives, in medicine as in other disciplines, often generates conflicts of outlook, and these, in turn, easily lead to extravagances of opinion. For extended periods, the sciences which later proved to be basic to medicine—chemistry in the eighteenth century and physiology in the next—were rudely rejected as plainly being of no value to medicine at all. At other times, they provided occasion for excessively enthusiastic hopes that they would clear up, once and for all, the still-unsolved problem of medicine. As Shryock describes the early eighteenth-century orientation toward therapeutics:

> Since no practical benefits seemed to result from the pursuit of pure medical science, questions about the utility of research were naturally raised and were difficult to answer. Of what avail was it after all "to know that the pancreas has a duct?" It is easy to observe that science, in the long run, was bound to enrich practice, but this was not obvious at the time. In any case this thought would have afforded small comfort to the sick, who could hardly wait a century or more for cures.[20]

Quite apart from historical analogies, which are properly suspect, there is, perhaps, an object lesson here for the contemporary role of sociology in the field of medicine. Difficult and uncomfortable as this policy is, it might be well to steer a course between the enthusiasts who optimistically make large, and still unjustified, claims about what sociology can contribute to the training of practitioners and to the practice of medicine, and the cynics who, impatient to see immediate results and noting that large gains from sociology have not accrued, insist that it is bootless to pursue this line of inquiry at all. There is no need to reproduce, in this field, the long history of cleavage between clinicians and laboratory scientists.

Uncritical enthusiasm and uncritical opposition work to reinforce one another, to the detriment of both medicine and social science. The excessive claim that social science is now prepared to make large contributions to the improvement of medical practice is probably related to the refusal by some medical educators and practitioners to allow any place to the social sciences. In turn, the more fixed and unthinking the opposition to any utilization of social science in medicine, the greater the tendency for some to make exaggerated claims for social science, if only by way of rebuttal.

Such an excess of sentiments, both pro and con, seems to be dwindling. Instead, many medical educators have adopted an attitude of guarded and critical receptivity to sociology, an attitude of benevolent skepticism.[21] This is reflected, for example, in the judgment of Dr. Howard C. Taylor, Jr., when he observes:

> The failure to associate medicine with sociology is perhaps the most obvious oversight in medical education . . . the physician [is] largely unprepared, unfamiliar even with the vocabulary of the sociologist, and without the basic knowledge of social principles enabling him to act or to recommend in this field.
>
> . . . the [medical] student could with benefit receive some instruction in formal sociology. Such work would provide a framework for the student's now considerable but unorganized observational data on social ideas.[22]

Didactic instruction in sociology would probably not do much to enable medical students to acquire the perspectives of sociology in medical practice. Much more work in medical sociology is required before such instruction can become truly useful. The medical student need not, of course, become a sociologist and psychologist as well as a physician. In the education of the medical student, it would presumably be with these fields as it has long been with the other sciences basic to medicine. At best, the student can be taught to grasp the fundamental principles rather than the full range of specific details of these disciplines, to acquire the frames of reference of psychology and sociology for understanding human behavior. Continued neglect of these subjects, on the other hand, means that physicians will tend to practice in terms of an uninformed, perfunctory, and amateurish psychology and sociology.

Historically, medicine has been a polygamist becoming successively and concurrently wedded to many sciences and practical arts. Nor has medicine lacked for additional would-be mates, the psychological and social sciences being the most recent and vocal of these. If they have at times seemed importunate and impatient, this may be because they feel themselves to have been left waiting too long. And if at other times they have acted overly diffident, this may be because it is a source of wonder to them that they are being considered at all. Moreover, as is often the case with polygamy, the first set of wives—say, the biological and chemical sciences—is reluctant at first to approve yet another addition to the ménage. But there is still hope. As the burden of work plainly becomes more than can be managed by the present members of the household, they become ready for new accessions to help carry the load of what needs to be done.

As medical educators have come to adopt a favorable view of the place of sociology in medical education, they have also come some distance toward developing an interest in sociological studies of medical education. Thus far, we have considered three sets of circumstances which have contributed to the emerging interest of medical educators in education as a social process: the continuing advancement of medical knowledge which must somehow be incorporated into the curriculum, the structurally determined competition for time among departments in the medical school, and the growing recognition of the social sciences as having a place in the practice of medicine. Yet this interest might well have continued to be confined to episodic, uncontrolled, and casual impressions on the part of medical educators of how one or another form of medical education is working out, just as the greater part of opinion about the workings of higher education in general is based on this kind of casual empiricism. Still other elements in the situation have served to convert this continuing concern with the problems of educating the medical student into provisional but methodical inquiries into the processes and results of distinct forms of medical education. One of these elements is the historically developing aversion of medicine to sheer empiricism.

Reduction of empiricism.   Medicine, in company with most of the other applied sciences, has experienced through the centuries an irregular alternation between periods of raw empiricism and periods of extreme rationalism. But the secular tendency, particularly in recent generations, has been toward repudiating these misleading alternatives. There has been a steady move toward reducing what Conant has called the "degree of empiricism"[23] in medicine and in the sciences upon which it draws. In this commitment to the scientific point of view, there is an insistent pressure to transform the empiricist "let's try it and see" kind of experimentation, little informed by prior theoretical formulations, into the kind of controlled observation and experiment that is guided by an explicit conceptual scheme. Like the sciences generally, medicine is engaged in a continuing effort to reduce the degree of empiricism in its body of knowledge by increasing the systematic empirical verification of logically connected sets of ideas.

It has long been tacitly assumed that this outlook is appropriate for the study of medicine but not for the study of medical education. More recently, the same perspective is being transferred to this latter sphere. Together with associates in psychology and sociology, some medical educators are turning to methodical study of the educational process, rather than relying upon casual impressions.

Innovations in medical education.   That newly emerging interest is, understandably enough, most marked in those schools which Dr. George Packer Berry has described as developing "provocative experiments . . . aimed at making revisions in our teaching programs which are consistent with a growing understanding of the whole patient rather than just a part of the patient." To be sure, most medical schools are continually engaged in revising their curricula. But it is especially when these involve changes of some magnitude that there develops a marked interest in systematic observation of how these changes are actually working out. The faculties of these schools seek, so far as is now possible, to apply scientific method to the study of the workings and consequences of these new arrangements, if only because they have been committed to that method in the development of medical knowledge itself.

Much else has no doubt brought about the current interest in processes of medical education. But in short retrospect, the sources of that interest in the sociological study of these processes among medical educators seem to have been principally these five:

1.   The great advances in medical knowledge which raise new problems of how to make that knowledge an effective part of the equipment of medical studies;

2.   Stresses on the allocation of the limited time available in the curriculum which lead to continued review of the bases for various allocations;

3.   Renewed recognition of the importance of the social environment in both the genesis and control of illness together with growing recognition of the role of the social sciences in providing an understanding of that environment;

4.   A commitment to scientific method which calls for replacing howsoever skilled empiricism by more systematic and rational analysis of the process of education; and

5.   As a precipitating factor, substantial innovations in medical education which call for systematic comparisons of the objectives and outcomes of the innovations.

Sources of Convergence in Sociology

Independent developments in the field of sociology have also been leading to a substantial interest in the study of medical education.

The sociology of the professions.   First among these is the marked growth of the sociology of occupations.[24] Studies of the social organization of occupations and of occupational roles, sporadically undertaken during the last generation,[25] have accumulated into a steady and growing stream. Occupations in general and the professions in particular have come to be recognized as one of the more significant nuclei in the organization of society. A great share of people's waking hours is devoted to their occupational activities; the economic supports for group survival are provided through the pooled work of socially interrelated occupations; the aspirations, interests, and sentiments of men and women are largely organized and stamped with the mark of their occupations.

The sociological study of the medical school affords a prototype for comparable studies in other professions. All inquiries into the comparative prestige of the professions in American society have uniformly found that medicine commands the greatest measure of public esteem. There is evidence also that the other professions frequently look to medicine as a model, albeit not as a model immune from criticism, for the directions their own development might effectively take. If systematic studies of the medical school should prove their worth, it seems likely that other professions will also undertake such studies.

Lending further particular interest to the sociological (as distinct from the psychological) study of medical schools[26] is the relative complexity of their social structure. Medical students must relate themselves to many and diverse groups in the course of their training; more so than students in any of the other professions (except, possibly, for social workers and nurses). They enter into relations not only with fellow students and faculty—these relationships they share with students in the other professions—but also with patients and a varied professional and technical staff, in the hospital and outside it—with nurses, social workers, medical practitioners, physical therapists, pharmacists, and administrative personnel. Schools of law and of engineering, for instance, have no parallel to these complex patterns of relationships with diverse individuals and groups during the course of training. Such networks of relationships—such complex role-sets—constitute important parts of the social environment of learning by the medical student, and therefore call for systematic study.

Collaboration of social science and health professions.   As we have noted, there has developed, in modern medicine, a distinct interest in examining the actual and potential connections between the medical and the social sciences. Interest in such collaboration has also become evident among social scientists.[27]

Just as laboratory and clinical research has had an essential part in radically reshaping medical practice and teaching throughout the century, so the social and psychological sciences, in their own necessarily limited fashion, bid fair to provide basic perspectives and knowledge during the last part of the century. This is not a prophecy or a mission but a summary description of tendencies now much in evidence and promising to become accumulatively more marked. As disciplined inquiry moves forward on the social, and not only the economic, contexts of illness and medical care, a body of knowledge is developing which can be drawn upon in the clinical training of medical students. Sociologists and psychologists are attached to the staffs of medical schools to develop the use of social science in helping to prepare physicians for their role in society.

The sociological study of organization.   From this interest in the sociological study of illness and medical care it is a short step to an interest in the sociological study of the medical school itself, for this links up with a long-standing tradition of sociological study of social institutions and formal organizations. During the past generation, this tradition has taken on a new vitality as empirical research based on systematic field observations, rather than only on documentary evidence, has begun to be developed.[28] In large part, these have been studies of industrial and business organizations, government departments, trade unions, and hospitals.[29] But the methods of inquiry and fundamental concepts are equally appropriate for study of the social organization of the medical school in its bearing upon the behavior and learning of those involved in it.

These developments have begun only during the past generation or so. Before then, it would not have been possible to conduct systematic empirical studies of the medical school as a social environment. The social sciences were distinctly not ready. Psychology, sociology, and social anthropology had first to develop additional skills and knowledge before they could consider, even programmatically, the pertinence of their disciplines for medical training and practice. Not, of course, that these social sciences are now in full maturity, needing only to be routinely applied. But they have reached a point, in the judgment of many who are both critical and informed, where they can be utilized to advance our understanding of illness, of medical training, and of medical care. A growing sense of these potentialities, among medical educators and social scientists, has led to field studies of the social environment which the medical school provides for its students.

The process of socialization.   Social scientists have long had an enduring interest in studying the process of "socialization," the process through which individuals are inducted into their culture.[30] It involves the acquisition of attitudes and values, of skills and behavior patterns making up social roles established in the social structure. For a long time, studies of socialization were largely confined to the early years in the life cycle of the individual; more recently, increasing attention has been directed to the process as it continues, at varying rates, throughout the life cycle. This has given rise to theoretical and empirical analyses of "adult socialization."[31]

From this standpoint, medical students are engaged in learning the professional role of the physician by so combining its component knowledge and skills, attitudes, and values, as to be able and motivated to perform this role in a professionally and socially acceptable fashion. Adult socialization includes more than what is ordinarily described as education and training. Most conspicuous in the process of medical learning is, of course, the acquisition of a store of knowledge and skills, which occurs to some extent even among the least of these students. Beyond this, it is useful to think of the processes of role acquisition in two broad classes: direct learning through didactic teaching of one kind or another, and indirect learning, in which attitudes, values, and behavior patterns are acquired as by-products of contact with instructors and peers, patients, and other members of the health team. It is particularly important to attend systematically to the less conspicuous and more easily neglected processes of indirect learning. For as with all educational institutions, it is natural for those far removed from the details of life and work in the medical school to assume that the great bulk, and the most significant part, of what the student carries away is learned through formal instruction—an assumption which is often remote from the actual facts of the case. Not all which is taught in medical school is actually learned by students and not all which is learned is taught there, if by teaching is meant didactic forms of instruction. Students not only learn from precept or deliberate example; they also learn—and it may often be, most enduringly learn—from sustained involvement in that society of medical staff, fellow students, and patients which makes up the medical school as a social organization.*

Our Columbia studies therefore include more than a sidelong glance at the informal and unpremeditated ways in which students come to acquire the attitudes and values by which some of them will presumably live as medical practitioners. We provisionally assume that students acquire the values which will be basic to their professional way of life in the course of their social interaction with others in the school, exchanging experiences and ideas with peers, and observing and evaluating the behavior of their instructors (rather than merely listening to their precepts). The ways in which these students are shaped, both by intent and by unplanned circumstances of their school environment, constitute a major part of the process of socialization.

Methods of social research.   The past generation has also witnessed distinct advances in the methods of collecting and analyzing sociological facts which have made empirical studies of organization possible. Detailed accounts of these methods of sociology are available in several books,[32] but an abridged summary may serve to indicate some of the principal ones.

FIRSTHAND OBSERVATION.   The procedures of field observation, as

---

*An observation emphatically borne out in the forthcoming memoir by Lewis Thomas, *The Youngest Science: Notes of a Medicine-Watcher* (New York: Harper & Row, 1982).

used in sociology, have been the least subject to change. These are much like the procedures adopted by the social anthropologist for observing "social processes under natural conditions." Although primarily qualitative in nature, direct observation of repeated and delimited situations—for example, among preceptorial groups of students—also provides data on social interaction which can be quantified.

In the Columbia studies, field observers conducted what is tantamount to a social anthropological study of the medical school and of associated sectors of the teaching hospital.[33] They observed the behavior of students, faculty, patients, and associated staff in the natural—that is to say, the social—setting. They made observations in lecture halls and laboratories; they accompanied physicians and students on rounds to note the social interaction there, and spent time observing the kinds of relationships which develop between student and patient and between student and teacher. These many hours of observation were recorded in several thousand pages of field notes, making up a detailed account of recurrent patterns of students' experience. Some examples of the types of situations selected for observation are these: occasions which proved especially stressful to students; the latent (as distinct from the expressly didactic) teaching of physician-patient relationships by faculty members who serve as role models for students; the emotional tone or social atmosphere of students at work in laboratories; the patterns of faculty-student interaction and of interaction among students themselves.

Early in one study, for example, observation was focused upon the teams of four students at work in the anatomy laboratory. Since students select their partners, we can learn from the composition of these teams the characteristics which students look for in their first work partners. We can then compare these with independent evidence on the relationships later established among students, to see how these change and how they are connected with the formation of attitudes. From the sociological perspective of the observer, it is sometimes possible to see implications of recurrent situations in the school which might go unnoticed by others. For instance, when witnessing the behavior of students at their first autopsy, the observer notes how the group operates to sustain certain reactions and to curb others, even though such "regulatory social processes" are ordinarily not perceived as such by those directly involved in them.

A principal purpose of direct observation of this kind is to identify aspects of the social environment which seem to have most direct bearing on processes of attitudinal and cognitive learning. Tentative hypotheses deriving from the observations then become a basis for deciding upon the more systematic data to be collected through other methods. This illustrates a major characteristic of the array of procedures used in the sociological study of so complex an institution as a medical school: no one set of data collected through a particular procedure (say, through direct observation) stands alone; it is, instead, typically interwoven with data, on the same subject, collected through other procedures (say, interviews and standardized questionnaires). This serves to reduce, if not to eliminate, the shortcomings of any one procedure by providing collateral evidence to test the implications drawn from a single body of data.[34]

SOCIOLOGICAL DIARIES AND FOCUSED INTERVIEWS. Direct observation permits researchers to take note only of what students and faculty do and say in particular situations. It does not necessarily furnish a sufficient basis for inferring how they perceive and evaluate the situation, for discovering what it means to them. Private definitions of the meaning of social situation are not always evidenced in outward and visible behavior. As a further basis for tentatively identifying at least part of the range of reactions to the same situation, students in each of four years of training kept detailed journals. These journals describe, often in formidable detail, daily routines of experience; reactions to these experiences; and developing attitudes toward fellow students, faculty, patients, family, and friends.

Such records of the subjective meanings of the events in which a small number of students have been involved do not, of course, indicate the entire range of meanings which students at large assign to the events in a school. But they do afford supplementary information which otherwise is largely lost to view. Moreover, these typically detailed and lively reports of responses to the environment provide tentative leads to the processes through which students develop their values, learn new orientations, gain recognition of the limits to their own individual competence and to the competence of current medical knowledge itself. Some of these leads in turn become the basis for developing hypotheses about the diversity of responses among students to what is ostensibly the "same" environment of learning.

As a short example of how the same episode involves contrasting definitions of the situation, consider these independent accounts by student-diarists in the same class:

> *Student A:* Monday, we got back our chem. exams. As I supposed, I did flunk it. The marks in general were good; most folks about me got high 80's and 90's. *I guess some of us are just naturally born stupid and careless.*
> *Student B:* Well, we got back our chemistry tests today. I didn't do as well as I should have, but I passed with a very high C. . . .

I really knew about a B's worth of material. . . . I seemed to see a lot of 100's and 90's floating around the lab, but what can you do about that? *So many of the fellows were chemistry majors and/or took elementary biochemistry in undergraduate school.*

In one respect, these divergent perceptions are in accord with the working assumptions of sociology that the meaning assigned to evaluations of one's performance will be *relative* to what the person perceives to be (or knows to be) the entire range of evaluations of peers. Self-images do not develop in a social vacuum; they are affected by comparisons with the performance of others who thus unwittingly compose the framework for self-appraisal. But this first approximation leaves untouched the further question of how it happens that the one student concludes from his comparative failure that he may not have the capacities needed for satisfactory performance whereas the other finds reassurance in contrasting the extent of his earlier preparation with that of his peers. Repeated evidence of such diverse definitions of situations which are outwardly much the same furnishes a basis for systematically exploring the roots of such divergences. Just as firsthand observation suggests hypotheses for ongoing inquiry, so do the volumes of diary materials.

The uses of diaries were enlarged by the use of interviews with students focused upon some of the implications of what they have recorded.[35] Weekly installments of the diaries were carefully studied by field workers as a source of tentative hypotheses about distinctive aspects of the social environment and their significance for processes of attitudinal and cognitive learning. Hypotheses were then explored through intensive interviews with the student-diarists which centered on experiences, responses, and concerns only briefly touched upon in the original entries.

On the basis of the observational and documentary materials, as well as lecture notes and syllabi, Dr. Renée Fox prepared what might be described as "a sociological calendar of the medical school." This is a detailed chronological account of the important attitudinal and cognitive learning that takes place in the classroom and outside of it, so far as it is possible to piece this together from such diverse materials. This sociological calendar provides a provisional overview of the major sequences of learning thus far identified and may be of interest to the medical educator as well as to the sociologist concerned with the processes of acquiring attitudes and values.

The field observations, student journals, and focused interviews thus provided the Columbia studies with hypotheses which would otherwise have been entirely overlooked. It should be repeated that in such sociological studies sound interpretations require the conjoining of data independently obtained by the use of differing methods of inquiry. No single set of materials is sufficient in itself.

THE PANEL TECHNIQUE.[36]   Since the late 1930s, social scientists have been developing a design for the longitudinal study of short-term changes in attitudes, values, and behavior known as "the panel technique." This technique uses repeated observations, interviews, or questionnaires for the same individuals over a period of time.

The major advantages of the panel procedure can be quickly summarized. It enables the investigator to identify persons who have changed (or remained constant) with respect to a wide variety of attitudes and behavior, instead of relying, as is necessary with other kinds of interviews, upon their often faulty and systematically biased memories. Ready comparisons can be made of the orientations expressed by the same people at successive times in the course of the inquiry. By appropriate analysis, it is also possible to learn *which types* of students—differing, for example, with respect to their social relations within (or outside) the school—are most likely to develop certain kinds of value-orientations. Finally, only through the use of the panel procedure is it possible to study, for a comparatively large number of persons, the mutual interplay of different attitudes in the course of time.

The panel technique provided us with systematic data, consisting of annual soundings of students' attitudes, experiences, social relations, expectations, and values. These were obtained through the use of standardized questionnaires, the content of which was largely designed on the basis of observations in the course of fieldwork and interviews with students. The periodically collected data enabled us to relate such developments in students' outlook to various evaluations of their performance by the faculty through the four years of undergraduate training in medicine. To repeat: reliable estimates of such patterns of development require repeatedly collected data about the *same* students. Such estimates cannot be soundly based upon comparisons of the attitudes or performance of differing students in different classes, if each of these classes has provided only a single set of measures at one point in time.

SOCIOMETRIC PROCEDURES.   Techniques for charting the interpersonal alignments that emerge within social groups and organizations in composite have come to be designated "sociometry."[37] A large body of research attests that this is a powerful tool for *systematically* identifying the structure of interpersonal relations in groups. The very simplicity of the basic procedures probably contributes to their utility. In brief, the now numerous sociometric techniques all depart from the same fundamental idea of having each member of a group "privately specify a number of other persons in the group with whom he would like to engage in some particular activity,"[38] or, by an obvious extension, with whom the individual has already elected to enter into some interpersonal relation (as, for example, a close friendship).

Procedures for the statistical analysis of these choices, both reciprocated and not, have been developed to represent the preferred structure of interpersonal relations in the group, which can, by similar methods, be compared with the actual structure. It has been found, for example, that the greater the discrepancy between the social relations which are prescribed by the formal organization of the group and those which would obtain if the complex of private preferences were carried out, the greater the social conflict and tension within the group.

The Columbia studies adopted such sociometric techniques to compare preferred with actual interpersonal relations among medical students and to discover how distinctive patterns of interpersonal relations foster or curb the acquisition of medical skills, knowledge, and values. Thus it was found that in one school a small minority of students believed that physicians ought to exercise firm authoritarian control over patients in the course of therapy. Analysis of data on friendships among students found that the students who held this view, which departed from the professional norm most commonly held in the school, were chosen by others as friends far less frequently than would be expected if this attitude played no part.

Sociometric data helped appreciably to trace some of the connections between unpremeditated and undesigned structures of social relations on the one hand, and the acquisition of knowledge and values on the other.

DOCUMENTARY DATA.   Until sociologists began to collect systematic data on their own initiative—and, on any substantial scale, this is largely the work of our own century[39]—they had to rely largely on the official statistics collected by governmental and other agencies, and on documentary records. As a result, particularly so far as quantitative data were concerned, sociologists worked with evidence which often had only tangential or fortuitous bearing on the theoretical problems with which they were concerned. This left a wide margin for error, as the statistics in hand were crudely reorganized in an effort to fit them into categories pertinent to the sociological hypotheses. Research had to wait upon the incidental and, at times, accidental availability of relevant data. This condition has greatly changed. Sociologists now take it as a matter of course that they will themselves try to collect much of the data which they require.

In the study of social organization and institutions, however, there is no occasion for a *total* shift from the exclusive use of pre-collected data assembled by the institutional agencies of society to the exclusive use of field data assembled by the sociologist. The two can be and should be systematically related.

Like other organizations, medical schools assemble a great deal of factual and evaluative information about their personnel. Some of this can be utilized in the sociological study of these schools and connected with the data collected by sociologists themselves. Thus, schools provide readily accessible estimates of the quality of performance by students as these are registered in grades. Such materials are a distinct asset. More importantly, these grades have further value in that they are an integral part of the institution itself. They comprise a system of evaluation which constitutes an important segment of the environment for students. Grading systems vary in many ways: in stringency or leniency, in the frequency with which students are formally evaluated ("tests," "examinations," and "quizzes"), in the types of examinations, in the observability of these ratings (by having them communicated privately to each student or by posting them so that they can become known to the class as a whole). We have found that such institutional variations in practices of evaluating students appreciably affect the nature of the environment as this is experienced by students.[40]

Official records of the medical school thus have a double pertinence for the sociologist. As part of the institution itself, the information and evaluation collected by the school and the ways in which they are collected constitute part of the environment for its personnel, both students and faculty. As a type of information about student performance, grades can be collated with field data to relate cognitive learning to social and attitudinal learning. It is possible, for example, to relate the data on changes of attitudes and orientations of students to those measures of performance which the school provides in the form of grades in each year, cumulative averages, scores on the Medical College Admissions Test, evaluations by members of the Admissions Committee, and qualities of students reported in letters of recommendation. Just as the various kinds of field data are interrelated to arrive at provisional conclusions, so these, in turn, are related with the documentary data provided by the school.

This short review may be enough to suggest how recent developments in methods of social research have made possible the systematic and empirical study of social institutions and organizations. When coupled with the other sources of interest in the professions generally and in the medical profession in particular, these advances in method have contributed, in their way, to the growing interest of sociologists in studying the medical school.

In the large, then, at least five coordinate developments in sociology have brought about the concerted beginning of sociological research on medical education:

1.   The marked and cumulating interest in the sociology of professions, which includes, as a major component, studies of professional schools;

2.   The growing utilization of social science as composing part of the scientific basis for the provision of health care in contemporary society;

3.   The recent growth in the empirical study of complex social organizations, among which schools constitute an important special class;

4.   The similar growth of interest in the process of adult socialization in general which, in application to the field of medicine, is concerned with the processes by which the neophyte is transformed into one or another kind of medical practitioner; and

5.   The recent advances in methods and techniques of social inquiry which make it possible to examine these subjects and problems by means of systematic inquiry.

Social historians of the future, looking back on this convergence of independent developments in medicine and in social science toward methodical investigation of the processes of medical education, will doubtless record countervailing tendencies which limit the character of these studies. They will perhaps note that in medicine, as in other institutional spheres, trial innovations meet with resistance. If they are wise, however, they will also note that not every disturbing innovation necessarily means improvement, that change is not invariably for the better. They will be interested, then, to see to what extent the prevailing responses to these developments were matters of prejudgment, pro or con, and to what extent matters of critical judgment suspended until enough of the evidence was in hand. Historians may also find some parallel between the reception of the social and psychological sciences by physicians in the mid-twentieth century and that accorded the laboratory sciences basic or ancillary to medicine in earlier centuries. But, in the main, as would appear from the review set out in these pages, they may conclude that reasonably adequate support, both in medical and in social science circles, was given to the beginnings of an analytical rather than only an empirical study of medical education.

PSYCHOLOGICAL AND SOCIOLOGICAL PERSPECTIVES

As we have noted, social science studies of medical education differ from technical evaluations designed to appraise the content and organization of curricula in terms of standards which are so nearly a matter of consensus in the medical profession that they are no longer under debate. There have been periodic evaluations of curricula, facilities, and staff—the renowned Flexner report being neither the first nor the last of these. Current research on medical education by social scientists, however, tends to be of a different kind. Some of it is designed to search out the extent to which medical schools achieve their announced purposes and to identify the circumstances which facilitate or curb achievement of these purposes. This provides part of the evidence for evaluation by medical practitioners. But other types of social science inquiry do not have such directly practical objectives.

The two main strands of methodical research on medical education have been psychological and sociological. We have intimated—for example, in reviewing Morgan's *Discourse*—that these represent distinctive points of view. To say that they differ is not, of course, to say that they are entirely at odds. On the contrary, we start from the supposition and shall try to show that they are largely complementary, meeting in a middle ground which has been described as social psychology (or, by some, as psycho-sociology).

To see how psychological and sociological studies of medical education relate to one another, we must identify their distinctive approaches, the questions which they characteristically raise, and the concepts in terms of which they organize their inquiries. For this purpose, we first examine the theoretical orientations of psychology and sociology, recognizing that each of these fields includes a variety of them. We then compare a few problems involved in the systematic study of medical schools which have been or can be studied from the standpoints of both psychology and sociology.

General Orientations of Psychology and of Sociology[41]

Any attempt to set out the theoretical relations between psychology and sociology is subject to at least three misunderstandings. First, it may be assumed that an effort is being made to fix the boundaries of inquiry which should obtain for each of the two disciplines; that it is an effort to advocate jurisdictional boundaries.

Second, it may be taken to claim that each of the two fields of inquiry is homogeneous, with no significant divergences of theoretical outlook, focus on problems, and ways of work. Third, and most extravagantly, it will sometimes be inferred that the effort is concerned with appraising the jurisdictions and comparative merits of the two fields, claiming that one or the other has a greater capacity to identify and account for regularities of human behavior. These three assumptions do not hold here; more, they would be irrelevant if they did hold.

Our aim is more modest and less invidious than such misunderstandings would allow. Psychologists and sociologists have begun inquiries into medical education. For many, and not only among medical educators, the distinctive concerns, problems, theories, and methods of these two fields are not easily distinguished. Since both are concerned with enlarging our understanding of that great complex whole which is medical education, the relations between the theoretical orientations of each are easily blurred. A short examination of these orientations will suggest how they can be consolidated into an overarching body of knowledge.

However much they differ in other respects, the various approaches in psychology are alike in their focus *on the individual.* Gestalt theory, field theory, psychoanalysis, behaviorism of various types—to mention only a few—differ in many ways, but they are alike in attempting to account for certain aspects of the behavior of individuals. This general assertion, loose and subject to modification in detail though it is, will probably gain ready assent, not only because it is approximately the case but also because it has so often been made before. For our purposes, however, it is more useful to itemize some of the types of specific questions about human behavior which stem from each orientation. Even a small sample of such questions will serve to make the general formulations more widely understandable. Psychologists ask, for example:

> How is the personality of the individual to be conceived, what are its principal attributes, and how are these related?
>
> Which qualities of individuals enable them to perform certain tasks more or less well? The field of psychometrics is concerned with identifying and measuring these attributes.
>
> Which psychological processes result in one or another characteristic form of behavior, or in one or another type of personality? Are there, for example, self-regulating processes on the psychological plane as there are for the individual conceived as a biological organism?
>
> What are the regularities of sequence in the development of the individual self—what, for example, are the phases of life-cycle development?

How do organisms in general, and human beings in particular, learn?

What individuals perceive is evidently not determined wholly by the "objective" characteristics of what is "out there" to be perceived. What, then, are the determinants of perception?

The behavior of individuals can be usefully conceived as affected by various dispositions. What properties and processes of individuals affect their motivations?

This short list suggests that the distinctive orientation is that of identifying properties and processes of individuals which can be thought of as affecting the ways in which they perceive, think, feel, and act. The theoretical emphasis is upon individuals, although it is recognized that the properties and processes attributable to individuals have different behavioral consequences depending upon the situations in which they find themselves. The pervasive concern is with finding effective means of characterizing individual persons and their behavior, with interest in their environment obtaining only so far as it helps lead to this result.

In similarly general terms, also subject to correction in matters of detail, the correlative sociological orientation is directed toward characterizing the attributes, processes, structure, and functions of the *social and cultural environments* in which individuals find themselves. The parallel is fairly close. What the psychologist seeks to discover systematically about individuals, provisionally abstracted from their environments, the sociologist seeks to discover systematically about the environments, abstracted temporarily from the particular individuals in them. Just as psychologists seek to identify the significant attributes of individuals, so sociologists seek to identify significant attributes of social and cultural environments. A short list of questions raised by sociologists may serve to amplify what is meant by the general statement. Sociologists ask, for example:

How is social organization to be conceived, what are its principal attributes, and how are these connected?

Which properties and structures of social organization enable individuals to operate with greater or less effectiveness within their social contexts?

What processes in an organization foster or curb the achievement of the goals of individuals within them, enabling these to be realized with greater or less stress?

What are the regularities in sequences of social status to be assumed by individuals within the organization or society? What are the effects of discontinuities and continuities in these status-sequences?

The culture of a society incorporates the values people in that society live by. How does the structure of the society facilitate or hamper the efforts of persons variously located in that structure to act in terms of these cultural values?

This specimen list of sociological questions, like the list of psychological questions, only touches upon some general problems characteristic of the field of inquiry. But taken in conjunction, the two lists indicate that however much these distinctive problems differ, they are complementary. In the main, psychology treats of the qualities of *individuals,* of the processes through which they perceive their environment and learn to modify or cope with it, of the motives governing their behavior, of their development and growth as a function of both learning and maturation. Throughout, the analytical focus is upon the individual, with the social surroundings being regarded as a given which is not within the theoretical competence of the psychologist to analyze. In the main, *sociology treats of the social environment,* the conditions under which one or another form of social organization comes about, the attributes of organizations and their interrelations, the development of social values and norms, their functions in governing the socially patterned behavior of individuals, and the forces making for changes in social structure. Here, the analytical focus is upon the structure of the environment, with the attributes and psychological processes of individuals being regarded as given and not within the theoretical competence of the sociologist to analyze. And, as has been said, the middle ground in which an effort is made to relate the variability of individuals and the variability of the social environment constitutes the field of social psychology or psycho-sociology.

Psychological and Sociological Research on Medical Education

By and large, social science research in the field of medical education has been marked by three conspicuous characteristics. First, it has been largely confined to psychological studies of medical students and has largely neglected studies of the relations of students to the others in the medical school (medical faculty, associated paramedical personnel, patients). Second, studies of medical students have largely focused on identifying the qualities of applicants presumably qualifying them for admission and on the prediction of academic performance in medical school. Only a few inquiries have examined the responses of students to distinctive parts of the environment provided by the medical school. Third, these studies have been characterized by a strongly empiricist bent; that is, they are primarily designed to discover correlations between measurable qualities or traits of individual students and subsequent academic performance in medical school, primarily as measured by grades. They have not been analytical, designed to account for the correlations between individual traits and performance which are found to obtain.

This triple emphasis—upon students, upon their individual qualities, and upon empirical correlations of these with their later performance in school—was perhaps to be expected in the early stages of inquiry. Since it was almost entirely psychologists who first undertook these studies, it is understandable that they focused upon the qualities of individual students. The long-standing concern of medical schools with finding sound criteria for optimum selection among numerous applicants only reinforced the tendency to try to discover the properties of applicants which best qualify them for medical study (and, it is provisionally assumed, for later medical practice). Finally, the interest in identifying these attributes of applicants leads directly to the search for correlations between these attributes and later academic performance.

Now that other kinds of social scientists have extended their interest in research on medical education, we suppose that the character of these inquiries will become broadened and more diversified. A short review will indicate a wider range of problems of medical education amenable to social science inquiry, and indicate the ways in which collateral problems are approached from distinctively psychological and sociological standpoints.

Research on selection and academic performance. We draw upon two reviews of the hundred or so studies concerned with identifying the attributes which make for academic success in medical school.[42] These reviews find that a great diversity of individual qualities and prior performance of students has been included in these studies:

high school and college grades;

aptitudes as measured by a variety of tests (including the Medical College Admission Test, the Moss Aptitude Test, and the Minnesota Aptitude Test);

intelligence (as measured by ACE, AGCT, CAVD, PMA, Kulhman, Otis, Stanford-Binet, and Terman Concept Formation tests, among others);[43]

achievement (as registered in tests of arithmetic, classification inventory, zoology, general chemistry, and so forth);

reading (in terms of speed, accuracy, and the like);

study habits;

occupational interests (especially as indexed by the Strong vocational interest blank);

personality (as indicated in the MMPI, TAT, Allport-Vernon, Bernreuter, Humm-Wadsworth, Rorschach, and Szondi tests);

various assessments of attitudes and behavior (based on interviews;)

and such status attributes of prospective students as age, father's (not mother's) occupation, marital status, and community of residence.

The design of these psychological studies is much the same, although they differ in detail. The design typically consists of (1) the measurement of qualities of prospective students by use of one or more standardized tests, or of selected experiences and academic performance before the students have entered upon their medical studies; and (2) the computation of correlations between these measures and measures of subsequent academic performance. The predictive value of these diverse measures has varied greatly. Gottheil and Michael conclude their critical review, for example, by saying:

> . . . the results . . . have not appeared to be highly impressive. Many psychological tests have been applied. . . . In general, these have not improved upon or even equalled the efficiency of premedical grades in predicting medical grades. Nevertheless, in those instances when attempts were made to assess, weight, and combine the various factors necessary for achieving satisfactory grades (such factors as ability, interest, personality, and achievement), the results were more encouraging. Multiple correlation coefficients have been reported ranging from 0.52 to 0.66 with an average of 0.58. . . . Thus despite the many limitations of the criteria and predictor variables used in the selection of medical students, it would appear that predictions may actually be considerably more efficient than they have been generally thought to be.[44]

Super and Bachrach come to much the same conclusion, but emphasize the following point:

> Studies of intellective factors have reached a plateau, with correlations between intelligence and achievement in medical school clustering in the .40's and .50's. Progress seems likely to be made in the affective areas rather than the intellective, for intelligence is not likely to account for more of the variation in achievement. A real need therefore exists for good measures of motivation of personality factors. . . . Again, socio-economic, cultural, and experience factors other than type of school course are largely overlooked in the investigations under review, although key persons have been superficially studied (why they become key figures and how key figures function in that capacity has not been considered).[45]

The dean of British experimental psychologists, Sir Frederic

Bartlett, having himself engaged in studies bearing upon the selection of medical students, summarizes the experience with intelligence and aptitude tests in these general statements:

> (a) Negative prognosis is safer than positive; or, more specifically, lack of success in intelligence and aptitude tests is a safer index of failure in life situations requiring intelligence and corresponding aptitudes than is success in the tests an index of success.
> (b) It is safer to predict moderate, or routine, success from test results than to foresee outstanding success.
> (c) Intelligence-test prognosis has a wider range than that of aptitude tests, but even the former cannot be made to cover all types of "problematic" situations.
> (d) Aptitude tests provide a less safe basis for prognosis, whether of failure or of success on all points, than intelligence tests.[46]

As these observations imply, there is also something of historical irony here. The more efficient these tests are in culling out probable failures among prospective students and the more widely the tests are used as a basis for selecting students, the less effectively they can predict varying degrees of academic success among the students who are admitted. As has been repeatedly indicated and as Gottheil and Michael have emphatically noted, "the magnitude of report correlation coefficients [between preadmission test scores and grades in medical school] has frequently been decreased by the effect of restriction in the range of cases" available for study in the school.[47] These and other artifacts of the current use of tests lessen their capacity to differentiate sensitively gradations of accomplishment as these are registered in academic grades or ranking in medical school.

Research on medical education has understandably focused on the personal qualities—intellective, affective, social—of the *individual student*. After all, it seems almost self-evident that the trained capacities of individual students will determine their effectiveness as medical students and presumably (though little is known of this in any systematic fashion) as physicians. Moreover, such research provides a basis for definite action: it can affect procedures of selection, and medicine, like all the other professions, is necessarily concerned with the problem of choosing the best recruits. Research has therefore centered on the qualities or attributes of individual students which seem to make for success in medical school. There remains the difficult problem of establishing sound criteria of "successful performance," and all those who have engaged in research on this subject recognize that this remains *terra incognita*. We have much to learn, for example, about the extent to which grades in medical school are related to the quality of later performance in the role of physician. In turn, the criteria of the "good physician" have yet to be formulated in a form sufficiently precise and valid for use in systematic inquiry.

Technical problems of measurement such as these set certain limitations upon the prediction of subsequent performance on the basis of psychological knowledge about the individual student. Beyond these technical problems are theoretical problems which have to do with the conceptual framework adopted in these inquiries. Adopting the contrary-to-fact premise that the technical problems have been resolved and that reasonably satisfactory criteria and measures of the quality of performance, as student and as physician, have been established, there still remains the distinctively sociological matter that behavior is a result not merely of personal qualities but of these in interaction with the patterned situations in which the individual behaves.[48] It is these social contexts which greatly affect the extent to which the capacities of individuals are actually realized. Yet intensive study of the social environment of learning by medical students has been largely neglected, even as the study of the psychological attributes of medical students has been intensified.

Technical limits upon the predictive value of various tests of individual qualities and personality therefore need to be distinguished from theoretical limits. Learning to be a physician, like complex learning of other kinds, is not a function only of intelligence and aptitude, of motivations and self-images; it is also a function of the social environments in which learning and performance take place. The sociological perspective therefore calls for systematic study of the socially patterned situations occurring in the medical school. From that perspective, we would expect to find, as we do find, substantial differences in the extent and effectiveness of medical learning among students of approximately the same intelligence and aptitude. For learning and performance vary not only with the individual qualities of students but also with their places in distinctive climates of value and in the organization of relations among students, between students and faculty, and between students and patients.

Though systematic evidence on this has only begun to be assembled in our Columbia studies, we assume that the learning environments afforded by different medical schools differ appreciably. This impression is confirmed by medical educators who have moved from one school to another. What is perhaps less immediately evident but, from the sociological standpoint, quite as significant, is that the learning environment constituted by each medical school differs for the individual students and groups of students within it. Only first appearances run to the contrary. In the large, students in a particular medical school have presumably been exposed to the same members of the faculty, the same textbooks, the same laboratory and clinical experience, the same values—in short, the same environment. But this is so only in a first, gross approximation. On further, more exacting inquiry, this "same environment" turns out to be internally differentiated. It comprises a variety of distinct environments for various types of students. Some students, for example, are more socially isolated than others. Some enter as lone individuals, others as engaged in a social network of friends. The Columbia studies have found that the requirements of the medical school are experienced as less stressful by the students who are incorporated into networks of personal relations than by the relatively isolated students. The extent to which students can realize their potentialities may thus be appreciably affected by their social status within the school. As another example, the studies have found that the environments constituted by medical fraternities in one school differ greatly for their members. The fraternities are composed of students of differing types (as these have been previously and, of course, confidentially rated by the committee on admissions). A student of high academic potential, as measured by antecedent tests, who becomes a member of a fraternity including many of like kind, will to this extent presumably be in a different social environment, and subject to differing social stress and support, than a student in another type of fraternity, in which individuals of this capacity are in the distinct minority.

Moreover, the criteria and procedures for selection of medical students have distinct sociological implications. *They help to shape the interpersonal environment which the school provides for each of its students.* For, as the criteria of admission vary, the composition of the student body will manifestly vary. If the admissions committee in one school, for example, assigns prime importance to intellective qualities of students, the composition of students in that school will of course be skewed toward the upper reaches of intelligence. As a result, students of any particular degree of intelligence will find themselves in an environment of peers distinctly different from that found in a school using another set of criteria for selection.

Next to nothing is known about the ways in which such differences in the composition of the student body present individual students with significantly differing environments and affect the social processes of their learning. One type of student body, for example, may induce a large measure of competitive stress; another, a more relaxed atmosphere for learning. But whatever the consequences of these differences, and they remain to be identified, it can be seen that the criteria and procedures for admission have not only the manifest function of selecting applicants more or less suited to the role of the physician, but also the indirect and latent consequence of producing distinctive local environments for students. In other words, procedures and criteria of selection involve not only the psychological consideration of the personal qualities of each student but indirectly the sociological consideration of the composition of the total student body as well.

These few observations may be enough to indicate the distinctive but complementary standpoints of psychology and of sociology in examining this one matter of connections between the personal qualities of incoming students and their later academic performance. As things now stand with regard to this type of problem:

The psychologist tries, in effect, to identify and to measure the personal qualities of incoming students which are significantly related to their performance in medical school.

The sociologist tries, in effect, to identify the various positions and social relationships in which students with particular kinds of personal qualities are involved, in order to see how these are related to academic performance of students having the same qualities but occupying differing positions in the social system constituted by the medical school.

Motivations of medical students, and sources of stress and support in the medical school environment. All organizations confront the functional problem of encouraging their members to fulfill their roles, of reinforcing their motivations to do so, and yet of avoiding that "excess" of motivation which subjects members to "undue stress." This connection between motivation and potentiality for stress is widely recognized. Medical students, for example, who have no great involvement in their work may do poorly, but they are also more likely to be exempt from acute distress over their poor performance. There is, so to say, an optimum zone of intensity of motivation. Below the lower limit of this zone, students will not be sufficiently motivated to live up to the requirements of their roles, beyond the upper limit, students will invest each new situation they face with undue significance and experience even fairly routine situations as stressful. The medical school thus faces the formidable problem of providing a "sufficiency" of incentives to medical students for fulfilling their roles without enlarging and intensifying these incentives to the point where they tend to produce that excess of anxiety and preoccupation with role performance which keeps students from realizing their potentialities.

Students presumably vary in the intensity of their fear of failure, in their capacity to tolerate stress, in their characteristic responses to anxiety. Apart from such individual variability, however, medical schools, and particular divisions of a medical school, vary in the extent to which they confront students with stressful situations. Differences in the structure of social relations among students and faculty also serve to reduce or to increase the frequency of anxiety states. Under some social conditions, anxious students work upon one another to intensify anxieties; under others, the anxieties of individually disturbed students are more readily contained by social mechanisms operating within the group. To the extent that this is so, the cognitive performance of students will be affected not only by their vulnerability to anxiety, but also by the group structure, which can operate to cushion or to intensify the impact of stressful situations in the school.

Like the problems of recruitment, the problems of motivation, anxiety, and stress have their distinctively psychological and sociological aspects. Some medical educators have recognized this in varying degree. Indeed, some innovations of curriculum and organization in medical schools are addressed to these very problems.

The design of the numerous psychological studies of motivation, stress, and anxiety has been adapted to the study of medical students.[49] Much of this research centers on the systematic changes of behavior under acute stress, commonly leading to a disruption of organized action or to rigidity and inflexibility of behavior. This type of inquiry also examines the responses of students with differing types of personalities to varying degrees of stress. The preeminent problem here is that of individual variability in the definition of what is considered threatening and in the type of responses to stress situations.

As we have seen, the collateral questions, from the sociological standpoint, deal with the characteristics of the environment which make for greater or less frequency of varying degrees of stress and support. Here the primary interest is not with personality differences in the vulnerability to stress, but in the social arrangements which produce varying patterns of exposure to stress. A prime, fine-grained objective is to identify those aspects of the environing social structure which produce more or less stressful situations rather uniformly for all students and those which differentially expose some, rather than other, groups of students to these stresses.

One may begin, for example, with the socially emphasized fact that the immediate future of medical students largely depends upon the appraisals of their performance by the faculty. This serves to deepen the affective concern of students with teachers. They are motivated to *know* what is expected of them by the faculty and to *know* in what measure they are meeting those expectations. This, of course, is one source of anxieties about grades in courses. When the pattern of periodically reporting grades to students is curtailed or eliminated, there develops a marked concern to find substitute bases for answering the institutionally generated question: "How am I making out?" Students tend to search for clues to the instructor's judgment of their performance. The most casual remarks by instructors become imbued with deep evaluative meanings. Changes in the system of evaluating students thus seem to have consequences, of largely unknown magnitude and kind, for the extent and intensity of stresses induced by the environment.

There are, in short, sociological as well as psychological dimensions of motivation, stress, and anxiety, and these need to be examined jointly.

Career decisions of medical students. What is considered occupational choice from the standpoint of the individual becomes the process of recruitment from the standpoint of the profession and the allocation of personnel in various occupational statuses from the standpoint of the society. What the individual defines as a promising opportunity afforded by the labor market, the profession defines as an "acute shortage" (say, of doctors or engineers or nurses), and the society defines as an imbalance of occupational distribution. These all patently refer to the same facts from the different perspectives of the individual, the occupational group, and the society. Articulating these three systems so that the flow and distribution of occupational choices are such as to meet the aspirations of individuals, the requirements of the profession, and an optimum balance among the occupations is a functional problem which is still poorly understood. But again, to state the problem is at least to *specify the nature of our ignorance* and to suggest interrelations between psychological and sociological analysis.

Career decisions exhibit the complementary nature of these two modes of analysis. Once again, each kind of inquiry has its distinctive kinds of questions. The psychologist will ask, for example, what types of students, as distinguished by personality tests, tend to elect the general practice of medicine, or one or another specialty. Although there is little firm evidence of a connection between personality and the choice of different kinds of medical careers, this has not prevented the emergence of a distinct student lore about the type of personality best suited to each kind of specialized practice. To some unknown extent, this lore itself seems to enter into the process of arriving at a decision, after the fashion of a self-fulfilling prophecy.* Some students engage in a fairly continual process of trying to match up their own personalities with the alleged personality requirements of various specialties. In contrast to general practice, many students are convinced, surgery and radiology require relatively little ability to reason. "It takes a certain personality to become a surgeon," says

*See Chapter 10, "The Self-Fulfilling Prophecy," in this volume—editors' note.

one student. "You have to be dashing and aggressive and full of energy. I've talked to a lot of doctors about this and they all say this is true. Why, just look at all the surgeons you know; I can think of only one exception to this rule and I've worked with a lot of them." Pediatrics, says another, requires "the non-aggressive, non-assertive, kind, understanding, yet strong, type. This is generally agreed upon." As for "x-ray men, eye, throat, and ear doctors," reports a third, they are "all of the businessman type running their practice very much like a business with rigid hours and fees." As these few of many such statements imply, students engage in appraising the skills, knowledge, performance, and personalities of faculty members as representatives of a particular specialty. There develops more or less of a consensus among students about the types of psychological qualities required by the different kinds of practice. It remains to be seen whether these images of the various medical roles affect the career choices which students actually make.

In effect, psychologists attempt to discover the actual truth of what these students assume to be known: they try to find out whether there is a distinct association between personality, the psychological requirements of each kind of professional role, and the choice of a particular field of practice. Sociologists ask, correlatively, how it is that students of the same personality type elect differing kinds of practice while students of differing personality types sometimes elect the same kind. From the standpoint of sociology, each decision—to go no further back than the decision to enter medicine as a lifework and the later decision to enter a particular specialty—is in part contingent upon the reactions of others with whom the individual student is socially related. As each decision in this sequence of decisions is being considered, it is reinforced or countered by others, and this reacts upon the stability of the decision and the satisfaction with it. Successive decisions progressively commit the student to pursuing one or another career, narrowing the range of subsequent alternatives. Each decision meets with greater or less social support, depending upon the values of the medical school in which the student is enrolled, the position one occupies in the eyes of faculty and peers, the constellation and values of one's family. These provide social contexts which operate to make the student's "personal decisions" variously contingent upon group affiliations, the culture and structure of these groups, and the positions within them. And once having entered a specialty, the students may find their social personalities conforming to the demands of the particular professional role; not only may decisive students elect to enter the field of surgery but, whatever their previous bent, once having begun the practice of the specialty, their personalities may be further shaped by the requirements of the specialized role.

The social process of career decisions involves far more than the end result of entering a particular field of medical practice. The social context affects the degree of stress attending these decisions. It has been found, for example, that students perceive the various medical specialties as differing in prestige and status.[50] Internists and surgeons are commonly assigned higher standing than, say, obstetricians and psychiatrists. Within such a climate of evaluation, the student who proposes to become a psychiatrist seems, from the preliminary data in hand, to be subject to greater stress than the student who plans to enter the more highly approved field of internal medicine. These climates of evaluation may vary substantially among medical schools. In that event, the student who decides to specialize in psychiatry at one school, where great value is attached to this field, will be in a substantially different social and psychological situation from that of the *same kind* of student making the same decision at another school in which psychiatry is often derogated. If only by way of tentative illustration, this suggests that the same career decisions will have differing psychological significance depending upon the social context.

Once again, psychological and sociological approaches to a particular problem prove to be complementary. Moreover, each approach can be taken a considerable distance before the two are brought together. In the illustrative case, it will then become possible to establish the probabilities of various kinds of career decisions being made by medical students of differing types of personality in various kinds of social environments.

The spectrum of medical values and norms.   One last illustration may bring out a further distinctive focus in the sociology of medical education, without comparing this focus with that of psychology. This is the value-environments afforded by medical schools.

The profession of medicine, like other occupations, has its own normative subculture, a body of shared and transmitted ideas, values, and standards toward which members of the profession are expected to orient their behavior. The norms and standards define technically and morally allowable patterns of behavior, indicating what is prescribed, preferred, permitted, or proscribed. The subculture, then, refers to more than habitual behavior; its norms codify and specify the values of the profession. This extends even to the details of language judged appropriate by the profession. Like other occupations, medicine has its distinctive vocabulary and like the vocabularies of other occupations, this one is often described derisively as jargon by outsiders and appreciatively as technical terminology by insiders.[51] The medical subculture covers a wide range—from matters of language to matters of relations with patients, colleagues, and the community—and it is the function of the medical school to transmit this subculture to successive generations of neophytes.

The composition of values involved in the medical subculture probably varies in detail and in emphasis among medical schools but there nevertheless appears to be a substantial consensus among subsets of schools. Our field observations suggest that in the 1950s appreciably the same values and norms obtained with varying emphasis in the medical schools of Cornell, Pennsylvania, and Western Reserve, and these, in turn, were similar to the values and norms codified in a report of a committee of the Association of American Medical Colleges.[52]

The system of values and norms can be thought of as being organized or patterned in at least two major respects. First, for each norm there tends to be at least one coordinate norm, which is, if not inconsistent with the other, at least sufficiently different as to make it difficult for the student and the physician to live up to both.[53] Alan Gregg, for example, speaks of the "readjustment" that takes place "between the detachment of the nascent scientist and the none too mature compassion of the beginner in therapy."[54] From this perspective, medical education can be conceived as facing the task of enabling students to learn *how to blend* incompatible or potentially incompatible norms into a functionally consistent whole.[55] Indeed, the process of learning to be a physician can be conceived largely as learning to blend seeming or actual incompatibles into consistent and stable patterns of professional behavior.

Second, the values and norms are defined by the profession in terms of how they are to be put into effect. They come to be defined as requirements of the physician's role. And since many physicians will find themselves in situations where it is difficult to live up to these role requirements, it becomes the more important that they thoroughly acquire the values which are to regulate their behavior.

For convenience, a list of values and norms in the practice of medicine will be itemized in three broad classes: those governing physicians' self-images, their relations to patients, and their relations to colleagues and to the community.

VALUES GOVERNING THE PHYSICIAN'S SELF-IMAGE
1. Physicians should continue their self-education throughout their careers in order to keep pace with the rapidly advancing frontiers of medical knowledge.

But: they also have a primary obligation to make as much time as possible available for the care of their patients.

2. Student-physicians should be interested in enlarging their medical responsibilities as they advance through medical school.
   But: they must not prematurely take a measure of responsibility for which they are not adequately prepared (or, at least, are not legally qualified to undertake).

3. Physicians must maintain a self-critical attitude and be disciplined in the scientific appraisal of evidence.
   But: they must be decisive and not postpone decisions beyond what the situation requires, even when the scientific evidence is inadequate.

4. Physicians must have a sense of autonomy; they must accept the burden of their responsibility and act as circumstances, in their best judgment, require.
   But: autonomy must not be allowed to become complacency or smug self-assurance; autonomy must be coupled with a due sense of humility.

5. Physicians must have the kind of detailed knowledge which often requires specialized education.
   But: they must not become narrowly specialized; they should be well rounded and broadly educated.

6. Physicians should have a strong moral character with abiding commitments to basic moral values.
   But: they must avoid passing moral judgments on patients.

7. Physicians should attach great value to doing what they can to advance medical knowledge; such accomplishments deserve full recognition.
   But: they should not express a competitive spirit toward their colleagues.

VALUES GOVERNING THE PHYSICIAN-PATIENT RELATIONSHIP

8. Physicians must be emotionally detached in their attitudes toward patients, keeping their emotions "on ice" and not becoming "overly identified" with patients.
   But: they must avoid becoming callous through excessive detachment, and should have compassionate concern for patients.

9. Physicians must not prefer one type of patient over another, and must curb hostilities toward patients (even those who prove to be uncooperative or who do not respond to therapy).
   But: the most rewarding experience for the physician is the effective solution of a patient's health problems.

10. Physicians must gain and maintain the confidence of their patients.
     But: they must avoid the mere bedside manner which can quickly degenerate into expedient and self-interested salesmanship.
11. Physicians must recognize that diagnosis is often provisional.
     But: they must have the merited confidence of patients who want "to know what is really wrong."
12. Physicians must provide adequate and unhurried medical care for each patient.
     But: they should not allow any patient to usurp so much of their limited time as to have this be at the expense of other patients.
13. Physicians should come to know patients as persons and devote substantial attention to their psychological and social circumstances.
     But: this too should not be so time-consuming a matter as to interfere with the provision of suitable care for other patients.
14. Physicians should institute all the scientific tests needed to reach a sound diagnosis.
     But: they should be discriminating in the use of these tests, because they are often costly and may impose a sizable financial burden on the patient.
15. Physicians have the right to expect a "reasonable fee," depending upon the care given and the economic circumstances of the patient.
     But: they must not "soak the rich" in order to "provide for the poor."
16. Physicians should see to it that medical care is available for their patients whenever it is required.
     But: they, too, have the right to a "normal life" with their families.

VALUES GOVERNING THE RELATION TO COLLEAGUES AND THE COMMUNITY

17. Physicians must respect the reputations of their colleagues, not holding them up to obloquy or ridicule before associates or patients.
     But: they are obligated to see to it that high standards of practice are maintained by others in the profession.
18. Physicians must collaborate with others on the medical team (nurses, social workers, technicians) rather than dominate them.

But: they have final responsibility for the team and must see to it that their associates meet high standards.

19. Physicians should call in consultants whenever needed.
    But: they should not add unnecessarily to the costs of medical care.

20. Physicians, as responsible professionals, should take an active role in their communities.
    But: they should not get involved in political squabbles or spend too much time in activities unrelated to their profession.

21. Physicians must do all they can to prevent, and not only to help cure, illness.
    But: society more largely rewards physicians for the therapy they effect as practitioners and only secondarily rewards those engaged in the prevention of illness, particularly since prevention is not as readily visible to patients who do not know that they remain healthy because of preventive measures.

This list of values and norms is of course far from exhaustive, but it may be sufficient to illustrate the principal point. It is not that the values, or the value and practical exigency, in each pair are necessarily at odds; they are only potentially so. The ability to blend these potential opposites into a stable pattern of professional behavior must be learned, and it seems from the data in hand that this is one of the most difficult tasks confronting the medical student.

Contrary to widespread opinion, the effective acquisition of these values by medical students is not a matter only of "medical ethics," which attaches significance to these values in their own right. They can also be considered, quite neutrally and without reference to their undoubted ethical aspect, in terms of their instrumental significance for the effective provision of health care. They are not absolute values, prized for their own sake; they are, presumably, values which serve as effective means to a socially important end. Just as cognitive standards of knowledge and skill in medicine have a manifest function in facilitating sound medical practice, so the moral standards have the same, though often less readily recognized, function. In short, we are considering primarily sociological rather than ethical aspects of the place of values in the professionalization of the medical student.

As centers of research, medical schools put students more fully in touch with the frontiers of medical knowledge than many, if not most, of them are apt to be in their later years of practice. This is widely recognized. What seems to have received less notice is the correlative fact that medical students are also being systematically exposed to professional values and norms which are probably "higher"—that is, more exacting and rigorously disinterested—than those found in the run of medical practice.[56] Medical schools are socially defined as the guardians of these values and norms. The schools thus have the double function of transmitting to students the *cognitive* standards of knowledge and skill and the *moral* standards of values and norms. Both sets of standards are essential to the proficient practice of medicine.

The functional significance of these values and norms is greatly reinforced by the social organization of medical practice. Students may be imbued with values and standards which can be more or less readily lived up to in the special environment of the teaching hospital, where the "right way of doing things" may be strongly supported by precept, example, and recognition. But once they have entered upon their own practice, some of these physicians will find themselves working under conditions which are far less conducive to ready conformity with such norms. Many of them will be independent practitioners, in a situation structurally different from that of the medical school. There, students and faculty alike are, in effect, under the continued scrutiny of other medical experts, who set store by critical appraisal of what is being done. This need not be wholly a matter of plan or of acknowledgment, but the structural pattern is so plain as to be generally acknowledged: to some extent, peers and superiors in the teaching hospital often serve in what amounts to the role of monitors of medical practice.[57]

In contrast, physicians in their private offices are largely subject to the controls only of the values and norms they have acquired and made their own. The medically uninformed patient is not in a position to pass sound judgment upon the normative adequacy of what the physician does. Medically informed colleagues are not in a position to know what is being done. These structural facts, therefore, put a special premium on having these values and norms instilled in the student during the course of professional socialization in the medical school. If this is not thoroughly achieved under the optimum conditions provided by the medical school, it is unlikely that it will be achieved under the usually less favorable circumstances of private practice.

Further reinforcing the functional significance of value-assimilation for effective medical practice is the sociological fact—known and experienced by physicians everywhere—that the expectations of some patients may in effect invite physicians to depart from the standards of good medical care. After all, sick people do not necessarily live up to the strict etymology of the word "patient." They are not necessarily long-suffering and forbearing, or "calmly expectant, quietly awaiting the course of events." On the contrary, the etymology of the term and the psychology of the patient are often poles apart.

Suffering people are disposed to want a nostrum, in the realm of health as in the realms of politics and, sometimes, of religion. It requires cultural training in self-discipline to accept the fact, when it is a fact, that a prompt solution to one's troubles is not possible. Not all cultures and societies provide that training. That is one reason why magical beliefs and practices flourish. When sick people have not formed the disciplined attitudes required by the social role of the patient, they may unwittingly exert considerable psychological pressure upon physicians to promise more than they responsibly can promise or even to engage in what one practitioner describes as "senseless and reprehensible treatment." Many patients will thus insist on being relieved of suffering, as soon as possible, and preferably immediately. Physicians are urged to do, not as they ought, but as their patients would have them do. In time, some physicians find themselves motivated to acquiesce in the expectations of patients who, having made a firm self-diagnosis, insist on one or another type of treatment. As one troubled practitioner put his dilemma, "If I don't do the operation she wants, it would not be [only] a matter of losing her, but all she might refer"[58]—a marvelously instructive reversal of roles in which the practitioner plaintively abandons his professional commitments, surrenders the authority of his presumed expertise, enters into collusion with the anxious patient, and blames the victim for this composite delinquency, all in the unquestioned interest of maintaining a profitable practice.

Since private practitioners in particular are subject to such incentives and opportunities for departing from what they know to be the appropriate kind of medical care, it becomes functionally imperative that they acquire, in medical school, those values and norms that will make them less vulnerable to such deviations. It is in this direct sociological sense that the acquisition of appropriate attitudes and values is as central as the acquisition of knowledge and skills to training for the provision of medical care.

SOCIALIZATION: A TERMINOLOGICAL NOTE

Ratified by more than two generations of use in psychology and sociology, the technical term *socialization* designates the processes by which people selectively acquire the values and attitudes, the interests, skills, and knowledge—in short, the culture—current in the groups of which they are, or seek to become, a member. It refers to the learning of social roles. Here, socialization refers to the processes through which the medical student develops a professional self, with its characteristic values, attitudes, knowledge, and skills, fusing these into a more or less consistent set of dispositions which govern behavior in a wide variety of professional (and extraprofessional) situations. Socialization takes place primarily through social interaction with people who are significant for the individual—in the medical school, probably with faculty members above most others, but also with fellow students, associated personnel (nurses, technicians, caseworkers, and so forth), and patients. Since the patterns of social interaction between medical students and these other people are only similar and not identical, the variations result in different kinds of medical practitioners emerging from what may at first seem to be the "same" social environment.

The *fact* that socialization occurs, that people acquire the culture and subculture of the groups with which they are affiliated, has been noticed for so long that the memory of man runneth not to the contrary. But the social and psychological processes through which socialization comes about, so that different individuals in the same group variously assimilate the established culture, have become, only in recent years, the object of methodical and sustained inquiry.[59] Just as all of us, even Macaulay's schoolboy, know by the repeated evidence of our own eyes that objects fall when they lack support and know this without recourse to the law of inertia, so we all know without recourse to sociology and psychology that individuals brought up in a Japanese, or American, or Bantu culture tend to acquire the speech, values, and ways of life current in their culture. As attention shifts to less commonplace, less gross matters of socialization, however, even the unexplained *facts* may not be easily available. Is it the case, for example, that as they move through successive years of medical school, students acquire a greater, or diminishing, preference for patients who express their appreciation of the physician's services? Does the value placed upon such responses by patients vary in the cultural climates of different schools? Familiarity with some of the gross events is of course only a specious substitute for more detailed knowledge of the processes through which socialization comes about or fails to occur. In considering the "socialization of the medical student," then, we consider the processes by which neophytes come to acquire, *in patterned but selective fashion*, the attitudes and values, skills, knowledge, and ways of life established in the professional subculture.

The sociological and psychological concept of socialization is central to our inquiry into the making of physicians. We therefore want to distinguish *this* concept of socialization from the concept of socialization as it is understood in economics and politics and, derivatively, in the vernacular. The economic and political usage of the word socialization stems from the doctrine which advocates ownership and control of the apparatus of production by the community as a whole, and its administration by political agencies of the community. Loosely speaking, it refers to the "nationalization" of industry, business, or professional services. It is this sense of the word, of course, which is current in medical circles in the form of that stock phrase, "the socialization of medicine." In the course of generations of controversy—at least since the days of Bismarck in Germany, Lloyd George in England, and Wilson, if not Theodore Roosevelt, in the United States—the words "socialized medicine" have become fighting words. Indeed, "socialized" medicine has become so much the stereotyped phrase that, in some quarters, the first word almost invariably produces the second, among both those who oppose and those who support certain kinds of arrangements for the distribution of medical care by physicians. To recognize this tendency in the use of language may perhaps be enough to nullify it—or, less optimistically, to put it in question. When we say that "medical students are being socialized" in the professional culture, we plainly do not mean that they are being "nationalized" or imbued with a belief in the virtues of socialism. For it should be clear, by now, that the technical term *socialization* as employed since early in this century by sociology and psychology has nothing whatever to do with the technical term *socialization* as employed in economics and politics since the middle of the last century.

In the context of sociology and psychology, "to socialize" means to render *social,* to shape individuals into members of groups (whatever they may be—familial, religious, or professional); in the context of economics and politics, "to socialize" means to render *socialistic,* to modify political or economic systems according to the doctrines of socialism. The first of these is a wholly descriptive concept, devoid of implicit or explicit preferences; the second is often an optative concept, advocating or rejecting as well as describing. The one is generally confined to use as a technical term, neutral and emotionally unexciting; the other is frequently extended into an invective, a signal for attack or support. In psychological and sociological usage, *socialization* refers to ways in which *individuals* are shaped by their culture; in economic and political usage, it refers to ways in which an *organization* of human activities is shaped into a designated kind of structure. In short, all that the two words now have in common are their sound and spelling.[60]

All this is simply a reminder that *socialization* is a member of that large class of words which are called homonyms. In spite of their superficial family resemblance and their common etymological ancestor in the distant past, *socialization*₁ and *socialization*₂ are semantically neither kith nor kin. This kind of case is familiar enough: the vocabularies of science have a large stock of homonyms, quite distinct words which happen to be, as Fowler puts it, "like in look but unlike in sense." A few examples must stand for the many that make up the imposingly long list of technical homonyms that turn up in the various branches of science. The bacteriologist, come of age since the days of Pasteur and Koch, does not hesitate to use the term *culture* simply because the anthropologist, from the days of Tylor and Kidd, has utilized *culture* in quite another sense. Nor, rightly enough, does the anthropologist hesitate to speak of *material culture*, by which he means generally the physical artifacts produced by people-in-society, for fear that this might be confused, in the minds of some, with a *bacterial culture*. The parallel, which is not apparently the result of borrowing, indeed runs to specialized formations of the basic homonym: both bacteriologist and anthropologist, for example, speak, in their several ways, of *subcultures*. And neither avoids the term because "culture" is colloquially still understood as fastidious self-cultivation or, after the fashion of Matthew Arnold, as the "disinterested search for sweetness and light." As is generally the case with language, the context aptly enough shows which meaning of the homonym is intended and, in a language shot through with homonymous constructions, words of the same outward appearance are bound to appear in quite unrelated fields of inquiry.[61]

Perhaps a closer parallel to the case of *socialization* is the case of *rationalization*. Economists use the term to refer to "the scientific organization of industry to ensure minimum waste of labor, standardizing of production and, presumably, a resulting maintenance of prices at a constant level" even though Ernest Jones had introduced the term into psychoanalysis to signify those morally or rationally elevated explanations of one's conduct which are plausible and unwittingly false. And again, the homonym rationalization,[62] firmly rooted in both economics and psychology, is anything but misleading, except to those who are bent on misunderstanding. The report that "Smith is rationalizing his own inadequacy as a supervisor when he describes his staff as uncooperative" is not likely to be understood as an oblique allusion to Smith's plans for industrial reorganization, even by those trained wholly in economics and untutored in the intricacies of psychoanalysis.

And so it goes with a multitude of homonyms, scientific and colloquial. Homonyms may lead more than a double life. The physician uses *percussion* diagnostically; the musician, esthetically; the gunman, destructively. A *section* is one thing for the surgeon and anatomist, another for the botanist, and still a third for the mathematician; just as the geologist, printer, soldier, college teaching assistant, real estate broker, and railway worker have each their own technical meaning for this versatile word. *Remission* may denote a decrease in the violence of a disease in pathology and relief of quite another kind in theology. The word *mass* takes on distinct and severally useful meanings in physics, politics, and pharmacy, in mining, fine arts, military science, and Catholic ritual. *Force* carries lightly the burden of its varied significance as "unlawful violence" in the sphere of law and as a collective term in the vernacular for police officers engaged in maintaining law and order, just as it stands for quite different matters in physics, ethics, and literary accounts of lovemaking.

If only on the basis of ample precedent, it would seem that the widespread currency of the economic and political meanings of *socialization* in debates over appropriate arrangements for distributing medical services need not rule out the use of the psychological and sociological homonym, as in the phrase "socialization of the medical student," to refer to the processes through which the student is being inducted into the professional culture of medicine. This review of usages would be unnecessary were it not for two things.

First, the "socialization of medicine" is a matter of great and acrimonious controversy, which for many is charged with intense feeling and passion. Such affect-laden words seem to have a way of driving their affectively neutral and therefore dull homonyms out of circulation.[63] It is therefore necessary to emphasize the particular technical sense in which we have employed the term socialization throughout our sociological studies of medical education.

Second, technical homonyms seldom result in misunderstandings since the readers of writings containing these terms are ordinarily themselves at work in the same technical field, and consequently share a common universe of discourse. Readers in the same field at once supply the appropriate, rather than the extraneous, meanings of the homonym, since they are socially insulated from the like-appearing word of quite different meaning. But when, as in the present instance, a technical term, such as *socialization,* comes to the attention of those in other fields, quite the contrary is apt to occur. Readers will naturally enough supply the meaning with which they are most familiar, and some may actively resist the thought that it may have an equally well-established though different meaning in the technical field previously unknown to them. And since "the socialization of medicine" has entered as a stock phrase into the vernacular, it is likely that the psychological and sociological meaning of socialization will be repeatedly subordinated to its economic and political meaning, unless this tendency is countered in advance.

That is why it has been emphasized throughout this essay and in other papers reporting our studies that the terms *socialization, socialize,* and *socialized* are employed almost without exception in their psychological and sociological sense.

NOTES

[1]No later treatise on the subject has the scope and detail of Theodor Puschmann, *A History of Medical Education from the Most Remote to the Most Recent Times,* translated and edited by Evan H. Hare (London: H.K. Lewis, 1891). See also W.F. Norwood, *History of Medical Education in the United States Before the Civil War* (Philadelphia: University of Pennsylvania Press, 1944).

[2]This pioneering document is available in a photo-offset reprint of the first edition by The Johns Hopkins Press in 1937. Appropriately enough, this reprint contains an introduction by Abraham Flexner.

[3]Abraham Flexner, *Medical Education in the United States and Canada: A Report to the Carnegie Foundation for the Advancement of Teaching,* Bulletin Number Four (New York: Carnegie Foundation, 1910).

[4]This is a paraphrase and application of conceptions set forth by Paul F. Lazarsfeld and Robert K. Merton, "Mass Communication, Popular Taste and Organized Social Actions," in *Communication of Ideas,* Lyman Bryson, ed. (New York: Harper and Brothers, 1948), pp. 95–118, especially pp. 102–103.

[5]A summary of this experience is found in the memoirs of Abraham Flexner, *I Remember* (New York: Simon and Schuster, 1940), Chapter 9.

[6]Richard Harrison Shryock, "The Interplay of Social and Internal Factors in the History of Modern Medicine," *The Scientific Monthly* 76 (1953):226.

[7]There is evidently a long history of debate on the amount of time required for an "adequate" education in medicine. In the first century B.C. Thessalos held that six months were quite enough; in the second century the great Galen argued that in light of the immensity of knowledge required by the physician, no fewer than eleven years were needed.

[8]To a more limited extent, the same kind of competition operates among the departments in the other divisions of the university. But some reflection will show that these often loosely connected departments experience a great difference in the degree of such competition, if not in kind. There is not much direct competition, for example, between a department of fine arts and a department of physics.

[9]Similar observations have been made by many physicians with a capacity for considering the practice of medicine as itself a social system, variously relating physicians to their patients and the community. This particular phrasing is by the physician-biochemist-and-sociologist, L.J. Henderson, *The Study of Man* (Philadelphia: University of Pennsylvania Press,

1941), pp. 12–13. Elton Mayo is another physician-and-sociologist who has developed this hypothesis in some detail: *Some Notes on the Psychology of Pierre Janet* (Cambridge, Mass.: Harvard University Press, 1938), Appendix, pp. 111–126. This importance of continuity of medical care has often been appreciated by laymen. In Chapter 3 of *Janet's Repentance,* for example, George Eliot has someone remark that ". . . it's no trifle at her time of life to part with a doctor who knows her constitution."

¹⁰The World Medical Association, *Proceedings of the First World Conference on Medical Education* (London: Oxford University Press, 1954), p. 39.

¹¹Ibid., p. 405.

¹²Ibid., pp. 671–672.

¹³Ibid., p. 385.

¹⁴Ibid., p. 672.

¹⁵Reported by Morris Fishbein, *A History of the American Medical Association, 1847 to 1947* (Philadelphia: W. B. Saunders Company, 1947), p. 483.

¹⁶The World Medical Association, *Proceedings of the First World Conference on Medical Education,* p. 747. When Auguste Comte invented that "convenient barbarism," the word sociology, he could scarcely foresee the connotations which would be foisted upon it. As we shall see in the concluding part of this chapter, the confusion is worse confounded* by the fact that the word "socialization" is a technical term in sociology and psychology which is far removed from its meaning in such phrases as "the socialization of medicine."

¹⁷As indicated, for example, by Henry E. Sigerist, *Medicine and Human Welfare* (New Haven: Yale University Press, 1941), p. 101.

¹⁸L.J. Henderson, "The Practice of Medicine as Applied Sociology," *Transactions of the Association of American Physicians* 51(1936):8–22.

¹⁹Willard C. Rappleye, *Report of the Dean of the Faculty of Medicine* (New York: Columbia-Presbyterian Medical Center, 1955), p. 19. Dean Rappleye goes on to say that ". . . these considerations need not and should not substitute for a thorough education in the basic disciplines, but rather should supplement and vitalize it."

²⁰Richard Harrison Shryock, *The Development of Modern Medicine* (New York: A.A. Knopf, 1946), p. 21.

²¹See Mary E. W. Goss and George G. Reader, "Collaboration Between Sociologist and Physician," *Social Problems* 4(1956):82–89.

²²Howard C. Taylor, Jr., in *Trends in Medical Education,* Mahlon Ashford, ed. (New York: The Commonwealth Fund, 1949), p. 103. See other comments to the same effect by F.W. Jackson, Thomas A.C. Rennie, and Thomas D. Dublin, ibid., pp. 227, 260, 290–291.

²³James B. Conant, Foreword to *Harvard Case Studies in Experimental Science* (Cambridge, Mass.: Harvard University Press, 1950).

²⁴For a recent short overview, see Ernest O. Smigel, "Trends in Occupational Sociology in the United States: A Survey of Postwar Research,"

*Again prompted by an editor, I cite the source of a familiar phrase: Milton's *Paradise Lost,* Bk II, line 996.

American Sociological Review 19(1954):398–404; see also Theodore Caplow, *The Sociology of Work* (Minneapolis: University of Minnesota Press, 1954).

[25]Robert E. Park did much to initiate the sociological study of occupations at the University of Chicago in the 1920s. This was developed further by his colleague, Everett C. Hughes, who turned his attention in part to studies of professions. At Harvard University, Talcott Parsons contributed theoretical formulations which did much to enlarge interest in the sociological study of the professions. And during the 1950s, studies in this field were carried forward at Columbia University.

[26]The next part of this chapter distinguishes distinctively psychological and distinctively sociological approaches to medical education and indicates their connections.

[27]On this convergence of interest, see Leo W. Simmons and Harold G. Wolff, *Social Science in Medicine* (New York: Russell Sage Foundation, 1954). The Health Information Foundation has been issuing an inventory of *Social and Economic Research in Health* which bears witness to a growing volume of sociological research in this field, year by year.

[28]This phase in the empirical study of organization was significantly generated by the work of Elton Mayo and his associates of the Harvard Business School. See, for example, Elton Mayo, *The Human Problems of an Industrial Civilization* (New York: The Macmillan Company, 1933), and for the major report on these studies, Fritz J. Roethlisberger and William Dickson, *Management and the Worker* (Cambridge, Mass.: Harvard University Press, 1939). For theoretical statements, see Talcott Parsons, "Sociological Approach to the Theory of Organization," *Administrative Science Quarterly,* June and September 1956; Herbert A. Simon, *Administrative Behavior* (New York: Macmillan, 1947).

[29]Again, only a few among the many can be cited here: Philip Selznick, *TVA and the Grass Roots* (Berkeley: University of California Press, 1949); Alvin W. Gouldner, *Patterns of Industrial Bureaucracy* (Glencoe, Ill.: The Free Press, 1954); Peter M. Blau, *The Dynamics of Bureaucracy* (Glencoe, Ill.: The Free Press, 1955); S.M. Lipset, M. Trow, and J. Coleman, *Union Democracy* (Glencoe, Ill.: The Free Press, 1956); R. G. Francis and R. C. Stone, *Service and Procedure in Bureaucracy* (Minneapolis: University of Minnesota Press, 1956); A.H. Stanton and M.S. Schwartz, *The Mental Hospital: A Study of Institutional Participation in Psychiatric Illness and Treatment* (New York: Basic Books, 1954). (In view of the greatly differing connotations of "bureaucracy" current in medical and in sociological circles, it should be remarked that for the social scientist, "bureaucracy" is a technical term designating a formal, hierarchic organization of statuses, each with its sphere of competence and responsibility. In the social science vocabulary of organization, "bureaucracy" is not a pejorative.)

[30]As implied earlier in this chapter, the word "socialization" has a quite different and long-standing connotation in medical circles. This historical fact cannot be exorcized; it must, instead, be taken into account if we are not to become involved in semantic confusions and controversies. With this in mind, I have appended a detailed terminological note on the concept of socialization in the hope of forestalling such bootless conflicts of meanings.

[31]See Talcott Parsons, *The Social System* (New York: The Free Press, 1951), Chapter 6 and, in particular, the remarks on adult socialization on pp. 207–208; John Dollard, "Culture, Society, Impulse, and Socialization," *American Journal of Sociology* 45 (1939):50–63. See also Irwin L. Child,

"Socialization," in *Handbook of Social Psychology*, Gardner Lindzey, ed. (Cambridge, Mass.: Addison-Wesley, 1954), which includes an extensive bibliography.

[32]Among these, see William J. Goode and Paul K. Hatt, *Methods in Social Research* (New York: McGraw-Hill, 1952); Paul F. Lazarsfeld and Morris Rosenberg, eds., *The Language of Social Research: A Reader in the Methodology of Social Research* (New York: The Free Press, 1955); Leon Festinger and Daniel Katz, eds., *Research Methods in the Behavioral Sciences* (New York: Dryden Press, 1953); Marie Jahoda, Morton Deutsch, and Stuart W. Cook, *Research Methods in Social Relations* (New York: Dryden Press, 1951), 2 vols.; John Madge, *The Tools of Social Science* (London: Longmans, Green and Company, 1953). For comparison with how matters stood a generation earlier, see Sidney and Beatrice Webb, *Methods of Social Study* (London: Longmans, Green and Company, 1932).

[33]At Cornell, Mary E. W. Goss and Dr. Renée Fox, and at Pennsylvania, Dr. Samuel Bloom engaged in observational studies; at Western Reserve, Dr. Milton J. Horowitz independently observed preceptorial groups in particular.

[34]This short review of method does not report the procedures adopted to cross-check and dovetail the various kinds of experience.

[35]This procedure was developed by the field-workers themselves, largely on the initiative of Dr. Renée Fox. For a statement of procedures adapted to this purpose, see R.K. Merton, Marjorie Fiske, and Patricia L. Kendall, *The Focused Interview* (New York: The Free Press, 1956).

[36]See Lazarsfeld and Rosenberg, eds., *The Language of Social Research*, pp. 231–259.

[37]This set of techniques was originated by J.L. Moreno and first comprehensively reported in his treatise, *Who Shall Survive?* (Washington, D.C.: Nervous and Mental Disease Monograph, No. 58, 1934; new and enlarged edition, Beacon, N.Y.: Beacon House, 1953). It has since been greatly developed by Moreno and his associates, and by a considerable number of psychologists and sociologists. For an extensive bibliography, see the 1953 edition of Moreno's book; for a compact summary of inquiry making use of this set of procedures, see Gardner Lindzey, ed., *Handbook of Social Psychology*, Chapter 11.

[38]Lindzey and Borgatta, in *Handbook of Social Psychology*, p. 407, go on to point out that the procedure also provides for specifying persons with whom each individual would prefer not to associate in one or more activities.

[39]This will be recognized as a general statement which holds in the large, not in detail. There were, of course, important beginnings in the nineteenth century. Most notable, no doubt, is the detailed field work, more than a century ago, by Frédéric Le Play, particularly as recorded in his extraordinary six-volume work, *Les Ouvriers Européens* (1855). The monumental survey by Charles Booth, *Life and Labour of the People of London*, reported in 17 volumes between 1889 and 1903, will also come to mind. The point is, however, that these are notable precisely because they were such distinct exceptions. See Frédéric Le Play, *Les Ouvriers Européens* (Paris: Imprimerie Impériale, 1855); and Charles Booth, *Life and Labour of the People in London* (London: Macmillan, 1902–1903).

[40]For example, see the brief report on the number of graded examinations and its connection with the climate of competitiveness among stu-

dents. Robert K. Merton, Samuel Bloom, and Natalie Rogoff, "Studies in the Sociology of Medical Education," *Journal of Medical Education* 31(1956):557.

[41]For a more detailed statement, see the two essays on the theoretical relations between sociology and psychology by Talcott Parsons and Theodore M. Newcomb in *For a Science of Social Man: Convergences in Anthropology, Psychology, and Sociology,* John Gillin, ed. (New York: Macmillan 1954), pp. 67–101 and 227–256.

[42]Donald E. Super and Paul Bachrach, "The Physician," in *Review of the Literature on Choice and Success in Scientific Careers,* Scientific Careers Project, Teachers College, Columbia University, Working Paper No. 1, November 16, 1956 (hectographed), Chapter 4; Edward Gottheil and Carmen Miller Michael, "Predictor Variables Employed in Research on the Selection of Medical Students," *Journal of Medical Education* 32(1957):131–147. These comprehensive reviews, independently conducted and covering much the same ground, come to the same general conclusions.

[43]Since these numerous tests are more definitely indicated in the two review papers, this list identifies them only by title.

[44]Gottheil and Michael, "Predictor Variables," p. 141.

[45]Super and Bachrach, "The Physician," p. 12.

[46]Frederic Bartlett, "Use and Value of Intelligence and Aptitude Tests," *Proceedings of the First World Conference on Medical Education* (London: Oxford University Press, 1954), p. 200.

[47]Gottheil and Michael, "Predictor Variables," p. 141. In addition, as Bartlett notes ("Use and Value of Intelligence and Aptitude Tests," p. 205), in England "it seems to be the case that the distribution of successes in the final medical examinations is so widely different from that which is normally secured in any known intelligence test that it seems as if one can say straight off that there could never be any significant statistical relation between the two. It may, of course, be the case that if we succeed in finding any satisfactory criterion of professional efficiency we shall find that our initial tests come out rather better as compared with that."

[48]This distinctly sociological component of the problem has of course been periodically recognized by psychologically oriented investigators, even when it has not been methodically incorporated into the research design. For example, consider this clear formulation of the theoretical issue: "A chronic problem in all studies of the prediction of human behavior . . . lies in the uncertainty about the situation into which prediction is to be made. Particularly is this true of life circumstances in which knowledge of all the conditions and the precise demands they make on individuals varying in personality is usually unavailable. In large measure this accounts for the limited efficiency of our prognostic psychiatric indices." Harold Basowitz et al., *Anxiety and Stress: An Interdisciplinary Study of a Life Situation* (New York: McGraw-Hill, 1955), p. 285. David C. McClelland makes a correlative observation: "Often a particular [performance] test is processed by machine scoring and yields only a collection of standard scores which are not of very much assistance in trying to characterize an individual's behavior. Neither the problems with which the person was faced nor the particular kinds of successes or failures he made are evident to the observer: all he has is the outcome of a complex, unanalyzed behavior process." David C. McClelland, *Personality* (New York: William Sloane Associates, 1951), p. 168.

[49]As some among many pertinent reports, see H.G. Wolff, *Stress and*

Disease (Springfield: C.C. Thomas, 1953); Basowitz et al., *Anxiety and Stress;* Leo Postman and J.S. Bruner, "Perception Under Stress," *Psychological Review* 55 (1948):314–323; O. Diethelm and M. R. Jones, "Influence of Anxiety on Attention, Learning, Retention and Thinking," *Archives of Neurology and Psychiatry* 58 (1947):325–336; D.P. Ausubel, H.H. Schiff, and M. Goldman, "Qualitative Characteristics in the Learning Process Associated with Anxiety," *Journal of Abnormal and Social Psychology* 48 (1953):537–547; E.L. Cowen, "The Influence of Varying Degrees of Psychological Stress on Problem-Solving Rigidity," *Journal of Abnormal and Social Psychology* 47 (1952):512–519.

[50]Merton, Bloom, and Rogoff, "Studies in the Sociology of Medical Education," pp. 563–564.

[51]Being human, physicians in their status as outsiders often regard the distinctive vocabularies of other professions—say, the profession of law—as largely composed of superfluous jargon. It seems to be fairly uniform that one group's language is another group's jargon. (See Chapter 4, "Our Sociological Vernacular," in this volume—editors' note.)

[52]"The Objectives of Undergraduate Medical Education," *Journal of Medical Education* 28 (1953):57–59.

[53]On the general conception', see Robert K. Merton, *Sociological Ambivalence* (New York: The Free Press, 1976), pp. 3–105—editors' note.

[54]Alan Gregg, "Our Anabasis," *The Pharos of Alpha Omega Alpha* 18 (1955):22. This short, brilliant examination of the life of the medical student is virtually a paradigm for future studies.

[55]For a study based on this conception, see Gene N. Levine, "The Good Physician: A Study of Physician-Patient Interaction," Working Paper Number 3, Evaluation Studies of the Cornell Comprehensive Care and Teaching Program, Columbia University (Bureau of Applied Social Research, 1957).

[56]This is, of course, only the statement of an impression, but one often reported in the medical profession. It will remain an impression until systematic comparisons are made between practice in medical schools and among medical practitioners at large.

[57]The general matter of varying organizational bases for the "observability" of role performance is basic to an understanding of the workings of social structure. Some organizations—the medical school and hospital are cases in point—are so arranged that, apart from intent, the behavior of each member is subject to observability by others with continuing appraisals of that behavior. Other structures—and much of private medical practice is a case in point—are such that there is relatively little visibility of this kind. Sociologically, this is a variable of social structure, independent of the further fact that individuals may be motivated to conform with the requirements of the social role, even when they are structurally insulated from direct observation and appraisal. On the concept of observability, see Robert K. Merton, *Social Theory and Social Structure,* enlarged ed. (New York: The Free Press, 1968), pp. 390–410, 428–429.

[58]W.R. Cooke, "The Practical Application of Psychology in Gynecologic Practice," *Nebraska Medical Journal* 25 (1950):371.

[59]The annals of science—physical, biological, and social—are crowded with instances of the premature suspension of curiosity because a commonsense knowledge of gross phenomena had precluded interest in the mech-

anisms through which these phenomena came to be. Out of this indefinitely large class of cases, one example will perhaps suffice: as Köhler has pointed out, everyone knows that we come to forget many experiences, and many take it for granted that this decay of memory is simply the result of passage of time. Yet recent experimental work in psychology has shown how much more complex are the processes which make for faulty memory; that forgetting is less a case of old experience fading from memory than of "the interference, inhibition, or obliteration of the old by the new." It might also be said that it is the office of systematic study to question the "self-evident" commonplaces of human experience and to show, often if not invariably, that these are not what they seem. On this general issue, see Wolfgang Köhler, *Dynamics in Psychology* (New York: Liveright Publishing Corporation, 1940), pp. 30–31; on the role of sociology (as of other disciplines) in examining widely held, "obvious" beliefs, some of which turn out to be plausible untruths, see Chapter 2, "Notes on Problem Finding in Sociology," in this volume.

[60]And a common etymological lineage. It is idle, of course, to debate matters of priority or "correct" usage when the same collocation of letters happens to have quite distinct and unrelated meanings. In some contexts, the psychological and sociological meaning of socialization is appropriate; in others, the economic and political meaning. To assert that one, rather than the other, meaning is correct would be to legislate in a realm where laws which collide with the folkways are notoriously ineffective; to confuse the two meanings is to border on the grotesque. But it is of passing interest that such a basic repository of word meanings as the *Oxford English Dictionary* first cites the psychological and sociological sense of the term "socialize," and only then turns to its economic and political sense.

[61]That the same technical word within a discipline may come in the course of events to have several related meanings is a fact which has nothing to do with scientific homonyms. See the extensive monograph on such a case of multiple meanings by A.L. Kroeber and Clyde Kluckhohn, *Culture: A Critical Review of Concepts and Definitions* (Cambridge, Mass.: Peabody Museum of American Archaeology and Ethnology, 1952). As Kroeber and Kluckhohn observe, "The word culture with its modern technical or anthropological meaning was established in English by Tylor in 1871, though it seems not to have penetrated to any general or 'complete' British dictionary until more than fifty years later—a piece of cultural lag that may help to keep anthropologists humble in estimating the tempo of their influence on even the avowedly literate segment of their society", (p. 9). By the same token, the degree of humility due from psychologists and sociologists is profound beyond measure: the word socialization in its technical sense had yet to find its way into general dictionaries in the 1950s.

[62]It is perhaps best to say nothing here of the use of the word *rationalization* in mathematics to refer to the process of clearing from irrational quantities.

[63]This would be somewhat akin to the process, noted by students of language, through which words "go to the bad" ("pejoration"). For example, the modern English word "silly" stems from the Middle English word self. This originally meant "blessed" (Anglo-Saxon *soelig*, Modern German, *selig*, etc.). But "since the 'children of this world are in their generation wiser than the children of light', and since the good will not stoop to the tricks of the evil, the latter regard them as lacking intelligence and as mere fools to have such scruples. . . ." For this and other examples of pejoration, see

Louis H. Gray, *Foundations of Language* (New York: Macmillan, 1939), p. 259ff.

Just as there are cultural patterns of change in the meanings of words, so there are psychological patterns of supplying one, rather than another, meaning to homonyms, depending on temperamental characteristics of the individual. Thus, L.L. Thurstone has developed a "homonyms test" in which subjects are asked to respond with a synonym or definition to each word in a list of forty. The words have at least two common associations, one of these being physical and literal, the other more nearly human and emotional. For examples: lead, fire, taste, strike, slight, exhaust, push, revolution, nerve, pull. The responses of subjects, who are of course unaware of the nature or purpose of the test, are classified and counted to find out the ratio of emotional connotations to physical or literal connotations. This yields an objective score which is then related to other known temperamental characteristics of the subject. See L.L. Thurstone, *A Factorial Study of Perception* (Chicago: University of Chicago Press, 1944), p. 78ff.

Patterns of associations with homonyms would presumably relate not only to psychological characteristics, such as temperament, but also to social characteristics, such as occupation. It is assumed in our discussion that, in a test, most physicians would spontaneously supply the economic and political meaning to the homonym *socialization,* and most sociologists, the psychological and sociological meaning.

CHAPTER 7

Functions of the Professional Association*

The professional association is an organization of practitioners who, having been judged to be professionally competent, are banded together in pursuit of their own common and public interests. The association is usually a voluntary association, but the extent to which this is so differs greatly from profession to profession. At the one extreme in the legal profession are states with an "integrated bar" which require all practitioners to be members of the bar association. Just short of such explicit compulsory membership are the ostensibly voluntary associations where the option not to join is small since the penalties for not belonging are great, as in the case of county medical societies. Toward the other extreme, the option not to join the association is large since the penalties for not belonging are negligible, as in the case of the more than seventy-five engineering societies.

Professional associations also differ in their structure. Some are closely controlled by a central office; others grant much autonomy to local branches. But variations of structure need not concern us here, for it is not so much its structure as its functions which distinguish the professional association.

In a word: the professional association *is* as the professional

*Reprinted with permission from the *American Journal of Nursing* 58 (1958):50–54.

association *does*. Its manifest and latent social functions, not the structures designed to put these functions into effect, constitute its social excuse for being.

ORGANIZATIONAL AIMS

Just as function must be distinguished from structure, so must functions be distinguished from the stated objectives of the association. Professional associations typically put into their statements of purpose a strong claim to being designed, in the first instance, to work through their specialized competencies for the welfare of the community in general and of their respective clienteles in particular. Thus, the American Medical Association announces as one of its principal aims the steady improvement of health care;[1] the American Bar Association, promotion of the administration of justice;[2] the American Nurses' Association, improvement of nursing care for all the people. Similar statements are made by the hundreds of professional associations, great and small.

What associations profess as their aims may coincide with what they actually attempt to do—but again, they may not. Still, statements of public and private purpose do provide guidelines for assessing the measures to be undertaken by the association. This is true for declarations designed not only to reach the general (that is, the professionally uninstructed) public but also, as everyone connected with such associations knows, to reach the membership of the organization itself. Declarations of high purpose need not be merely window dressing, although they are in perpetual danger of becoming so. This is particularly the case when the profession confronts a crisis in which the interests of its members seemingly or actually conflict with the interests of the public.

Nevertheless, it would be facile and often mistaken to assume that such statements of public purpose invariably render only lip service to social values. Even when neglected in practice, they afford a potentiality of control over actions contemplated by the association and help bring these actions more nearly into line with announced purposes.

Occasional or sometimes sustained departures from publicly declared purposes can result from multiple and not always easily reconcilable functions of the association. For example, the association is committed to look out for the economic and social welfare of practitioners in the profession, for if the membership organization does not do so, who will? Again, it is typically dedicated also to the objectives of raising the standards of professional education, for if the organized body of informed professionals does not take on this task, who else can? Yet objectives such as these, principled as they are, at times collide, or may seem to collide, with the interests of the public. A profession largely persuaded that its members are not receiving incomes commensurate with their worth may press for higher salaries which many in the public will judge excessive. (This sort of thing helps form the image of professions so energetically propagated by Bernard Shaw as a "conspiracy against the public.") Or the association, on behalf of its apparently unimpeachable purpose of improving the competence of practitioners, may call for a great increase in public funds to advance professional education. This capitalization of brain power may raise the cost of (possibly more effective) professional service. This, too, may alienate the public, who feel themselves twice penalized; once, by taxation, and again, by higher fees for professional care. They can tell when the fiscal shoe pinches, but they cannot so easily distinguish excellent professional care from good care, and good from mediocre or inferior care.

Beyond these potential sources of conflict, a professional association may fall into the hands of those who conscientiously put the interests of the profession above all other interests, if only because they identify themselves strongly with their profession.

All apart from such extreme episodes of professional deformation, there is a structural basis for conflicts of interest between a profession and its public. Much as we might like it to be so, the social world, with its differentiations and stratifications, is not organized into a natural harmony of interests in which "all things work together for good." At least in the short run, it is not the case that what is good for the profession of medicine, law, social work, or nursing is necessarily best for the community, and conversely. Only if potential and actual conflicts are recognized and admitted, rather than put aside as a severe embarrassment and systematically denied, can they be mitigated and worked out. "Irreconcilable conflict" can be reconciled when the sources of conflict are understood, continually reappraised, and dealt with through the exercise of power tempered with shared notions of equity. This will not achieve (theoretically unachievable) optimum solutions, but it can mitigate titanic "solutions" based solely on the exercise of power.

Every professional association faces the difficult task of trying to maintain a delicate balance between fulfilling its functions for its professional constituency and for the community. The not-too-distant days in which the nurse was rewarded for her dedication to high purpose by a dismally low income remind us that the balance can be lost at the expense of the professional group, just as innumerable other instances remind us that it can be lost at the expense of clientele.

For these various reasons, the objectives affirmed by a professional association need not coincide with its actual functions. If structure provides only the machinery for the performance of functions and if stated objectives provide only a guide to the selection of functions, what, then, are the basic functions which the professional association actually performs? Or, to substitute momentarily for the many-meaninged word "function," what do professional associations actually *do* and what are some of the ramified consequences of what they do?

TYPES OF SOCIAL FUNCTIONS

The professional association does so many things that, if they are to be understood, we must find a way of sorting them out into their several kinds. For this purpose, we can draw upon a way of thinking about the social functions of an organization which sociologists have found helpful. This involves designating the human units for which these activities are functional: individuals, subgroups, the organization, and the larger society.[3] Some functions of the professional association primarily affect individual members of the profession (and indirectly their clientele); others have consequences primarily for the profession as a whole and for the association as its corporate expression; and still others primarily affect the larger social system in which individuals and organizations find themselves. This notation of kinds of multiple functions has the further merit of sensitizing us to the possibility that some activities of professional associations which are functional for one or more of these units can be dysfunctional for others—that is, can interfere with their purposes and adaptations—a possibility already noted.

Functions for Individual Practitioners

Perhaps the most pervasive and far-reaching function of the professional association for individual practitioners consists in giving them social and moral support to help them perform their roles. The organization helps see to it that professionals need not cope with their professional problems alone. This supportive function does not require that the organization cater to the weaknesses of individual practitioners; rather, it can serve to reinforce their strengths.

Particularly in the salaried professions, as distinct from the prevalently free-lance, fee-paid professions, lone practitioners cannot effectively safeguard their social and economic welfare. Economic theory notwithstanding, there is held to be a considerable gap between the prevailing schedule of salaries and the schedule which, in all equity, should obtain.[4] For generations, this has been true of the salaries of nurses. Whether through collective bargaining or through the less direct pressure of appealing to public opinion, the association works to increase salaries.

The protective functions of the association for the individual practitioner are not limited to the narrowly economic matter of salaries. Others operate indirectly to improve conditions of work. They are designed to enable practitioners to do their professional job more effectively, to the further benefit of clients. (The clientele, typically, has no awareness of such benefits they derive from the work of the professional association.)

In the professions, as in all other forms of activity, sustained motivation is necessary for superior performance of roles. These motives to do well must be harnessed to the institutionalized system of rewards. This is another function of associations, particularly of salaried practitioners, which press for the provision of opportunities for advancement in accord with the growth of professional experience and competence.

The association works also to help prepare practitioners for the more effective discharge of professional roles. It acts on the philosophy that professional education is a lifelong process; establishes institutes to advance the education of practitioners; protects both them and the public by working toward legally enforced standards of professional competence; and helps motivate practitioners to develop their skills and to extend their knowledge. These and related functions can be summed up by observing that, in the professions, each practitioner is a brother's (or sister's) keeper. Each is expected to live up to or to exceed acceptable standards of practice and to see to it that others also do so. This means that, in varying degrees, the professions develop social and moral ties among their members who enter into a community of purpose.

This review has dealt with the functions of the professional association for members of the profession rather than for the members of the association only. This was not a lapse. It was meant to emphasize the point that members of the profession who are not members of the association typically receive an unearned increment of social, moral, and economic gain from the work of their professional colleagues in the association. In the not inappropriate idiom, those who remain outside are "freeloaders": they do not pay their way, either in dues or in kind. True, the freeloaders in a profession often do not see themselves as such. They often fail to realize that they are nonpaying and nonparticipating beneficiaries of the sustained work done by the dues-paying members of the profession. They are like those citizens who avoid paying taxes and taking part in public service while benefiting from the taxes and activities of those who contribute to the commonwealth. Professional associations try to convert freeloaders into members, preferably actively participating members, who will do their share of the work which the organized profession needs to have done and will have their voices heard when the association formulates its policies.

Functions for the Profession

We can now drop the first tier of functions—those for the individual practitioner—and proceed to the second, composed of functions for the profession as a whole. Although the same organizational activities tend to have both types of functions, some of these operate primarily for individual practitioners and others primarily for the profession as a collectivity.

The foremost obligation of the association is to set rigorous standards for the profession and to help enforce them: standards for the quality of personnel to be recruited into the profession; standards for the training and education of the recruits; standards for professional practice; and standards for research designed to enlarge the knowledge on which the work of the profession rests. The effective association is in the vanguard. The standards it sets are more exacting than those with which the lay public might be content. After all, only informed practitioners can know the potentialities and not merely the current realities of professional practice. They are the custodians of professional traditions; through their constituted organizations, they can try to anticipate the future and continually raise their sights.

To say that the effective professional association is engaged in pressing for higher standards of personnel, education, research, and practice is to say that it is committed to being dissatisfied with the current state of the profession. At least in its charter of purposes, the professional association needs to repudiate that final smugness which assumes that everything possible has already been attained. It thereby becomes committed to keep members of the profession from resting easily on their oars, even when they feel so inclined.

In this sense, the professional association can serve as a kind of organizational gadfly, stinging the profession into new and more demanding formulations of purpose. It must therefore be prepared to become a target for hostile criticism by those members of the profession who feel themselves disadvantaged by the forward thrust toward raising the standards of the profession.

This is only another instance of the "noncontemporaneity of the contemporaneous," of the coexistence of generations and cohorts. At any moment in the history of a profession, strata of its members are variously trained and variously competent, if only because they have entered the field at different times. Some of the less highly trained, naturally enough, look with displeasure, if not despair, at rising standards of qualifications for professional practice. To cope with this familiar problem, organizations have adopted the device of the "grandfather clause," which exempts current members from having to meet newly instituted and more rigorous standards of the profession. Even so, there typically remains a residue of resistance and hostility toward the policy of raising standards.

This is inherent in the process of growth of a profession, and the staff of the professional association should know it. They should know that the life of an officer in a forward-moving professional association is not a tranquil one. They should realize that an excess of tranquility may only register the growth of complacency in the profession and the decline of responsible criticism among its constituted representatives. They should sense that the quiet organizational life may only mean that the profession is not living up to the commitments in effect made when it accepted the monopoly of rights and immunities conferred on it by society. If the obligation to raise standards for the profession makes life difficult at times, it is the price which the truly professional association must be prepared to pay.

Since the dynamic of professions is provided by the growth of their specialized knowledge, the professional association has the further function of advancing research in its field, either directly through research agencies of the association or, more often, indirectly through help to other groups in the profession. It can provide a clearinghouse of professional knowledge; it can help make the research career feasible and esteemed; it can work toward the expansion of opportunities for research. In this respect, the professional association incorporates elements of the learned society, just as in some of its protective functions for individual practitioners, it incorporates elements, more or less regulated by a professional ethic, of the trade unions.[5]

The function of facilitating research does not stand alone. If the results of research are not disseminated among the profession, they are inert, powerless to move the profession forward. The professional association therefore establishes journals devoted to reporting and spreading new knowledge, as well as ancillary house-organ journals presenting information on the changing role of the profession in society.

By working to raise the standards of personnel, education, practice, and research, the association serves a latent function for the profession, a function not directly contemplated in these activities which are judged to have worth in their own right. To raise these standards tends to improve the social standing of the profession. It lays the groundwork for a rise in social esteem. Rising public esteem for a profession is not merely the result of what is often described as "public relations," of persuading the public that the profession should be highly regarded. As publicists know, the development of a public relations program is no adequate substitute for the reality to be reported.

By providing authentic information to the public about what is actually taking place in the profession, the association can narrow or close the gap between actual advances and the public understanding of what these mean for the quality of professional service. If the public face of the profession is too heavily made up, any temporary rise in social esteem becomes only the prelude to a great fall. It is the task of the association to improve the effectiveness of the profession, the task of its department of public relations to see to it that the degree of improvement becomes highly known. The art of meiosis— that is, of sustained understatements—is the art appropriate to the public relations arm of the professional association.

Functions for the Society

The functions of the professional association for individual practitioners and for the profession are, in the main, conspicuous. But one of its principal functions for society is far from evident; it has often gone wholly unnoticed. This is its function, as one of the great intermediate associations, to help prevent the atomization of society into a sand heap of individuals intent on pursuing their own private interests. Such an atomized condition is a step toward totalitarianism, which consolidates power over socially disconnected individuals into a single center. As one thoughtful observer described this process:

> The destruction of the independent labor unions in Nazi Germany was followed by the prohibition of independent economic organizations of every kind. It was not the fact of labor that was central; it was the social fact of *union*. All autonomous organizations were destroyed and made illegal: professions, service clubs, voluntary mutual aid groups, fraternal associations, even

philatelist and musical societies. Such organizations were regarded, and correctly, by the totalitarian government as potential
sources of future resistance, if only because in them people were
brought together for purposes, however innocent, that did not
reflect those of the central government. As organizations, they
interposed themselves between the people as a society and the
people as the masses.[6]

In a word, the professional association is one of those intermediate organizations which furnish the social bonds through which
society coheres. It provides unity in action and social cohesion without
contiguity of its members. It mediates between practitioner and
profession, on the one hand, and, on the other, between practitioner
and social environment, of which the most important elements, apart
from clientele, are allied occupations and professions, the universities, the local community, and the government.

The association relates each profession to allied professions.
These relations may be conflictful and faulty—they often are—but
they are less faulty than they would be were it not for the many
organizational liaisons which typically develop. The association also
works to justify the scope, not infrequently the expanding scope, of
the jurisdiction of the profession and to safeguard it against the rival
claims of neighboring professions and technical occupations.

The pressure toward expansion, which derives in part from
advancement of professional knowledge, often strains relationships
with neighboring professions. This problem only underscores the
importance of instituting and maintaining effective liaison between
professions, for only when this is firmly established can the relationship bear the stresses which conflicting claims to jurisdiction impose
upon it. Even so, it is wise to expect residual conflicts of interest
between professions that will remain unresolved. This is one of the
costs of a pluralistic society in which decisions about the appropriate
division of professional work are not imposed from above.

The many-sided relations of the profession to the government
are also mediated in part through the professional association. To
do more than mention this fact would be to enter upon a long and
complex account. It is enough, perhaps, to refer to the continuing
role of the association in formulating policies for legislative enactment
and in monitoring proposed legislation which bears upon the work
and goals of the profession.

In its relation with the varied groups which compose the social
environment of the profession, the association seeks to develop a
sufficient consensus to be able to speak authentically and authoritatively on behalf of the profession. Were a profession such as nursing
to be heard through a million separate voices, with each profes-

sional nurse proclaiming her own views and sentiments, the result would be cacophony. The association seeks instead to create a concert of purpose.

This representative role presents the professional association with the great problem of achieving a flexible consensus of values and policies. It must not only appear to speak for the profession; it must stand on firm ground in doing so. Yet it must also provide for dissent, without having dissent end in noise. To achieve this goal— that is, an adaptable consensus with full opportunity for responsible dissent—requires formidable feats of organization. A few general observations are in order.

One is the tried, trite, and true proposition that the association can provide two-way avenues for communication: ideas, problems, prospects, experiences, and objectives can come to the association from members of the profession, and these, having been examined by democratically elected representatives of the association, then go back to the constituency for review. Local constituent groups can provide a forum where issues can be threshed out before action on them is taken nationally.

The professional association, like other large-scale organizations committed to democratic procedure, is confronted with the enduring temptation to transform the channels of communication into one-way conduits, with information and decisions moving from the top of the organization. Unless the structure provides for reciprocal communication, the association works through control from above, whatever its pretensions to the contrary.

Two-way communication exacts an organizational price; at times, a heavy price. To wait upon the informed comment, and not merely the reluctant assent, of a far-flung and varied constituency often slows down the work of the profession. Although waiting is at times a heavy drag on change, more often, I suspect, it only seems so. For until the great majority of the profession are themselves persuaded of the merits of proposed changes, changes which are instituted are apt to be nominal rather than genuine. Only the men and women doing the work of the profession can translate proposals for improvement into social reality.

To be able to speak effectively for the profession, the association must represent as many members of the profession as possible. This means that the association must strive for what the sociologist describes as "completeness,"[7] meaning that all those eligible for membership actually are members. Of course, no professional association has achieved completeness, and associations differ greatly in the extent to which they have approximated it. After its first half-century, for example, the American Medical Association could count among its members only 9 percent of the 100,000 physicians then in practice; by the late 1950s, more than a century after its founding, somewhat more than two-thirds of the almost 450,000 physicians were enrolled.

Associations of about the same size differ substantially in the degree to which they approximate completeness and, consequently, in the extent of the authority and influence they can exercise. That is why professional associations are in principle committed to the effort to enroll as large a proportion as possible of those eligible for membership. As spokesman for the profession, the association strives to move ever closer to completeness, knowing that this will remain an asymptotic goal—one that can only be approximated, not fully reached. In this way, the association can better fulfill the multiple functions which are both its obligation and its reward.

NOTES

[1] Morris Fishbein, *A History of the American Medical Association, 1847–1947* (Philadelphia: W.B. Saunders Co., 1947).

[2] Albert P. Blaustein and Charles O. Porter, *The American Lawyer: A Summary of the Survey of the Legal Profession* (Chicago: University of Chicago Press, 1954).

[3] Robert K. Merton, *Social Theory and Social Structure* (New York: The Free Press, 1968), pp. 106–108.

[4] Theodore Caplow, *The Sociology of Work* (Minneapolis: University of Minnesota Press, 1954), Chapter 8.

[5] Bernard Goldstein, "Some Aspects of the Nature of Unionism Among Salaried Professionals in Industry," *American Sociological Review* 20 (April 1955):199–205.

[6] Robert A. Nisbet, *The Quest for Community* (New York: Oxford University Press, 1953), pp. 202–203.

[7] Merton, *Social Theory and Social Structure*, pp. 342–346, 368–369.

PART III

Social Research Applied to Public Policy

Basic Research and Potentials of Relevance*

Science has become one of the dominating social institutions of our time, directly or indirectly affecting the lives of men and women everywhere. A wider range of problems than ever before is now tackled from the perspectives of science. Through the technologies to which it has given rise, science has comprehensively changed the world in which we live and how we live in it just as it now goes far toward determining when and how we shall die.

The enterprise of science is now so widely accepted that we are apt to forget the long historical process through which it acquired widespread social and moral legitimacy. A short three centuries ago, the physical and biological sciences were very much on trial. They were granted legitimacy not as values in their own right but only by being linked with other widely accepted values. That is why efforts were made on every side to show that the new science served the purposes of God and religion, the needs of the economy and the military, and the general well-being of the population.[1] As Galileo put it, when he was under fire for his Copernican ideas, "I find it necessary to justify myself in the eyes of all men whose judgment in matters of religion and reputation I must hold in great esteem."

*Reprinted from *American Behavioral Scientist* 6 (May 1963): pp. 86–90, by permission of the Publisher, Sage Publications, Beverly Hills.

Later, Robert Boyle found it advisable to argue for the practical value of the new science in his tract, symptomatically entitled the *"Usefulness* of Experimental Natural Philosophy." The primary case for science was made by showing that it can help society achieve objectives other than knowledge itself: power, comfort or pecuniary gain, health, repute, efficiency, or almost anything other than the advancement of knowledge for its own sake.

This dependence of science upon other institutionalized values began to change. Science gradually acquired an increasing degree of autonomy, claiming legitimacy as something good in its own right, just as much so as literature and the other arts, as the quest for physical well-being or for personal salvation. The attitude is reflected in Ben Franklin's reply to the question put to him about the use of a new discovery: "What good is a newborn baby?"—a reply echoed by Pasteur and Faraday in the century to come. This attitude expresses a double confidence: that fundamental scientific knowledge is a self-contained good and that, in any case, it will in due course lead to all manner of useful consequences serving varied interests in society. There has developed both an intrinsic and utilitarian rationale for basic science. As we shall see, the two rationales are bridged by the concept of "potentials of relevance" of basic scientific research for interests other than knowledge itself.

COMPONENTS OF BASIC AND APPLIED RESEARCH

The growth of science has invited debates over the distinctive character of basic or fundamental research and applied research and development. These dialogues seldom result in full agreement on the meanings of the principal terms, just as they seldom result in such full disagreement as to cut off further discussion. Rather than enter still another pair of definitions into the lists, we identify the bases of agreement at the core and of disagreements at the periphery of these concepts.

Basic research discovers uniformities in nature and society and provides new understandings of previously identified uniformities. This conception departs from a prevailing tendency to define basic research in terms of the purposes of the investigators. It is a functional, not a motivational, definition. It refers to what basic research objectively accomplishes, not to the motivation or purposes of those engaged in that research. To be sure, the purposes of investigators greatly affect the actual conduct and outcome of the investigation: the aim to discover new understandings makes it probable that the research will be fundamental rather than practical, just as an applied orientation more often results in simply utilizing basic knowledge to achieve practical outcomes. Nevertheless, in the behavior of scientists, as with human behavior generally, subjective purpose and objective consequence are analytically separate, coinciding at times and differing at times.[2] Just as inquiries aimed at fundamental knowledge have repeatedly turned up unsuspected applications, so inquiries aimed at application have, though perhaps less often, turned up unsuspected understandings of uniformities in nature and society.

Abandoning the aim or intent of scientific inquiry as the exclusive criterion, we can distinguish applied from basic research as that which makes use of existing knowledge, fundamental or empirical, to achieve practical outcomes in new ways. Basic and applied research are alike in developing new knowledge by drawing upon past knowledge. They differ in that the new knowledge developed by basic research is of a kind that adds to general understanding of uniformities that go beyond any particular class of applications; it adds to the cognitive capital that comprises basic science. Applied research draws primarily upon that capital to arrive at new methods of achieving a practical objective that is itself outside the sphere of basic knowledge.

Three components distinguish basic from applied research. Purpose can be loosely classified as the "personal component" in research and the actual cognitive consequences of investigation as the "cultural component" (the increments accruing to the stock of knowledge and implements that make up part of the scientific and technological culture). The third component is "social," referring to the social roles assigned investigators engaged in scientific research. The role of workers in basic research has distinctive characteristics: (1) it provides them with relative autonomy in selecting the problems on which they will work; (2) it gives them more latitude for deciding to shift from these initial problems to others turning up in the course of the inquiry, which they find more interesting or promising; and (3) the role provides the primary "reference groups," the individuals and groups whose appraisal of their work they regard as central, made up primarily of fellow scientists, with nonscientists entering only at a distant remove. In describing these as elements of the social *role* of scientists engaged in basic research, I mean to emphasize that they have social grounds for claiming these as rights and that others tend to honor these claims. I do not mean to say that, in any concrete case, there is full agreement on these role-defined rights or that particular scientists are not exposed to strains when others exert pressure to have them depart from this role.

In all three respects, the role of workers in applied research tends toward the other extreme: (1) although the investigator may at times select the problem, the choice tends to be constrained by the particular practical outcomes which others judge worth achieving; (2) once launched on the inquiry, the investigator is the more often expected to stay with it; and (3) to a far greater degree, the most significant judgments of that work are made by an institutionalized reference group comprised of people outside the field of science who are charged with the responsibility for making practical use of the results.

The array of scientific researches probably involves differing mixes of personal intent, cultural consequences, and social role. The three components are probably correlated, but the extent of the correlation is unknown. Much of present-day research, varying perhaps by discipline, probably falls between the extremes of the pure type of basic research and the pure type of applied research. Whether this is so cannot be gauged even from the best estimates of resources allocated to basic and applied research in the United States, for the categories employed in these estimates are at best gross. The National Science Foundation estimated that for 1981, 12.7 percent of the approximately $69 billion devoted to scientific research and development was for basic research, with 67.5 percent of this amount provided by the federal government, 16.5 percent by industry, 10.1 percent by colleges and universities, and 5.9 percent by other nonprofit institutions.[3] It can be inferred that some unknown part of the work described as "development" is oriented toward basic research (by the criteria we have proposed), just as some unknown part of work classified as basic is in fact oriented to development.

INTERDEPENDENCE OF SCIENCE AND OTHER SOCIAL INSTITUTIONS

The historical fact that science has become a major national resource means more than ever that the other social institutions must take up some position—sometimes only by default—on their relations to science. This is only a special case of the general sociological premise that the institutional orders coexisting in a society—the family, economy and polity, science, religion and education—are variously interdependent while each still retains a measure of independence. Total social structures can be distinguished in part by the degree of independence accorded each institutional sphere, as we see by contrasting the polar extremes of a totalitarian and a free society.

Like other social institutions, science is a citadel of values and interests protecting the functions distinctively discharged by that institution. Like that of government officials, business and labor leaders, religious leaders and educators, the institutional role of scientists leads them to resist developments which they see as invading their sphere of autonomy, so that they lose in independence what they seem to gain from new forms of social support. For science, the core of autonomy is found in scientists' commitment to basic research. This, as we have seen, is comprised in its pure form of the *personal purpose* to search out new understandings of uniformities in nature and society, the *social role* assigned the scientists to select their own problems for investigation and to follow their own bent in conducting that investigation, and the *cultural consequences* which enlarge fundamental knowledge, all apart from its serving other purposes. Many scientists may accord greater value to basic than to applied research not only because of its function of extending fundamental knowledge but also because it symbolizes the distinctive claims to autonomy of science. Any policy governing the relations of science to other social institutions which fails to take account of this quest for autonomy is apt to be self-defeating.

The relations between business (or labor or government or other sponsoring agencies) and basic scientific research can now be seen as a special case of the relations between two connected but independent types of social institutions. Any policy governing these relations would do well to recognize this composite of interdependence *and* independence. It calls for arrangements which serve the distinctive interests of both science and business, and do not alienate large numbers of people in the ranks of the two groups. Under such arrangements, scientists engaged in basic research are not to be required to abandon their role-commitments by turning exclusively to applied and developmental research, just as the managers of sponsoring organizations are not to be required to abandon fiduciary obligations to their constituencies by supporting research that apparently has no bearing on the principal purposes of their organizations. On this view, the objective is to design arrangements which connect basic science and practice-oriented organizations while maintaining the integrity of both. That their diverse interests collide at the edge need not mean that they must collide at the core. That, at least, is assumed by the concept of the potentials of relevance of basic research for diverse organizations and institutions.

POTENTIALS OF RELEVANCE

The concept of the potentials of relevance directs attention to the obvious and important fact that different sectors of the spectrum of *basic research* have differing probabilities of being germane to certain kinds of practical outcomes. The concept relates to a policy of research support for those lines of inquiry of basic research which, so far as can be judged, will have the greatest degree of relevance for the supporting enterprise. (This is distinct from the policy of only supporting applied and developmental research focused on the solution of specific problems.)

The policy of supporting basic research with potentials of relevance has several interesting properties. First, it preserves a substantial freedom of choice of problems by scientists. This makes it more probable that they will be thoroughly committed to their research and that, through self-selection, they will be investigating those problems they are best equipped to investigate. The process of self-selection is of course not infallible; it does involve a margin of error in matching scientists and research problems. But, in the large, it is apt to summon the deepest motivations of investigators and to draw upon their distinctive skills and capacities.

Second, the policy preserves a substantial freedom of choice for supporting organizations—whether business, labor, operative government agencies, or voluntary associations—to select from the spectrum of basic research those lines of inquiry which hold the most promise of yielding fundamental *and* relevant knowledge.

These two aspects of the policy can be summed up in a third; it provides for a negotiable relationship between scientists devoted to basic research and supporting organizations. They meet on the comparatively neutral ground in which each retains its central commitments while allowing for a degree of benefit to the other.

Fourth, it is evident that a prevailing policy of support for basic research having maximum potentials of relevance for each kind of supporting institution will, in the aggregate, make only for selective apportionment of resources to many, but far from all, kinds of basic research. No invisible hand works to ensure that every type of basic science will receive needed support. Imbalances are bound to develop. Certain types of basic science having great practical potentials receive a good deal of support while others receive very little.

This leads directly to the fifth observation: basic science which has little apparent potential of relevance for the purposes of organizations, in and out of government, business, and labor, is precisely the kind which needs to receive its primary support from institutions that have evolved to help advance basic knowledge, all apart from anticipated practical outcomes. Over the long run, the major institution evolving to support this kind of basic science has of course been the university. Another type of institution able, though not always ready, to serve the same function of supporting scientific inquiries with little potential of "practical" relevance is the great private foundation. And, more recently, such government establishments as the National Science Foundation and sectors of other government agencies supporting scientific research have helped to fill in the interstices in those sciences which, here and now, hold small promise of serving purposes other than the advancement of knowledge itself. It is the *distinctive* function of such agencies of society to take up the slack by supporting types of basic research not supported under the canons of practical relevance.[4]

On this view, the interdependence of basic science and other social institutions is segmental rather than uniformly distributed throughout the social structure. Each class of organizations, with its distinctive interests and functions, can provide support for that sector of ongoing and prospective basic research which, so far as we fallible mortals can judge, has the greatest potentials of relevance for it. Specialized organizations and agencies have evolved which could deliberately work to correct the major imbalances resulting from the policy of potentials of relevance. They can support that part of basic research which would otherwise fall, largely unnoticed, into the interstices between institutionalized public and private interests.

BASIC SOCIAL RESEARCH AND POTENTIALS OF RELEVANCE

To concretize these general observations, we examine potentials of relevance in basic *social* research for a sector of the business world not widely known for supporting basic research of any kind: the American life insurance industry. If potentials of relevance can be identified in that domain of business, then *a fortiori* they will be found elsewhere in the so-called private sector of the economy and society. In this sketchy account, basic social research is taken as a special case of basic scientific research, just as the business of life insurance is taken as a special case of very big business. It may be enough to trace the main outlines of problems in basic social research which have been supported on grounds set forth in the concept of potentials of relevance.

From the standpoint of potentials of relevance, the life insurance business needs to be concerned primarily with selected portions of basic *social* research, just as, by the same logic, the telephone business is concerned primarily with selected portions of basic research in physics and chemistry, the aircraft industry with selected portions of basic research in aerodynamics and many related specialties, and the pharmaceutical business with selected portions of basic research in chemistry and biology.

Within the broad spectrum of social research, however, not every part has the same potential of relevance for problems distinctive to life insurance as a business enterprise. The most immediately relevant field of basic research is, of course, demography. But research in that field ramifies into other spheres of basic social research. If patterns of change in the composition and distribution of populations are to be understood, they must be linked with patterns of social organization and of associated attitudes and motivations that make for those changes. Various kinds of research on the family thus becomes plainly relevant. After all, if people had no sense of obligation to the members of their families or if they came to assume that the financial basis for discharging that obligation would be amply provided by other institutional arrangements, they would of course have less occasion to invest in life insurance. An historically evolving and latent family structure is presupposed by the very institution of life insurance. Yet we have only begun to map out and to understand the dynamics of change in the reciprocal obligations that are institutionalized in the American family.

Or consider the potentials of relevance hidden away in basic research on social time.[5] We know next to nothing, in a fundamental, systematic way, about the mechanisms shaping the time perspectives of various categories of people. Which categories, for example, accent the future as the time of greatest concern to them, which the past, and which the short-run present? How do these perspectives differ among age strata and socioeconomic classes? Does the long future look vague and undifferentiated to comparative youth, with their negligible past, so that only the present and immediate future appears significant to them? How do differing time perspectives link up with basic dispositions toward security and risk taking?

Or again, consider the sociology and social psychology (and not merely the biology) of death. What is the range of variation in the images of death and the attitudes people take toward it? What leads to its being regarded as an inevitability to be assiduously ignored for as long as possible and what to its being regarded, precisely because it is inevitable, as something that should be taken into account in current economic and social decisions? The concept of potentials of relevance suggests that the life insurance industry has ample grounds for supporting basic social research on this long neglected and, in some quarters, tabooed subject.[6]

A final example must suffice to illustrate types of problems in basic social science having distinctive potentials of relevance for this particular industry. A spate of basic sociological and psychological studies examining the dynamics of small groups has direct relevance for understanding those small groups which characteristically make up the local agencies of large life insurance firms. These investigations are basic in the strict sense that their findings are not confined, in their implications, to a narrow band of application to practice. They deal with basic mechanisms of social interaction, group formation, and corresponding outcomes. Here, perhaps, is another occasion for ostracizing a widespread and thoroughly erroneous assumption about one kind of distinction between basic and applied social research. It is often supposed that it is the character of groups of people being observed which determines whether social research is basic or applied. Put more concretely, this mistaken assumption would hold that if research on small groups happens to deal with, say, life insurance agents, this signifies at once that the inquiry is of an applied sort and can have significance only for this one occupational category. But that, of course, is not the case. The notorious fact that a large fraction of the many investigations of behavior in small groups has been confined to readily accessible students being observed under laboratory conditions does not signify that the general findings hold only for such students[7] (although this, of course, lessens the range of variability and sets still unidentified constraints on the social scope of those findings). Occasional (and still far too infrequent) replications of some of these investigations which deal with people drawn from industry and the military, for example, indicate that uniformities of behavior patterns uncovered in the studies with students are not peculiar to that population. The import of this for our own subject is evident: if the small groups under observation were to be composed of life insurance agents (rather than those ubiquitous college students), the research would not thereby become applied rather than basic. The difference between the two kinds of research resides not in the particular populations under study but in the formulation of the research questions and the corresponding design of investigation. There is no reason why such basic problems as the relations between communication networks in a group, its state of morale, and its effectiveness in task performance could not be investigated to as much scientific advantage in groups of life insurance agents as in groups of college students.[8]

Applied social research has been used in government, industry, business, labor, voluntary organizations, city planning, social work, medicine, public health, and agriculture for a comparatively long time. The support of *basic* social research by these special sectors of American society has only begun. We need only grant that "whatever is, is possible" in order to conclude that the concept of potentials of relevance can serve as a guide to policy governing relations between basic social science and business or other spheres of practice. For in the early 1960s, The Equitable Life Assurance Society did precisely that by establishing an Office of Social Research, under the direction of the sociologist John W. Riley, that has since been given over to basic social research with distinct potentials of relevance for the life insurance industry. There is reason to suppose that this can be taken as one prototype for distinguishing effectively between the functions of basic and applied social research while drawing upon the distinctive potentials of each.

All this can one day make obsolete the old story told by Francis Bacon almost four centuries ago:

> Nor can I tax or condemn the morigeration or application of learned men to men in fortune. For the answer was good that Diogenes made to one that asked him in mockery, How it came to pass that philosophers were the followers of rich men, and not rich men of philosophers? He answered soberly, and yet sharply, Because the one sort knew what they had need of, and the other did not.[9]

NOTES

[1]For one detailed account of how the legitimacy of the new science came to be established, see Robert K. Merton. *Science, Technology and Society in Seventeenth-Century England* (New York: Howard Fertig [1938]1970), Chapters 4–9.

[2]Merton, *Social Theory and Social Structure*, pp. 77–79, 660–662.

[3]*National Patterns of Science and Technical Resources* (Washington, D.C.: U.S. Government Printing Office, 1981), p. 8.

[4]The history of science is of course replete with cases in which basic research having no immediately discernible practical implications proved eventually to have widesweeping technological consequences. The point is, however, that, all apart from such windfalls, basic science lays claim to social support simply because it advances our fundamental knowledge of nature and society.

[5]See, for now ancient examples, P.A. Sorokin and R.K. Merton, "Social Time: A Methodological and Functional Analysis," *American Journal of Sociology* 42 (1937):615–629; and P.A. Sorokin, *Sociocultural Causality, Space, Time* (New York: Russell, [1943] 1964). After a lapse of scientific interest in social time, a new spate of research has begun: see, for example, Eviatar Zerubavel, *Patterns of Time in Hospital Life* (Chicago: University of Chicago Press, 1979) and *Hidden Rhythms: Schedules and Calendars in Social Life* (Chicago: University of Chicago Press, 1981); Barry Schwartz, *Queuing and Waiting* (Chicago: University of Chicago Press, 1975); and the ample bibliographies in those monographs.

[6]See William A. Faunce and Robert L. Fulton, "The Sociology of Death:

A Neglected Area of Research," *Social Forces* 36 (1958):205–209; James C. Diggory and D.Z. Rothman, "Values Destroyed by Death," *Journal of Abnormal and Social Psychology* 63 (1961):205–210. Since this was first written in 1963, sociologists and social psychologists have of course produced a copious research literature on death. At least one of the major life insurance companies, through its Office of Social Research, has sponsored basic research on the subject.

[7]As is generally known, a sizable fraction of psychological and sociological experiments deals with students in colleges and in secondary and elementary schools. But the investigators are not trying to develop a social psychology or sociology of the student; the choice of experimental subjects is largely dictated by accessibility. That is why, we must suppose, 20 of the first 26 researches reported in an excellent anthology of small-group research deal with students, the rest with accessible groups in industry and the military. See Paul Hare, Edgar F. Borgatta, and Robert F. Bales, eds., *Small Groups: Studies in Social Interaction* (New York: A.A. Knopf, 1955).

[8]For another range of basic social research bearing on this industry not foreseen at the time this article was first put in print, see Viviana A. Rotman Zelizer, *Morals & Markets: The Development of Life Insurance in the United States* (New York: Columbia University Press, 1979).

[9]Francis Bacon, *The Two Bookes of the Proficience and Advancement of Learning* (London, 1605), as reprinted in *The Works of Francis Bacon*, collected and edited by James Spedding, R.L. Ellis, and D.D. Heath (Boston, 1863), Vol. 6, p. 116.

CHAPTER 9

Social Knowledge and Public Policy*

Commissions—in the broad sense of a collegial body of persons charged by an authority with a designated activity and purpose—have long been an element in governance. Perhaps the most famous and the most effective have been the Royal Commissions of Inquiry in Britain, which came into their own in the nineteenth century as "favored instruments leading to major advances in social legislation, such as the Factory Acts."[1] And perhaps the most generous and surely the most notable tribute to the character and accomplishments of the royal commissions is found in these familiar words:

> The social statistics of Germany and the rest of Continental Western Europe are, by comparison with those of England, wretchedly compiled. But they raise the veil just enough to let us catch a glimpse of the Medusa head behind it. We should be appalled at the state of things at home, if, as in England, our governments

*Reprinted by permission of the publisher from Mirra Komarovsky, ed., *Sociology and Public Policy: The Case of Presidential Commissions*, pp. 153–177. Copyright 1975 by Elsevier North Holland, Inc. The writing of this chapter was supported in part by the Center for Advanced Study in the Behavioral Sciences and in part by a National Science Foundation grant to the Program in the Sociology of Science, Columbia University. Helpful criticism was given me by Robert Dahl, Cynthia Epstein, and fellow Fellows at the Center: Graham Allison, Robert Darnton, Irving Janis, Martin Krieger, James March, Arnold Thackray, Edward Tufte, and Harriet Zuckerman.

and parliaments appointed periodically commissions of inquiry into economic conditions; if these commissions were armed with the same plenary powers to get at the truth; if it was possible to find for this purpose men as competent, as free from partisanship and respect of persons as are the English factory inspectors, her medical reporters on public health, her commissioners of inquiry into the exploitation of women and children, into housing and food.[2]

This unstinted praise of the composite integrity, truth-telling, and capability for social investigation of commissions of inquiry appears in Karl Marx's *Capital*—in the celebrated preface to the first German edition. Evidently, the founder of modern Communism, the prime contributor to an early sociology of knowledge, and the pitiless critic of bourgeois society thought it possible "to get at the truth" about social and economic conditions obtaining in that society and to record part of that truth in the form of "social statistics." As Marx explains, the truth was being searched out by royal commissions and others at work in the service of that dispossessing instrument of the ruling class, the bourgeois English State.

Not, of course, that Marx ascribed the integrity of these critical investigators to lofty motives. What is more interesting and more nearly in accord with his general doctrine is that he saw this institutionalized pattern of truth-telling as itself socially induced. It is identified as an expression of class interest in a particular historical context. The American Civil War had "sounded the tocsin for the European working class," just as the American War of Independence had done for the European middle class.

In England the progress of social disintegration is palpable. . . . Apart from higher motives, therefore, their own most important interests dictate to the classes that are for the nonce the ruling ones, the removal of all legally removable hindrances to the free development of the working-class.[3]

In short extension and paraphrase, Marx is, in effect, advancing the interesting idea that under certain conditions, self-interest, collective and individual, can make for truth-seeking and truth-telling just as, under other conditions, it can and notoriously does make for deliberate lying as well as unwitting deception, both of self and of others.

Commissions of inquiry have not been confined to England. From the beginning, presidents of the United States have also had their commissions. Washington began with a commission to look into the Whiskey Rebellion; ever since, presidents or Congress have instituted one or another kind of commission, at first sporadically and then, in this century, at a greatly quickened pace.[4]

Mansfield has instructively proposed three conjoint criteria for sorting out types of commissions. *First,* in terms of duration, ranging from "bodies convened ad hoc to deal with a specific situation" to those permanently established. *Second,* in terms of their varying overt purposes, among them arbitration; regulation; operation of public enterprise; advice-giving; investigation of a major historical event (for example, assassination of a president); and, of most immediate interest to us, the study, planning, and recommendation of public policy. *Third,* in terms of their "latent functions, notably, bargaining [among disparate interests], public education, delay, patronage, appeasement, frustration of opposition to current policy, and rubber-stamping."[5] From the standpoint of structure, as Mansfield also notes, the commission form is admirably suited to serving a representational function, by providing for voice in its deliberations to a diversity of distinct and often opposed interests. The extent to which commissions have actually been made up of members strongly opposed in interests and values is quite another, politically significant matter.

This essay considers a quartet of American presidential commissions, appointed for a limited time for the announced purpose of formulating plans and recommendations for public policy bearing on four distinct sets of socially defined problems in American society. Beyond their announced purpose, as we will see, these ad hoc commissions had a variety of latent functions and dysfunctions for diverse social formations. To meet its charge, each of the commissions arranged for research projects and programs, consisting principally of social research of one description or another.

This practice of social investigation is in direct continuity with what had become a tradition for the British royal commissions. These regularly provided for inquiry that would "make for a definitive determination of controversial facts and [so it was said] for a trustworthy judgment on a complex public problem."[6] In turn, the royal commissions had an emerging tradition of empirical social investigation to draw upon. As Stephen Cole has shown, the statistical and social science associatons in Britain that had come into being before the middle of the nineteenth century were largely activated by concern with social reform. With increasing regularity, they fostered or actually mounted empirical investigations of crime, poverty, prison life, factory conditions, and kindred problems. Even before applied social research became more fully institutionalized in the form of providing for a trained, full-time, paid staff, such research was being carried forward by a variety of (sometimes voluntary and often self-taught) investigators: actuaries, army officers, businessmen, civil servants, clergy, physicians, and, tellingly enough, early in the period, only a sprinkling of professors. Cole goes on to observe that most of these de facto social researchers were in professions that provided them with access to statistics institutionally generated by hospitals, philanthropic organizations, the courts, prisons, and various other agencies of government.[7]

Marx was thus merely being observant when he praised the social statistics and other social data being compiled before his eyes in England. It was these data that would enable him and others to reconstruct crucial aspects of the English social reality, to get "upon the right track for the discovery of the natural laws of its movement." It was for reasons such as this, writes Marx, that "I have given so large a space in this volume to the history, the details, and the results of English factory legislation."[8] And an abundant space it is. No one has yet inventoried the whole of the official reports by commissions of inquiry, factory inspectors, public health inspectors, and other official bodies, which Marx drew upon in the *Capital.* But his careful citation practices, more meticulous than those adopted by most of us pedantically inclined academicians, afford a clue to the scale on which he made use of the researches stemming from these sources. A small sampling of his liberal citations is enough to serve us here.

The 60,000-word monograph entitled "Machinery and Modern Industry," which constitutes the celebrated Chapter XV of the first volume of *Capital,* contains some 240 footnotes. About a sixth of these are given over to developing points in the text or to demolishing *bêtes noires* (such as Malthus and Ure); the remaining 200 or so are used to indicate the sources of the evidence and ideas that he introduces in the text.[9] The arithmetic of these citations summarizes the copious extent to which Marx drew upon the investigations recorded in those reports of parliamentary commissions and other official bodies, known from their dark blue paper covers simply as the Blue books.

Of the approximately 200 citations of all sources, including ancient, medieval, and modern writings, 138 (or more than two-thirds) referred to Blue books of one sort or another: 70 to Reports of Inspectors of Factories, 45 to Reports of Royal Commissions, 11 to Reports on Public Health, 9 to the Census (primarily of 1861), and 3 to other Blue books (such as the Statistical Abstract of the United Kingdom).[10]

Never before, surely, and probably never since, have the reports of government commissions been put to more consequential use.

These few scattered observations on commissions of inquiry in an earlier time and another place are perhaps enough to provide perspective and distance as we examine the use of research by commissions in our own time and place. The observations remind us of the following:

1.   Government commissions of inquiry are themselves a his-

torically evolving social form for discovering or systematically
describing selected aspects of a social reality.

2.   Commissions are both producers and consumers of social
      research.

3.   The institutionalization of procedures for undertaking re-
      search on behalf of commissions engaged in recommending
      public policy began some time ago and is presumably still in
      process.

4.   The use of that research need not be confined to its utilization
      by the commissions inaugurating it.

5.   As the historic case of Marx emphatically proclaims, the re-
      sults of authentic social inquiry can be utilized by people
      whose political commitments differ sharply from those of the
      commissioners or the investigators.

FOUR PRESIDENTIAL COMMISSIONS OF INQUIRY

As a sociological understanding of social institutions and collective behavior would lead us to expect, national commissions of
inquiry are created by the president or the Congress or both in response to their reading of the social and political temper of the times,
current and prospective. Commissions are usually established in
Times of Trouble. (That is, one supposes, why there have been so
many of them.) The public troubles are sometimes acute, sometimes
chronic, and the one kind is frequently superimposed upon the other.

Acute troubles often lead to the formation of commissions to
investigate the unique event (as in the case of the Warren Commission). Occasionally, specific events trigger the appointment of a commission to inquire into the enduring problem dramatized by the
particular event, as with the National Commission on Violence, instituted in the grim hours after the assassination of Robert Kennedy.
When commissions are created to formulate new policies on chronic
problems even though there has been no sudden, visible change in
actual circumstances, this presumably represents a threshold phenomenon of accumulated troubles (as, for example, with the belated
public and institutionalized response to the deterioration of our human and natural environments). Finally, a combination of chronic
and acute troubles apparently led to a commission to examine the
socially defined problems of obscenity and pornography, when that
age-old continuity of interest in matters judged unchaste was coupled
with a conspicuous growth in scale. In all cases, it appears, national

commissions are in origin and outcome deeply affected by both actual and perceived climates of public opinion and action.

Whatever their historical origins and their manifest and latent functions, commissions of inquiry are—commissions of inquiry. That is, they are publicly committed to make a search or investigation directed toward uncovering germane information and knowledge; they are, in short, institutionally committed to research. The research may turn out to be sound or specious, wide-ranging or parochial, deeply significant or inconsequential, inspired or pedestrian. But the public commitment being what it is, research there must be. Yet, surprisingly little seems to be systematically known about the ways in which research programs and projects are brought into being by these policy-formulating commissions, how the research is conducted, and most of all, how the results of research relate to the formulation of proposed policy.

It is therefore a rare opportunity to have circumstantial accounts about these matters prepared by sociologists who have played a major role as members of presidential commissions: Otto Larsen, Lloyd Ohlin, James Short, and Charles Westoff.

Their accounts, written from the perspective of participant-observers, exhibit an interesting symmetry, with a methodological aesthetic all their own. In their role as *participants,* the authors deal principally with sociology *in* the commissions (that is, with the use, nonuse, misuse, or pointed absence of sociological knowledge). In their role as *observers,* they deal principally with the sociology *of* the commissions (that is, with their origins, structure, dynamics, evolution, and aftermath). That division of the subject provides a ready format for my observations on their reports.

THE SOCIOLOGY OF COMMISSIONS

The variety of social processes, structures, and functions observed in the behavior of the commissions can be related to the variegated problematics of the sociological discipline itself.

Plainly, the commissions exhibit the operation of power structures in the production, use, abuse, and nonuse of sociological knowledge. Composed of representatives of various (not, of course, all) constituencies, each commission was bound to exhibit some degree of internal conflict. From the standpoint of structural analysis, this observed pattern of conflicting perspectives among the commissioners is no mere happenstance. For in a society structurally differentiated as ours is, conflict *must* result from the ground plan of a commission that authentically represents citizens located in diverse strata and sectors of the social structure, with their distinctive and often incompatible interests and values.

To the extent that the membership of a commission represents the spectrum of major interest groups, this guarantees a structurally induced strain toward initial conflict and subsequent compromise or continuing stasis. Apparently, it is with commissions as it is with food: the effort to cater to all tastes makes for blandness. Yet, on more than one occasion, through a sociologically interesting process of trade-offs, the commissions came out with strong collective recommendations that individual commissioners were surprised to find themselves endorsing. Some recommendations of the Commission on Pornography, for example, were in this special sense spicy rather than bland.

In part, this results from small group processes in continuing or intermittent operation. Processes of polarization, conflict, and mutual accommodation were at work under varying, sometimes ill-understood conditions. But the principal group-induced pressures were generally for compromise. As one observer summed this up, there is apparently nothing like an implacable deadline, as distinct from an ideology, to move *a task-oriented group* toward consensus. In seeming paradox, the commission format providing for minority reports may make for wider consensus than would otherwise obtain. Knowing that the minority can openly dissent, the visible majority may be more agreeable to modifying their position to avoid a scatter of contested recommendations. In turn, the minority report as an avenue of public expression becomes a structural device for avoiding the stasis condition of a hung jury.

Another aspect of the behavior of commissions can be identified from the perspective of a structural sociology focused on organizational constraints and processes of differentiation in groups. One constraint derives from what some of us take to be important variables in group structure and individual membership in groups. These variables can be described as the *socially expected* (not only the actual) *duration* of a group or organization and the expected duration of the occupancy of a status within a group or organization. Groups differ significantly in this aspect; many have an expectation of indefinite duration; some have an assigned life span. Memberships in groups differ in the same way: some, as in the case of tenure positions, carry the expectation of indefinite duration; others, as in the case of office holding, have a known pending termination. Such socially shared expectations of duration greatly affect the orientations and behavior of members of the group, the workings of authority and power within it, and the social environment in which the group finds its place.[11]

Consequences of the two types of expected duration are repeatedly implied and sometimes expressed in the description of the commissions' behavior. Thus, Lloyd Ohlin notes that "The Chairman, Executive Director . . . and many staff members [of the Crime Commission] were acutely conscious of the fact that a Presidential Commission has no enduring life and must rely on other established institutions and agencies to implement the results of its work."[12] This sense of the short, more-or-less unhappy life of the Crime Commission, this sense of its expected brief duration, led to a strategy of attempting to involve states and localities in a continuing program. In another connection, Otto Larsen reports that "confidentiality began to disappear completely toward the end of the [Pornography] Commission's life as drafts of reports were circulated,"[13] a result that might follow as much from the stage of the work as from the short, remaining duration of the commission. James Short refers to the substantial effects on the Commission on Violence of Lyndon Johnson's lame-duck incumbency, requiring the research to be carried out and a progress report to be submitted before a new president was inaugurated.[14] The lame-duck pattern is the classical archetype in which the known duration of occupancy of a status operates to affect policy formation and to make for the decreasingly effective exercise of authority.

Still, if it produces a body of research, the socially consequential life of a commission can extend well beyond its existence as a formally convened body. Long after it has been discharged with presidential (or parliamentary) thanks, the inquiries mounted by the commission can remain consequential, as we noted in the case of the Blue books that the British Museum made available to Marx, and as we can note now, for example, in the case of the Crime Surveys that the Crime Commission made available to the public.

Another important constraint upon the utilization of social research by the commissions was the discordant pacing of empirical social inquiry and of decision-making. The participant-observers uniformly note that the comparatively slow pace of much social research was out of phase with the urgent timetable by which national commissions work. In this regard, nothing much seems to have happened since at least the 1940s (and, one suspects, long before), when a study of policy-oriented research reported that "the tempo of policy decisions and action is often more rapid than the tempo of applied [social] research."[15]

This temporal disjunction between research and policy formation sets severe limits upon the possibility that the commissions could draw upon social research for many pertinent problems emerging in their deliberations. All this raises several questions about the relations of commissions to research programs. As we have seen, ad hoc commissions of inquiry are usually appointed in Times of Trouble. They are to seek out the sources of one or another of the currently defined troubles and to tell us what to do about them. For both manifest and latent political functions, commissions tend to be instituted in politically expedient or politically inevitable times. This leads us to ask whether those are the best times for investigating (not necessarily recommending modes of coping with) the problems in and of our society. It may be, as Edward Tufte has suggested, that the most effective political strategy is to exploit short-run pressures for long-run improvement;[16] the so-called crisis may provide the only chance that will present itself. But although a crisis mentality about a chronic problem provides a politically feasible basis for establishing a presidential commission, the same sense of urgency works against doing the careful and considerable research needed then and there. As we learn from the testimony of participant-observers, much of the research brought into being by an urgent commission must be piecemeal or otherwise limited by the exigencies of the public business to be transacted.[17]

Since considerations of political expediency—implying political feasibility—are bound to affect the timing of governmentally established commissions, there is reason to argue for *the more frequent creation of national commissions by other institutions and associations in the society.* Foundations do occasionally provide for such commissions and for programs of research, extending over a period of years, oriented to their requirements. Beyond that, there would seem to be a place for learned societies and professional associations in the social sciences to develop proto-commissions of their own, which would define public issues from their own theoretical stance and provide for associated programs of ongoing research oriented to those issues.

One more item in this incomplete inventory of observations on the sociology *of* commissions also links up with the role of sociology *in* commissions. Problems in both the microsociology and the macrosociology of scientific knowledge are implicated in the work of commissions.

The participant-observer accounts are rich in detail about the divergence of moral and intellectual perspectives of commissioners and staff drawn from different sectors of the society. Consider only the most conspicuous case: the interaction of the lawyers and the social scientists in trying to shape a knowledge-related set of recommendations.

As has always been the case since it became the capital, Washington is densely populated by lawyers. Presidential commissions are generally even more so. The Commission on Population is a rare exception. Of its twenty-four members, only a handful were lawyers, and these gained entry chiefly as members of Congress. The other three commissions more nearly reverted to type. Although the Commission on Pornography also had an unusual number of sociologists—Otto Larsen, Joseph Klapper, Marvin Wolfgang—a third of the eighteen commissioners had law degrees. Fifteen of the nineteen members of the Crime Commission were lawyers, as were fifteen of twenty-five of the task force directors of the Commission on Violence.

The preponderance of lawyers should come as no surprise: Max Weber had long since remarked on the special availability of lawyers for every arm and function of government. Nor is this merely a result of their lawyerly skills. It also has to do with the structure of their occupation. Far more readily than physicians or even academics, lawyers can detach themselves from their ordinary jobs to take on extraordinary assignments for longer or shorter periods. Eventually this tradition of public service within the guild of lawyers becomes self-perpetuating, in no little part because it is at times greatly rewarded. Lawyers also experience role-congruence between the requirements of their occupational roles and the demands of such ad hoc units as national commissions.

However, it is not the contrast between the detachability of lawyers and academic social scientists, but the differences between them in styles of work, intellectual perspectives, and, specifically, conceptions of evidence that must be noted here. The modes and loci of diverse and sometimes rival professional expertise are themes running throughout the reported behavior of staffs and commissioners. These are perhaps best crystallized in the preference of lawyers for use of sworn eyewitness depositions, and the contrasting preference of sociologists for use of interviews, social surveys, and other quantitative evidence. These preferences are sustained by a considerable professional apparatus and a not inconsiderable academic apparatus by which the evidence is evaluated. The reward system of science and learning, centered in peer review, reinforces the differential attachment to types of evidence.

An applied sociology of knowledge must take note of such structurally patterned differences in conceptions of what constitutes adequate evidence. It would be of no little interest to mount a research program that systematically compares the scope, relevance, validity, and utility of data that, collected in diverse ways, bear upon the same public issues considered by public commissions and other groups. A next step into the sociology of knowledge would require social scientists to compare the evaluation of these methods by experts drawn from disciplines that have institutionalized distinct methods of gathering and distinct criteria for assessing evidence.

At any rate, we can earmark the micro- and macro-sociology of knowledge as another basic context for that investigation of the behavior and consequences of commissions which constitutes the sociology *of* commissions.

SOCIOLOGY IN THE COMMISSIONS

Sociology *in* the commissions—that is, the actual role of sociological knowledge in the work and the conclusions of the commissions—provides its own microcosm of the discipline at large.

To the extent that the commissions drew upon sociological knowledge at all, that knowledge was evidently diverse in both general perspective and specific findings. None of the commissions, or their research staffs, confined itself to a single comprehensive and tight-knit paradigm that defined the range of problems and subjects to be investigated in detail and determined how they were to be investigated. Instead, the commissions, or at least their staffs, were tacitly committed to a pluralistic theoretical orientation. In some degree, this pluralism was probably built into the structure of the commissions through the appointment of members representing different constituencies with differing cognitive as well as value perspectives. But, in any case, it is apparent that the sociological research for the commissions did not uniformly or primarily derive from a single theoretical orientation—not functional analysis, symbolic interactionism, or social ecology; not structural analysis, exchange theory, or social dramaturgy; indeed, not even Marxism.

This kind of theoretical pluralism only reproduces in microcosm the actual and the cognitively appropriate state of the field of sociology itself—and of the behavioral sciences generally. Even to signal the grounds for this statement of preference for a pluralistic rather than monistic structure of sociological knowledge would require us to move far beyond the immediate subject.[18] But it can be argued that differing theoretical orientations are useful for understanding different kinds and aspects of sociological and social problems. Whatever the claim to the contrary by advocates of this or that theoretical stance, actual inquiry (and conspicuously so for inquiry aimed at dealing with concrete social problems) requires the use of complementary paradigms and conceptions.

In some quarters, "eclecticism" is an abusive epithet used to designate a shabby, incoherent collection of ad hoc interpretations of aspects of reality. The modifier, "mere," is unthinkingly introduced with such frequency that expression becomes telescoped into the composite "mereclecticism." Yet, the controlled and systematic use of complementary ideas drawn from differing orientations in the form of what can be called "disciplined eclecticism" characterizes much of social science today.[19]

Just as the aggregate of sociologists doing the research for the commissions adopted a plurality of theoretical orientations, so they also adopted a plurality of methods of inquiry. Different sorts of questions, derived from theoretical constructions or stimulated by empirical observations, call for different sorts of data acquired through diverse methods. The plurality of methods employed by the commissions' research staffs for the collection of data and for their ordering and interpretation also provides a replica of what is the collective practice in sociology at large.

The research programs of the commissions provide a miniaturized replica of sociology in still another aspect: the basic presuppositions involved in the imagery of the sociological knowledge thought necessary for formulating grounded recommendations for action. So far as one can tell, that imagery of the ambiguous relations between knowledge and the formulation of policy entertained by the researchers was not dominated by any of the various, at times simple-minded, positivisms: neither the scriptural version, "the truth shall make you free," nor the Comtean version, "from knowledge comes foresight; from foresight, the power to act" (which sounds rather more compelling when translated back into the French: *savoir pour prévoir, prévoir pour pouvoir*). Nor did the researchers adopt the positivistic slogan set out by Friedrich Engels in his nominally anti-positivistic tract, *Anti-Dühring*, when he wrote of the "leap of mankind from the realm of necessity into the realm of freedom."

The reports on the commissions contain few signs of such assumptions. Instead, they contain more than hints of concern with the basic, more modest question: Which forms of sociological and behavioral science knowledge made which kinds of difference to the recommendations adopted or rejected by the commissions? In place of reveling in an orgy of unconnected facts, the researchers focused on strategic concepts and facts that sometimes affected the formulation of policy. Consider only these examples in Charles Westoff's report on the Population Commission:

Item: One study concluded that "population growth played a minor role in the short run," as demographic time is counted (thirty to fifty years), when "compared with technological, economic, and governmental policy considerations." Why did this broad factual conclusion prove to be strategic? Because it seemed to have an almost direct policy implication calling for specified contingency analysis and indicating that, *for the time being,* population control is a comparatively "indirect and ineffectual policy lever for environmental problems."[20]

Item: Another strategic finding was the demonstration that "if women averaged 2.0 rather than 2.1 births [and, of course, anyone can see that this minute average difference could scarcely matter], zero population growth could be achieved near the same level and in almost the same time with *immigration continued at the current volume.* Although not a world-shaking scientific discovery, this bit of demographic intelligence was extremely important in the debate over immigration policy and was influential in defeating a recommendation to reduce the volume."[21]

These examples should not be taken to imply that sociological knowledge typically passes directy into social policy.[22] But to say more here about the gap between the two would only be redundant in view of Paul Lazarsfeld's close and informed analysis of the problem.[23]

This awareness brings us to a series of more detailed observations on the place of theoretical sociology in the research of the commissions. These observations take us somewhat afield to consider theoretical issues in sociology at large that are implied in that research.

THEORETICAL ORIENTATIONS

A Focus on Consequences

Throughout much of their work, we are told, the commissions focused on consequences: the consequences of existing practices and structures and the consequences anticipated from putting proposed policies into effect.

Charles Westoff: The Population Commission "focused on the economic, environmental, political, and social consequences of population growth."[24]

Otto Larsen: The "fateful" decision was taken in the Congressional Act establishing the Commission on Pornography to adopt the position that "knowledge about *the effects* [that is, the consequences] of exposure to explicit sex material [might be] relevant for making decisions about the forms of control that a society might exercise over obscenity."[25]

Lloyd Ohlin: "The most important inputs of social science knowledge to the Crime Commission were probably in the documentation of the harmful consequences of existing practices and policies and suggestions of a variety of persuasive theories and justifications for pursuing an alternative course."[26]

The focus on consequences should come as no surprise to sociologists aware of the pervasive character of functional analysis in sociology, not least those sociologists busily engaged in repudiating that mode of analysis. After all, research bearing upon general policies dealing with socially defined problems in and of society *must* focus on multiple functional and dysfunctional consequences of possible courses of action for a variety of social units (for example, varied groups, strata, regions) and the more comprehensive social systems. This is the case even though no scientific calculus exists for assessing, choosing among, and integrating such diverse consequences.

The four commissions played out a scenario composed of tacit and explicit theoretical orientations calling for them to examine the probable outcomes of alternative policies. What produced and maintained the reported conflicts in the commissions were principally the differences of interests, values, and ideologies affecting the weights to be assigned to selected consequences. So far as policy-oriented research is concerned, the critical conflict of interests and values centers on the question: What evidence of which consequences for which social systems, strata, and groups should be taken into account in the research?

In all of the commissions, the inescapable decision to select some, rather than other, types of expected consequences for investigation was basic to both the research program and the evolving rationale for alternative policies. To take only one instance, in the Population Commission it was this kind of value-charged, perspective-bound decision that divided the subgroup advocating the "unwanted fertility" perspective from the subgroup advocating the "ecological perspective."

Such conflicts highlight the untenable character of that long-forgotten positivism which, these days, is being revived by a small army of critics who promiscuously attribute caricatured versions of it to sociologists engaged in the empirical investigation of human problems in society. The research staff of the commissions evidently did not adopt the easygoing assumption that the sociological truth shall make it easy to choose among various courses of social action. Apart from much else, what makes such choices fundamentally underivable from sociological knowledge is the incommensurabilty of consequences that are in the interest of some sectors of the society and against the interests of others. This basic feature of comprehensive decisions, most marked in a highly differentiated society, leads inescapably to their acquiring a political character.

Thus, the overview of presidential commissions in action teaches us once again that when it comes to the formulation of public policy, one enduring problem facing sociologists is to clarify and to work out some way of analyzing "the aggregate of humanly relevant consequences." That problem has long been on the agenda of a certain kind of functional and structural analysis.

What Harold Lasswell presciently, and in a sense prematurely, described as "the policy sciences" in the 1940s referred chiefly to *social* research that is oriented to public and private policy.[27] Lasswell recognized that almost the entire spectrum of science could be drawn upon for investigations bearing upon the formation of policy, but he centered on the subset of the social sciences. Since his pioneering formulations, it has become possible to identify more of the distinctive contributions that social science can make to the formation of policy. Among these, consider the sociological perspective that examines latent social problems rather than the manifest problem defined for investigation by the institutional powers that be.

Latent Social Problems

Latent social problems refer to those unwanted social conditions that are at odds with some of the (often declared) values and interests of groups and strata in the society but are not generally recognized as being so. Sociologists do not impose their values upon others when they undertake to supply the knowledge about latent problems that often makes them manifest. Thus, when demographers working for the Commission on Population try to identify the social, economic, and cultural consequences of various rates of population growth, they in effect call the advocates of differing population policies to account for the results of putting one or another policy into practice. The demonstrated consequences of uncontrolled birth rates, for example, can then be seen as the aggregated result of people acting in accord with some of their values to produce outcomes that conflict with some of their other values.

This kind of latent social problem constitutes an important special case of the generic pattern of the unanticipated consequences of (individual or collective) social action.[28] Total commitments to values of every kind—whether rapid economic expansion ("growth"), rapid technological advance, rule-free communities, or full expression of self in which anything goes (analyzed by Lionel Trilling in the notion of "authenticity")[29]—have cumulative consequences that, if not counteracted, in due course undercut the originating values themselves.

This sociological perspective turns up repeatedly in the research programs of the several commissions. The same perspective is inherent in the newly developed intellectual and social movement dedicated to technology assessment. In effect, technology assessment focuses on the latent consequences of actual or proposed technological developments. It is designed to search out previously unknown or unconsidered social, ecological, and other humanly relevant consequences of existing or proposed technological complexes.[30]

The implications of this are significant for an evolving theory of policy-oriented social research because the emphasis upon discovering latent consequences of institutional or technological arrangements puts the current sociological accent on the subjective component of social action in its appropriate context.

The Hazards of Subjectivism

The idea of the subjective component in human action has a long history in sociology and had an even longer history before sociologists arrived on the historical scene. It is an idea, moreover, that has been formulated in several traditions of sociological thought: in Max Weber's notion of *Verstehen* (roughly: intuitive understanding), Robert MacIver's "dynamic assessment," Florian Znaniecki's "humanistic co-efficient," Talcott Parsons's "voluntaristic theory of action," and Alfred Schutz's "phenomenological perspective." The idea was succinctly formulated by W.I. Thomas in what is probably the single most consequential sentence ever put in print by an American sociologist:

> If men define situations as real, they are real in their consequences.[31]

Now, it is one thing to maintain, with Weber, Thomas, and the other giants of sociology, that to understand human action requires us to attend systematically to its subjective component: what people perceive, feel, believe, and want. But it is quite another thing to exaggerate this sound idea by maintaining that human action is *nothing but* subjective. That extravagance leads to sociological Berkeleyanism (the allusion being, of course, to the English champion of philosophical idealism, not to an American geographic or academic place). Such total subjectivism conceives of social reality as consisting *only* in social definitions, perceptions, labels, beliefs, assumptions, or ideas, as expressed, for example, in full generality by the criminological theorist, Richard Quinney, when he writes that "We have no reason to believe in the objective existence of anything."[32] A basic idea is distorted into error and a great injustice is visited upon W.I. Thomas when his theorem is thus exaggerated.

Exaggeration of a seminal truth produces its own brand of error. Total subjectivism, which in effect maintains that *only* social definitions of the situation (or other subjective equivalents) determine the character of human action and its consequences, manages to transform the Thomas Theorem into this fallacious maxim:

> If men do *not* define situations as real, they are not real in their consequences.

When the sufficient is thus transformed into the necessary, sociological error replaces sociological insight. Total subjectivism leads us astray by failing to provide a theoretical place for *systematic* concern with objective constraints upon human action. Those social, demographic, economic, technological, ecological, and other objective constraints are not always caught up in social definitions. To ignore those constraints is mistakenly to imply that they do not significantly affect both the choices people make and the personal and social consequences of those choices. It is to pave the road to Utopianism with bad assumptions. For, in the pithy phrasing by the sociologist Arthur Stinchcombe, which tempers the subjective emphasis of W.I. Thomas with the objective emphasis of Karl Marx, "People define situations, but do not define them as they please."[33]

The theoretical hazard of total subjectivism did not first turn up in exaggerations of the recent labeling perspective on deviant behavior.[34] It was potentially there in every voluntaristic paradigm of action and was skirted by Parsons a quarter-century ago. Then, as now, the position taken on total subjectivism seemed to me fundamental to sociological theorizing:

> When Mr. Parsons notes that the "social situation" must be analyzed with respect to "the various types of significance of situational facts to the actor," there is need for further strict clarification. Does this mean that sociology takes into account *only* those aspects of the objective situation to which the acting individual [or group] is oriented (cognitively, affectively, or through goal-definitions)? Does it imply that observable aspects of the situation of which the acting individual [or group] is *wholly unaware* are at once eliminated from the realm of facts pertinent for the sociologist? If so, one must register dissent . . . it is all the more important to clarify this formulation, else one might suppose that he [Parsons] advocates a basically idealistic or subjectivistic approach to sociological theories, in which *only* those aspects of the situation somehow taken into account by individuals are considered pertinent to the sociological analysis.[35]

To understand social life, we must indeed take account of how people perceive and define situations. But sociological theory can provide an adequate place for such perceptions without falling into the fallacy of total subjectivism. As formulated in the concept of the self-fulfilling prophecy,[36] for example, social definitions common in groups and collectivities *make up an important dynamic part of the social environment* in which anticipations help create the anticipated social reality. Thus, when schoolteachers decide in advance that children from certain ethnic or economic origins are apt to be substandard and treat them accordingly, they help bring about the retarded learning which they had anticipated. Subjective definitions of the situation therefore matter, and can matter greatly. But they do not alone matter.

To correct the imbalance that comes with total subjectivism and to restore the objective components of social situations to their indispensable place, we plainly need this counterpart to the Thomas Theorem:

> And if men do *not* define real situations as real, they are nevertheless real in their consequences.

The paired theorems serve as a continuing reminder of a truth that the sociologist must acknowledge (despite the idiomatic expression to the contrary): in society, as in other domains, what you don't know (or don't notice) *can* hurt you.

Indeed, it is precisely what you do not know that will often hurt you most, since you cannot take appropriate measures against the unknown. Whether their causes were socially defined as real or not, tuberculosis and Asiatic cholera managed to decimate many populations before Robert Koch discovered their pathogenic agents and laid the basis for their control.

A major function of science, and not only of research directly oriented toward public policy, is to provide an improved understanding of socially induced situations that are *not* generally defined as real, simply because of (sometimes motivated) ignorance. The geneticist Joshua Lederberg noted that it is ironic, but not surprising, that science comes to be penalized in the public estimation as the bearer of evil tidings about the dysfunctional consequences of economically or culturally preferred behaviors. As he observed,

> [There may be] some who wish we didn't know that radiation is mutagenic and carcinogenic. We could then use our atmosphere and other resources as sinks for our waste in that sphere, and get at least a short-term advantage of the economic utility of the procedures. Unfortunately, you cannot play those kinds of games with nature for very long. Those costs will be incurred to the extent that they are real . . . to the extent that there are actual health hazards . . . connected with them *whether you know about them or not.* Merely to be ignorant of them is simply to defer your recognition of them into the future—in no way to blunt . . . the actual impact.[37]

From the theoretical perspective being advanced here, it is of more than passing interest to learn of the emphasis on the interplay between subjective and objective aspects of the social reality found in the policy-oriented research conducted for the four commissions, which they variously used or ignored in arriving at their recommendations. Whatever else requires change in the future programs of research for national commissions and other policy-formulating groups, such an orientation does not.

Coda

The accounts by participant-connoisseurs of the national commissions advance the continuing effort to clarify the character and workings of policy-oriented sociological knowledge. They alert us to problems and prospects that we may not have previously considered. Among these are implications for concerted research programs that might be mounted by the national and international communities of sociologists.

All four observers report a common circumstance confronting the commissions. In each sphere of inquiry, there was a conspicuously insufficient backlog of the needed social research. Some new research had to be produced under forced draft; much of the rest could not be carried through at all within the time available.

This condition of ad hoc research under urgent pressure need not continue to be the typical condition. Sociologists attuned to structural and functional alternatives should remember that there really are public organizations besides government ones. Among these are the composites of professional association and learned society—the American Sociological Association, for example, and many another of like kind. Perhaps these organizations should, separately or in concert, initiate continuing research programs designed for use by functional equivalents of government commissions. Independent commissions centered upon social problems on the grand scale could be instituted—say, by the Social Science Research Council—without regard to the immediacies of political expediency. They, in turn, could generate terms of reference for programs of policy-oriented research in the sphere of the particular problem, without the strong pressures of urgency that have typically limited work done directly for congressional and presidential commissions.

In a word, we need not wait upon invitations from the White House or Congress to undertake continuing programs of policy-focused research of the kinds required by government commissions. Independent action by the community of social scientists in this domain would give added meaning to the social role of social science in the last quarter of our difficult century.

NOTES

[1]Charles J. Hanser, *Guide to Decision: The Royal Commission* (Totowa, N.J.: The Bedminster Press, 1965); see also Harvey C. Mansfield, "Commissions, Government," *International Encyclopedia of the Social Sciences,* (New York: Macmillan Co. and The Free Press, 1968), Vol. III, pp. 13–18.

[2]Karl Marx, *Capital,* (Moscow: Foreign Languages Publishing House, 1959), Vol. I, p. 9.

[3]Ibid., p. 9.

[4]No exhaustive counts exist, but it is said that Hoover appointed about sixty commissions and advisory boards during the first year-and-a-half of his presidency; Franklin Roosevelt, more than a hundred in his first two terms; Truman, a mere twenty or so during nearly eight years in office; with Eisenhower proceeding at a Truman-like rate during his first term. As we might suppose, the commissions were of varying scope, duration, intensity, and consequence, but little is known about them through systematic investigation. The estimates of numbers are assembled by Alan L. Dean, "Ad Hoc Commissions for Policy Formulation?", in *The Presidential Advisory System,* Thomas E. Cronin and Sanford D. Greenberg, eds. (New York: Harper & Row, 1969), pp. 101–116. However, these estimates evidently include a good many advisory bodies other than Presidential Commissions, strictly so-called. Popper has compiled a list of these in recent administrations: eleven for Truman, four for Eisenhower, four for Kennedy, twenty for Johnson, and five during Nixon's first two years in office. Frank Popper, *The President's Commissions* (New York: Twentieth Century Fund, 1970), Appendix 1.

[5]Mansfield, "Commissions, Government," pp. 13–14; see also Daniel Bell, "Government by Commission," *The Public Interest* 3 (1966):3–9.

[6]Hanser, *Guide to Decision,* p. 220. It should be emphasized that royal commissions and presidential commissions have only a cousinly resemblance, structural and functional. For contrasts as well as similarities between them, see Popper, *The President's Commissions,* pp. 50–54.

[7]Stephen Cole, "Continuity and Institutionalization in Science: A Case Study of a Failure," in *The Establishment of Empirical Sociology: Studies in Continuity, Discontinuity, and Institutionalization,* Anthony Oberschall, ed. (New York: Harper & Row, 1972), pp. 73–129; in the same volume see also the paper by David Elesh, "The Manchester Statistical Society: A Case Study of Discontinuity in the History of Empirical Social Research," pp. 73–129. As Paul F. Lazarsfeld reports in his foreword to that volume, these and other historical and sociological studies of the early period of empirical social research derived from a graduate seminar at Columbia which he and I gave jointly in the 1960s. But what Lazarsfeld characteristically does not go on to report is that his conviction about the potential significance of this subject ran deeper than mine. It was he, rather than I, who instituted a series of investigations of the subject by Oberschall, Bernard-Pierre Lécuyer, Terry Clark, Suzanne Shad, and others. For two other instructive inquiries, see

Nathan Glazer, "The Rise of Social Research in Europe," in *The Human Meaning of the Social Sciences*, Daniel Lerner, ed. (New York: Meridian, 1959); and Philip Abrams, *The Origins of British Sociology, 1834–1914* (Chicago: University of Chicago Press, 1968).

[8]*Capital*, pp. 9–10.

[9]His collaborator and editor was altogether aware of the diverse functions served by Marx's use of quotations and citations, principally in footnotes. In his preface to the English edition of *Capital*, Engels itemizes these functions, hinting at Marx's interest in what was to become the sociology of knowledge and at his deep commitment to the rights of private intellectual property. Following the style of Marx's own practice, one should fully quote Engels's observations to this effect: "A word respecting the author's [this being, of course, Marx's] method of quoting may not be out of place. In the majority of cases, the quotations serve, in the usual way, as documentary evidence in support of assertions made in the text. But in many instances, passages from economic writers are quoted [*n.b.*] in order to indicate when, where, and by whom a certain proposition was for the first time clearly enunciated. This is done in cases where the proposition quoted is of importance as being a more or less adequate expression of the conditions of social production and exchange prevalent at the time, and quite irrespective of Marx's recognition, or otherwise, of its general validity. These quotations, therefore, supplement the text by a running commentary taken from the history of the science." *Capital*, p. 5. Marx's practice generalized would greatly extend the current use of citation analysis for tracing genealogies of ideas.

[10]England, taken by Marx as "the classic ground" of "the capitalist mode of production" and therefore "used as the chief illustration in the development of my theoretical ideas," provided other sources of data about its social reality that could be utilized both by critics and defenders of that society. On a half-dozen occasions in the same Chapter XV, Marx drew upon papers and publications by the emerging societies for the advancement of social science. He notes in a "Report of the Social Science Congress, at Edinburgh," October 1863, that "In England women are still occasionally used instead of horses for hauling canal boats" (*Capital*, p. 394). Similarly, he refers the reader to "the speech of N.W. Senior at the seventh annual congress of The National Associaton for the Promotion of Social Science," 1863, which deals with "the very advantageous results of combining gymnastics . . . with compulsory education for factory children and pauper scholars." Marx thus provides eloquent testimony to the ways in which authentic social reportage and social science can provide subversive evidence about the social reality, a secular version of the biblical doctrine that the truth shall make you free.

[11]I have long argued that this is so. See Merton, *Social Theory and Social Structure*, pp. 365–366; and three of us found it to be so in a study of "planned communities" conducted some time ago: Robert K. Merton, Patricia S. West, and Marie Jahoda, *Patterns of Social Life: Explorations in the Sociology of Housing* (New York: Columbia University Bureau of Applied Social Research, 1948, mimeo.).

[12]Lloyd E. Ohlin, "Report on the President's Commission on Law Enforcement and Administration of Justice," in *Sociology and Public Policy*, Mirra Komarovsky, ed. (New York: The Free Press, 1975), p. 112.

[13]Otto N. Larsen, "The Commission on Obscenity and Pornography: Form, Function, and Failure," in ibid., p. 30.

[14]James F. Short, Jr., "The National Commission on the Causes and Prevention of Violence," in ibid., p. 77.

[15]Robert K. Merton, "The Role of Applied Social Science in the Formation of Policy," *Philosophy of Science* 16 (July 1949):161–181, reprinted in Merton, *The Sociology of Science* (Chicago: University of Chicago Press, 1973), pp. 70–98; the quotation is on p. 88.

[16]Edward Tufte, personal communication.

[17]James March (in a personal communication) has suggested that research does not always lag behind the knowledge and information requirements for formulating public policy. Research on the genetic effects of radiation, for example, has apparently outrun the pace of policy formation which takes that research into account.

[18]For a statement of these grounds, see Robert K. Merton, "Structural Analysis in Sociology," in *Approaches to the Study of Social Structure*, Peter M. Blau, ed. (New York: The Free Press, 1975), pp. 21–52.

[19]On "disciplined eclecticism," see Merton, ibid., pp. 47–52. Joseph J. Schwab has dealt with the "arts of Eclectic" in a series of evocative papers, among them: "The Practical Arts of Eclectic," *The School Review* 79 (August 1971):493–542; "What Do Scientists Do?", *Behavioral Sciences* 5 (January 1960):1–27.

[20]Charles F. Westoff, "The Commission on Population Growth and the American Future," in *Sociology and Public Policy*, Mirra Komarovsky, ed., p. 54.

[21]Ibid., p. 55.

[22]In reviewing this chapter, Irving Janis noted that the uses of pluralism could be formulated in terms of the quality of the planning and decision-making process: the extensiveness of search; openness to a variety of kinds of relevant information concerning the consequences of proposed solutions; the range of possible solutions considered; alertness to contingencies that require special planning; and other factors. For an extensive analysis of decision making in these terms, see Irving Janis and Leon Mann, *Decision Making: A Psychological Analysis of Conflict, Choice and Commitment* (New York: The Free Press, 1977).

[23]Paul F. Lazarsfeld and Jeffrey G. Reitz, *An Introduction to Applied Sociology* (New York: Elsevier, 1975).

[24]*Sociology and Public Policy*, p. 49.

[25]Ibid., pp. 12, 13.

[26]Ibid., p. 109.

[27]Daniel Lerner and Harold D. Lasswell, eds., *The Policy Sciences* (Stanford: Stanford University Press, 1951) provides an early summary of the Lasswellian perspective; Lasswell provided a more recent statement in *Pre-View of Policy Sciences* (New York: Elsevier, 1971). For other formulations of the field, see James F. Reynolds, "Policy Sciences: A Conceptual and Methodological Analysis," *Policy Science* 6 (1975):1–27; Laurence H. Tribe, "Policy Science: Analysis or Ideology?" *Philosophy and Public Affairs* (Fall 1972):66–110; and Yehezkel Dror, *Design for Policy Sciences* (New York: Elsevier, 1971).

[28]The interest in unintended and unrecognized outcomes of social

action has a long, discontinuous history from at least the time of Machiavelli, with contributions by such scholars as Vico, Adam Smith, Marx, Wundt, and, to approach our own time, Pareto. The problematics is sketched out in Robert K. Merton, "The Unanticipated Consequences of Purposive Social Action," *American Sociological Review* 1 (1936):894–904; is renewed and developed in the special case of "The Self-Fulfilling Prophecy," *The Antioch Review* (Summer 1948):193–210 [reprinted as Chapter 10 of this volume]; is linked up with concepts of "Manifest and Latent Functions" in Merton, *Social Theory and Social Structure*, 1968 (originally published in 1949); and is brought to bear on "latent social problems" in Chapter 3 of this volume.

[29]Lionel Trilling, *Sincerity and Authenticity* (Cambridge, Mass.: Harvard University Press, 1972).

[30]A penetrating article can serve as a root reference to the rapidly growing library on the subject: Laurence H. Tribe, "Technology Assessment and the Fourth Discontinuity: The Limits of Instrumental Rationality," *Southern California Law Review* 46 (June 1973):617–660.

[31]W.I. and Dorothy S. Thomas, *The Child in America* (New York: Knopf, 1928).

[32]Richard Quinney, *The Social Reality of Crime* (Boston: Little, Brown, 1970), p. 4.

[33]Audible in Stinchcombe's aphorism is the echo of Marx's famous second paragraph of *The Eighteenth Brumaire of Louis Bonaparte:* "Men make their own history but they do not make it just as they please." As Marx goes on to explain: "They do not make it under circumstances chosen by themselves, but under circumstances found, given and transmitted from the past." Arthur L. Stinchcombe, "Merton's Theory of Social Structure," in *The Idea of Social Structure*, Lewis A. Coser, ed. (New York: Harcourt Brace Jovanovich, 1975), pp. 11–33, quoted at pp. 15–16. On the sociological significance of the same passage from Marx, see Rose Laub Coser, "The Complexity of Roles as a Seedbed of Individual Autonomy," ibid., pp. 239 ff.

[34]As is often the case with the fate of ideas in the course of their diffusion, it is not so much in the work of the principal initiators of the labeling perspective as in that of their epigoni that extreme subjectivism appears. The seminal works include: Edwin M. Lemert, *Human Deviance, Social Problems and Social Control* (Englewood Cliffs, N.J.: Prentice-Hall, 1967); Howard S. Becker, *The Outsiders*, 2nd ed. (New York: The Free Press, 1973); Kai T. Erikson, "Notes on the Sociology of Deviance," *Social Problems* 9 (1962):307–314, and *Wayward Puritans* (New York: John Wiley, 1966); John I. Kitsuse, "Societal Reaction to Deviant Behavior," *Social Problems* 9 (1962):247–256; Aaron V. Cicourel, *The Social Organization of Juvenile Justice* (New York: John Wiley, 1968). For a thoroughgoing critical review, see Edwin M. Schur, *Labeling Deviant Behavior: Its Sociological Implications* (New York: Harper & Rowe, 1971); Nanette J. Davis, "Labeling Theory in Deviance Research: A Critique and Reconsideration," *The Sociological Quarterly* 13 (Fall 1972):447–474.

[35]Robert K. Merton, "The Position of Sociological Theory," *American Sociological Review* 13 (April 1948):167.

[36]See Chapter 10 in this volume, "The Self-Fulfilling Prophecy."

[37]Joshua Lederberg, *A Tenth Anniversary Event: Remarks on the Tenth*

Anniversary of the National Institute of General Medical Sciences (Washington, D.C.: U.S. Department of Health, Education and Welfare Publication No. [NIH] 74-274, 1974), p. 16, emphasis in original.

CHAPTER **10**

The Self-Fulfilling Prophecy*

As we have just taken note, it was W.I. Thomas, then the dean of American sociologists, who set forth that theorem basic to the social sciences: "If men define situations as real, they are real in their consequences."** Although that pregnant theorem appeared only once in Thomas's voluminous writings and although it was then and there elucidated in only a single paragraph, it has claimed the attention of many for it possesses the gift of deep sociological relevance, being instructively applicable to a wide range of social processes.

*Reprinted with permission from *The Antioch Review* (Summer 1948):193–210.

**What we have been describing as the Thomas Theorem appears on page 572 of the book he wrote with Dorothy Swaine Thomas in 1928: *The Child in America* (New York: Knopf). I ascribe the theorem to W.I. Thomas alone rather than to the Thomases jointly because Dorothy, who became Dorothy Thomas Thomas when they were married eight years after that book appeared, confirmed that the consequential sentence and the paragraph in which it was encased were written by him. Thus, nothing in this attribution smacks of "the Matthew Effect," which operates in cases of collaboration between scholars of decidedly unequal reputation to ascribe all credit to the eminent scholar and little or none to the collaborator(s)—supplementary note, 1982.

THE THOMAS THEOREM

There is all the more reason to assume that Thomas had hold of a crucial idea when we note that essentially the same theorem had been aperiodically stated by observant and disciplined minds long before. When we find such otherwise discrepant minds as the redoubtable Bishop Bossuet in his passionate seventeenth-century defense of Catholic orthodoxy; the ironic Mandeville in his eighteenth-century allegory, *The Fable of the Bees*, honeycombed with observations on the paradoxes of human society; the irascible genius of social science Marx, in his revision of Hegel's theory of historical change; the seminal Freud in works which have perhaps gone further than any others of his day toward modifying our outlook on men and women; and the erudite, dogmatic, and often sound Yale professor, William Graham Sumner, who lives on as spokesman for the middle classes—when we find this mixed company (and I select from a longer if less celebrated list) agreeing on the truth and the pertinence of what is substantially the Thomas Theorem, we may conclude that perhaps it is worth our attention as well.

To what, then, are Thomas and Bossuet, Mandeville, Marx, Freud, and Sumner directing our attention?

The first part of the theorem provides an unceasing reminder that we respond not only to the objective features of a situation, but also, and at times primarily, to the meaning this situation has for us. And once we have assigned some meaning to the situation, our consequent behavior and some of the consequences of that behavior are determined by the ascribed meaning. But this is rather abstract, and sociological abstractions have a way of becoming unintelligible if they are not occasionally tried to concrete data. What is a case in point?

A SOCIOLOGICAL PARABLE

It is the year 1932. The Last National Bank is a flourishing institution. A large part of its resources is liquid without being watered. Cartwright Millingville has ample reason to be proud of the banking institution over which he presides. Until Black Wednesday. As he enters his bank, he notices that business is unusually brisk. A little odd, that, since the workers at the A.M.O.K. steel plant and the K.O.M.A. mattress factory usually are not paid until Saturday. Yet here are two dozen workers, obviously from the factories, queued up in front of the tellers' cages. As he turns into his private office, Millingville muses rather compassionately: "Hope they haven't been laid off in midweek. They should be in the shop at this hour."

But speculations of this sort have never made for a thriving bank, and Millingville turns to the pile of documents upon his desk. His precise signature is affixed to fewer than a score of papers when he is disturbed by the absence of something familiar and the intrusion of something alien. The low discreet hum of bank business has given way to a strange and annoying stridency of many voices. A situation has been defined as real. And that is the beginning of what ends as Black Wednesday—the last Wednesday, it may be noted, of the Last National Bank.

Cartwright Millingville had never heard of the Thomas theorem. But he had no difficulty in recognizing a special case of its workings. He knew that, despite the comparative liquidity of the bank's assets, a rumor of insolvency, once believed by enough depositors, would result in the insolvency of the bank. And by the close of Black Wednesday—and Blacker Thursday—when the long lines of anxious depositors, frantically seeking to salvage their own, grew to longer lines of even more anxious depositors, it turned out that he was right.

The stable financial structure of the bank had depended upon one set of definitions of the situation: belief in the validity of the interlocking system of economic promises people live by. Once depositors defined the situation otherwise, once they questioned the possibility of having these promises fulfilled, the consequences of this unreal definition were real enough.

A familiar case this, and one doesn't need the Thomas theorem to understand how it happened—not, at least, if one is old enough to have voted for Franklin Roosevelt in 1932. But perhaps with the aid of the theorem the tragic history of Millingville's bank can be converted into a sociological parable which may help us understand not only what happened to hundreds of banks in the 1930s, but also what still happens to relations between blacks and whites, between Protestants and Catholics and Jews in these days.

VARIETIES OF SELF-FULFILLING PROPHECY

The parable tells us that certain kinds of definitions of a situation—we focus on the important class of *public* prophecies, beliefs, and expectations—become an integral part of the situation and thus affect subsequent developments. This is peculiar to human affairs. It is not found in the world of nature, untouched by human hands. Predictions of the return of Halley's comet do not influence its orbit. But the rumored insolvency of Millingville's bank did affect the actual outcome. The prophecy of collapse led to its fulfillment.

The self-fulfilling prophecy is, in the beginning, a *false* definition of the situation evoking behavior which makes the originally false conception come true. The specious validity of the self-fulfilling prophecy perpetuates a reign of error. For the prophet will cite the actual course of events as proof that he was right from the beginning. (Yet we know that Millingville's bank was solvent, that it would have survived for years had not the misleading rumor *created* the conditions of its own fulfillment.) Such are the perversities of social logic.[1]

The self-fulfilling prophecy works its ways in every sphere of human experience, *social or public and individual or private.* The *social type* involves prophecy-dominated interactions between individuals and between collectivities. Thus, the political leaders of hostile nations become persuaded that war between them is inevitable. Actuated by this conviction, they become successively more alienated from one another, apprehensively countering each "offensive" move of the other with a "defensive" move of their own. Stockpiles of armaments, raw materials, and armed men and women grow ever larger, and in due course the anticipation of war helps create the actuality. The examination neurosis provides a familiar case of the *individual or private type* of self-fulfilling prophecy. Groundlessly convinced that he is destined to fail, the anxious student devotes more time and energy to worry than to study and then, not altogether surprisingly, turns in a poor examination. The initially fallacious expectation makes for a seemingly confirming outcome.

It is the social or public self-fulfilling prophecy which goes far toward explaining the dynamics of ethnic and racial conflict in the America of today. That this is the case, at least for relations between blacks and whites, may be gathered from the 1,500 pages which make up Gunnar Myrdal's *An American Dilemma.*[2] That the self-fulfilling prophecy has even more general bearing upon the relations between ethnic groups than Myrdal has indicated is the thesis of the considerably briefer discussion that follows.

SOCIAL BELIEFS AND SOCIAL REALITY

As a result of their failure to comprehend the operation of the self-fulfilling prophecy, many Americans of goodwill (sometimes re-

luctantly) retain enduring ethnic and racial prejudices. They experience these beliefs not as prejudices, not as prejudgments, but as
irresistible products of personal observation. "The facts of the case"
permit them no other conclusion.

Thus, fair-minded white citizens strongly support a policy of
excluding blacks from their labor unions. Their views are, of course,
based not upon prejudice, but upon the cold, hard facts. And the
facts seem clear enough. Blacks, "lately from the nonindustrial South,
are undisciplined in traditions of trade unionism and the art of collective bargaining." Black workers are strikebreakers. With their "low
standard of living," the blacks rush in to take jobs at less than prevailing wages. The black workers are, in short, "traitors to the working
class," and should manifestly be excluded from union organizations.*
So run the facts of the case as seen by our tolerant but hard-headed
union members, innocent of any understanding of the self-fulfilling
prophecy as a basic process of society.

Our unionists fail to see, of course, that they have produced the
very "facts" which they sometimes observe. For by defining the situation as one in which blacks are held to be incorrigibly at odds with
principles of unionism and by excluding them from unions, the
unionists then invite a series of consequences which indeed make it
difficult if not impossible for many blacks to avoid the role of scab.
Out of work after World War I, and kept out of unions, thousands
of blacks could not resist strikebound employers who invitingly held
a door open upon a world of jobs from which they were otherwise
excluded.

History creates its own test of the theory of self-fulfilling prophecies. That some black workers were strikebreakers because they were
excluded from unions (and from a wide range of jobs) rather than
excluded because they were strikebreakers was shown in the last
decades by their virtual disappearance as scabs in industries where
they gained admission to unions.

The application of the Thomas Theorem also suggests how the
tragic, often vicious, circle of self-fulfilling prophecies can be broken.
The initial definition of the situation which has set the circle in motion
must be abandoned. Only when the originating assumption is questioned and a new definition of the situation introduced, does the
consequent flow of events give the lie to the assumption. Only then
does the belief no longer father the reality.

But to question these deep-rooted definitions of the situation

---

*This stands as written more than a generation ago. The far greater
extent to which blacks now take part in unions is one measure of social
change in this sphere—editors' note.

is no simple act of the will. The will, or for that matter, goodwill, cannot be turned on and off like a faucet. Social intelligence and goodwill are themselves *products* of distinct social forces. They are not brought into being by mass propaganda and mass education, in the usual sense of these terms so dear to the sociological panaceans. No more in the social realm than in the psychological realm do false ideas quietly vanish when confronted with the truth. No one expects a paranoiac to abandon hard-won distortions and delusions upon being informed that they are altogether groundless. If psychic ills could be cured merely by the dissemination of truth, psychiatrists would suffer from technological unemployment rather than over-work. Nor will a continuing "educational campaign" itself destroy racial prejudice and discrimination.

This is not a particularly popular position. The appeal to education as a cure-all for the most varied social problems is rooted deep in the mores of America. Yet it is nonetheless illusory for all that. For how would this program of racial education proceed? Who is to do the educating? The teachers in our communities? But, in some measure like many other Americans, the teachers share the same prejudices they are being urged to combat. And when they don't, aren't they being asked to serve as conscientious martyrs in the cause of educational utopianism? How long the tenure of elementary schoolteachers in racist communities who attempt meticulously to disabuse their young pupils of the racial beliefs they acquired at home? Education may serve as an operational adjunct but not as the chief basis for any except excruciatingly slow change in the prevailing patterns of race relations.

To understand further why educational campaigns cannot be counted on to eliminate prevailing ethnic hostilities, we must examine the operation of in-groups and out-groups in our society. Ethnic out-groups, to adopt Sumner's useful bit of sociological vernacular, con-sist of all those who are believed to differ significantly from "our-selves" in terms of nationality, race, or religion. The counterpart of the ethnic out-group is of course the ethnic in-group, constituted by those who "belong." Nothing is fixed or eternal about the lines sep-arating the in-group from out-groups. As situations change, the lines of separation change. For a large number of white Americans, Joe Louis was a member of an out-group—when the situation was de-fined in racial terms. On another occasion, when Louis defeated the nazified Schmeling, many of these same white Americans acclaimed him as a member of the (national) in-group. National loyalty took precedence over racial separatism. These abrupt shifts in group boundaries sometimes prove embarrassing. Thus, when black Amer-icans ran away with the honors in the Olympic games held in Berlin, the Nazis, pointing to the second-class citizenship assigned blacks in various regions of this country, denied that the United States had really won the games, since by our own admission the black athletes were "not full-fledged" Americans. And what could Bilbo or Rankin[3] say to that?

Under the benevolent guidance of the dominant in-group, ethnic out-groups are continuously subjected to a lively process of prejudice which goes far toward vitiating mass education and mass propaganda for ethnic tolerance. This is the process whereby "in-group virtues become out-group vices," to paraphrase a remark by the sociologist Donald Young.[4] Or, more colloquially and perhaps more instructively, it may be called the "damned-if-you-do and damned-if-you-don't" pattern in ethnic and racial relations.

IN-GROUP VIRTUES AND OUT-GROUP VICES

To discover that ethnic out-groups are damned if they do embrace the values of white Protestant society and damned if they don't, we turn to one of the in-group culture heroes, examine the qualities with which he is endowed by biographers and popular belief, and thus distill the qualities of mind and action and character which are generally regarded as altogether admirable.

Periodic public opinion polls are not needed to justify the selection of Abe Lincoln as the culture hero who most fully embodies the cardinal American virtues. As the Lynds point out in *Middletown*,[5] the people of that typical small city allow George Washington alone to join Lincoln as the greatest of Americans. He is claimed as their very own by almost as many well-to-do Republicans as by less well-to-do Democrats.[6]

Even the inevitable schoolboy knows that Lincoln was thrifty, hard-working, ambitious, eager for knowledge, devoted to the rights of the average man and eminently successful in climbing the ladder of opportunity from the lowermost rung of laborer to the respectable heights of merchant and lawyer. (We need follow his dizzying ascent no further.)

If one did not know that these attributes and achievements are numbered high among the values of middle-class America, one would soon discover it by glancing through the Lynds' account of "The Middletown Spirit." For there we find the image of the Great Emancipator fully reflected in the values in which Middletown believes. And since these are their values, it is not surprising to find the Middletowns of America condemning and disparaging those individuals and groups who fail, presumably, to exhibit these virtues. If it appears to the white in-group that blacks are *not* educated in the same measure as themselves, that they have an "unduly" high proportion of un-skilled workers and an "unduly" low proportion of successful business and professional men and women, that they are thriftless, and so on through the catalogue of middle-class virtue and sin, it is not difficult to understand the charge that "the black" is "inferior" to "the white."

Sensitized to the workings of the self-fulfilling prophecy, we should be prepared to find that the antiblack charges which are not patently false are only speciously true. The allegations are true in the Pickwickian sense that we have found self-fulfilling prophecies in general to be true. Thus, if the dominant in-group believes that blacks are inferior, and sees to it that funds for education are not "wasted on these incompetents," and then proclaims as final evidence of this inferiority that blacks have proportionately "only" one-fifth as many college graduates as whites,* one can scarcely be amazed by this transparent bit of social legerdemain. Having seen the rabbit carefully though not too adroitly placed in the hat, we can only look askance at the triumphant air with which it is finally produced. (In fact, it is a little embarrassing to note that a larger proportion of black than of white high school graduates have gone on to college; apparently, the black students who are hardy enough to scale the high walls of discrimination represent an even more highly selected group than the run-of-the-high-school white population.)

So, too, when Senator Bilbo, the gentleman from Mississippi (a state which then spent five times as much on the average white pupil as on the average black pupil), proclaimed the essential infe-riority of blacks by pointing to the per capita ratio of physicians among them as less than one-fourth that of whites, we are impressed more by his scrambled logic than by his profound prejudices. So plain is the mechanism of the self-fulfilling prophecy in these in-stances that only those forever devoted to the victory of sentiment over fact can take such specious evidence seriously. Yet the specious evidence often creates a genuine belief. Self-hypnosis through one's own propaganda is a not infrequent phase of the self-fulfilling proph-ecy.

So much for out-groups being damned if they don't (apparently) manifest in-group virtues. It is a tasteless bit of ethnocentrism, sea-soned with self-interest. But what of the second phase of this process? Are out-groups also damned if they *do* possess these virtues? They are.

*Again, this remains as written in 1948. Social change in this sphere continues—editors' note.

Through a faultlessly bisymmetrical prejudice, ethnic and racial out-groups get it coming and going. The systematic condemnation of the out-grouper continues largely *irrespective of what he does.* More: through a freakish exercise of capricious judicial logic, the victim is punished for the crime.[7] Superficial appearances notwithstanding, prejudice and discrimination aimed at the out-group are not a result of what the out-group does, but are rooted deep in the structure of our society and the social psychology of its members.

To understand how this happens, we must examine the moral alchemy through which the in-group readily transmutes virtue into vice and vice into virtue, as the occasion may demand. Our studies will proceed by the case-method.

We begin with the engagingly simple formula of moral alchemy: the same behavior must be differently evaluated according to the person who exhibits it. For example, the proficient alchemist knows that the word "firm" is properly declined as follows:

> I am firm,
> Thou are obstinate,
> He is pigheaded.

There are some, unversed in the skills of this science, who will tell you that one and the same term should be applied to all three instances of identical behavior. Such unalchemical nonsense should simply be ignored.

With this experiment in mind, we are prepared to observe how the very same behavior undergoes a complete change of evaluation in its transition from the in-group Abe Lincoln to the out-group Abe Cohen or Abe Kurokawa. We proceed systematically. Did Lincoln work far into the night? This testifies that he was industrious, resolute, perseverant, and eager to realize his capacities to the full. Do the out-group Jews or Japanese keep these same hours? This only bears witness to their sweatshop mentality, their ruthless undercutting of American standards, their unfair competitive practices. Is the in-group hero frugal, thrifty, and sparing? Then the out-group villain is stingy, miserly, and penny-pinching. All honor is due the in-group Abe for having been smart, shrewd, and intelligent, and, by the same token, all contempt is owing the out-group Abes for being sharp, cunning, crafty, and too clever by far. Did the indomitable Lincoln refuse to remain content with a life of work with his hands? Did he prefer to use his brain? Then all praise for his plucky climb up the shaky ladder of opportunity. But, of course, the shunning of manual work for brain work among the merchants and lawyers of the out-group deserves nothing but censure for their having chosen a parasitic way of life.

Was Abe Lincoln eager to learn the accumulated wisdom of the ages by unending study? The trouble with Jews is that they're greasy grinds, with their heads always in a book, while decent people are going to a show or a ball game. Was the resolute Lincoln unwilling to limit his standards to those of his provincial community? We should expect no less of a man of vision. But if the out-groupers criticize the vulnerable areas in our society, send 'em back where they came from. Did Lincoln, rising high above his origins, never forget the rights of the common man and applaud the right of workers to strike? This testifies only that, like all real Americans, this greatest of Americans was deathlessly devoted to the cause of freedom. But, as you examine the statistics on strikes, remember that this un-American practice is the result of out-groupers pursuing their evil agitation among otherwise contented workers.

Once stated, the classical formula of moral alchemy is clear enough. Through the adroit use of these rich vocabularies of encomium and opprobrium, the in-group readily transmutes its own virtues into others' vices. But why do so many in-groupers qualify as moral alchemists? Why are so many in the dominant in-group so fully devoted to this continuing experiment in moral transmutation?

An explanation may be found by putting ourselves at some distance from this country and following the anthropologist Malinowski to the Trobriand Islands.[8] For there we find an instructively similar pattern. Among the Trobrianders, to a degree which Americans, despite Hollywood and the confession magazines, have apparently not yet approximated, success with women confers honor and prestige on a man. Sexual prowess is a positive value, a moral virtue. But if a rank-and-file Trobriander has "too much" sexual success, if he achieves "too many" triumphs of the heart, an achievement which should of course be limited to the elite, the chiefs, or men of power, then this glorious record becomes a scandal and an abomination. The chiefs are quick *to resent any personal achievement not warranted by social position.* The moral virtues remain virtues only so long as they are jealously confined to the proper in-group. The right activity by the wrong people becomes a thing of contempt, not of honor. For clearly, only in this way, by holding these virtues exclusively to themselves, can the men of power retain their distinction, their prestige, and their power. No wiser procedure could be devised to hold intact a system of social stratification and social power.

The Trobrianders could teach us more. For it seems clear that the chiefs have not calculatedly devised this program for entrenching their power. Their behavior is spontaneous, unthinking, and immediate. Their resentment of "too much" ambition or "too much" success for the ordinary Trobriander is not contrived; it is genuine.

It just happens that this prompt emotional response to the "mis-placed" manifestation of in-group virtues also serves the useful ex-pedient of reinforcing the chiefs' special claims to the good things of Trobriand life. Nothing could be more remote from the truth and more distorted a reading of the facts than to assume that this con-version of in-group virtues into out-group vices is part of a deliberate plot of Trobriand chiefs to keep Trobriand commoners in their place. It is merely that the chiefs have been indoctrinated with an appre-ciation of the proper order of things, and see it as their heavy burden to enforce the mediocrity of others.

Nor, in quick revulsion from the culpabilities of the moral alche-mists, need we succumb to the equivalent error of simply upending the moral status of the in-group and the out-groups. It is not that Jews and blacks are one and all angelic while Gentiles and whites are one and all fiendish. It is not that individual virtue will now be found exclusively on the wrong side of the ethnic-racial tracks and individual viciousness on the right side. Conceivably there are as many corrupt and vicious men and women among Jews and blacks as among Gentile whites. It is only that the ugly fence enclosing the in-group happens to exclude the people who make up the out-groups from being treated with decency.

SOCIAL FUNCTIONS AND DYSFUNCTIONS

We have only to look at the consequences of this peculiar moral alchemy to see that there is no paradox at all in damning out-groupers when they do and when they don't exhibit in-group virtues. Con-demnation on these two scores performs one and the same social function. Seeming opposites coalesce. When blacks are tagged as incorrigibly inferior because they (apparently) don't manifest these virtues, this confirms the natural rightness of their being assigned an inferior status in society. And when Jews or Japanese are seen as having too much of the fruits of in-group values, it becomes plain that they must be securely controlled by the high walls of discrimi-nation. In both cases, the special status assigned the several out-groups can be seen to be eminently reasonable.

Yet this distinctly reasonable arrangement persists in having most unreasonable consequences, both logical and social. Consider only a few of these.

In some contexts, the limitations enforced upon the out-group— say, rationing the number of Jews permitted to enter colleges and professional schools—logically imply a fear of the alleged superiority of the out-group. Were it otherwise, no discrimination need be practiced. The unyielding, impersonal forces of academic competition would soon trim down the number of Jewish (or Japanese or black) students to an "appropriate" size.

This implied belief in the superiority of the out-group seems premature. There is simply not enough scientific evidence to demonstrate Jewish or Japanese or black superiority. The effort of the in-group discriminator to supplant the myth of Aryan superiority with the myth of non-Aryan superiority is condemned to failure by science. Moreover, such myths are ill-advised. Eventually, a world of myth must collide with a world of reality. As a matter of simple self-interest and social therapy, therefore, the in-group might be wise to abandon the myth and cling to the reality.

The pattern of being damned-if-you-do and damned-if-you-don't has further consequences for out-group members. Their response to alleged deficiencies is as clear as it is predictable. If one is told repeatedly that one is inferior, that one lacks any positive accomplishments, it is all too human to seize upon every bit of evidence to the contrary. The in-group definitions force upon the allegedly inferior out-group a defensive tendency to magnify and exalt "race accomplishments." As the distinguished black sociologist, E. Franklin Frazier, has noted, the black newspapers are "intensely race conscious and exhibit considerable pride in the achievements of the Negro most of which are meager performances as measured by broader standards." Self-glorification, found in some measure among all groups, becomes a frequent counter-response to persistant belittlement from without.

It is the damnation of out-groups for excessive achievement, however, which gives rise to truly bizarre behavior. For, after a time and often as a matter of self-defense, these out-groups become persuaded that their virtues really are vices. And this provides the final episode in a tragicomedy of inverted values.

Let us try to follow the plot through its intricate maze of self-contradictions. Respectful admiration for the arduous climb from office boy to president is rooted deep in American culture. This long and strenuous ascent carries with it a twofold testimonial: first, that careers are abundantly open to genuine talent in American society; second, that individuals who have distinguished themselves by their heroic rise are praiseworthy. It would be invidious to choose among the many stalwart figures who fought their way up, against all odds, until they reached the summit, there to sit at the head of the long conference table in the longer conference room of The Board. Taken at random, the saga of Frederick H. Ecker, once chairman of the board of one of the largest privately managed corporations in the world, the Metropolitan Life Insurance Company, will suffice as the prototype. From a menial and poorly paid job, he rose to a position of eminence. Understandably enough, an unceasing flow of honors came to this man of large power and large achievement. It so happens, though it is a matter personal to this eminent man of finance, that Mr. Ecker was a Presbyterian. Yet at last report, no elder of the Presbyterian church had risen publicly to announce that Mr. Ecker's successful career should not be taken too seriously, that, after all, relatively few Presbyterians have risen from rags to riches, and that Presbyterians do not actually "control" the world of life insurance or finance or investment housing. Rather, one would suppose, Presbyterian elders joined with other Americans imbued with middle-class standards of success to felicitate the eminently successful Mr. Ecker and to acclaim other sons and daughters of the faith who have risen to almost equal heights. Secure in their in-group status, they point the finger of pride rather than the finger of dismay at individual success.

Prompted by the practice of moral alchemy, noteworthy achievements by out-groupers can elicit other responses. Patently, if achievement is a vice, then achievements must be disclaimed—or at least, discounted. Under these conditions, an occasion for Presbyterian pride can become an occasion for Jewish dismay. If the Jew is condemned for educational or professional or scientific or economic success, then, understandably enough, many Jews will come to feel that these accomplishments must be minimized in simple self-defense. Thus is the circle of paradox closed by out-groupers busily engaged in assuring the powerful in-group that they have not, in fact, been guilty of inordinate contributions to science, the professions, the arts, the government, and the economy.

In a society which ordinarily looks upon wealth as a warrant of one kind of ability, an out-group is compelled by the inverted attitudes of the dominant in-group to deny that many men and women of wealth are among its members. "Among the 200 largest non-banking corporations. . .only ten have a Jew as president or chairman of the board." Is this an observation of an anti-Semite, intent on proving the incapacity and inferiority of Jews who have done so little "to build the corporations which have built America?" No; it is a response of the Anti-Defamation League of B'nai B'rith to anti-Semitic propaganda.

In a society where, as a survey by the National Opinion Research Center has shown, the profession of medicine ranks highest in social prestige among ninety occupations, we find some Jewish spokesmen maneuvered by the attacking in-group into the position of announcing their "deep concern" over the number of Jews in medical practice, which is "disproportionate to the number of Jews in other occupations." The oversupply of Jewish doctors becomes a deplorable situation meriting deep concern, rather than a joyous accomplishment meriting applause for their hard-won acquisition of knowledge and skills and for their social utility. Only when the New York Yankees publicly announce deep concern over their numerous World Series triumphs, so disproportionate to the number achieved by other major league teams, will this self-abnegation seem part of the normal order of things.

In a society which consistently judges professionals as higher in social value than even the most skilled hewers of wood and drawers of water, the out-group finds itself in the anomalous position of pointing with defensive relief to the large number of Jewish painters and paperhangers, plasterers and electricians, plumbers and sheet-metal workers.

But the ultimate reversal of values is yet to be noted. Each succeeding census finds more Americans in the city and its suburbs. Americans have traveled the road to urbanization until fewer than one-fifth of the nation's population live on farms. Plainly, it is high time for the Methodist and the Catholic, the Baptist and the Episcopalian to recognize the iniquity of this trek of their coreligionists to the city. For, as is well known, one of the central accusations leveled against Jews is their heinous tendency to live in cities. Jewish leaders, therefore, find themselves maneuvered into the position of defensively urging their people to move into the very farm areas being hastily vacated by city-bound hordes of Christians. Perhaps this is not altogether necessary. As the Jewish crime of urbanism becomes ever more popular among the in-group, it may be reshaped into transcendent virtue. But, admittedly, one can't be certain. For in this daft confusion of inverted values, it soon becomes impossible to determine when virtue is sin and sin, moral perfection.

Amid this confusion, one fact remains unambiguous. The Jews, like other peoples, have made distinguished contributions to world culture. Consider only an abbreviated catalogue. The field of creative literature (with acknowledgment of large variations in the caliber of achievement) includes Heine, Kraus, Borne, Hofmannsthal, Schnitzler, Kafka. In the realm of musical composition, there are Meyerbeer, Mendelssohn, Offenbach, Mahler, and Schonberg. Among the musical virtuosi, consider only Rosenthal, Schnabel, Godowsky, Pachmann, Kreisler, Hubermann, Milstein, Elman, Heifetz, Joachim, and Menuhin. And among scientists of a stature sufficient to merit the Nobel prize, examine the familiar list which includes Bárány, Mayerhof, Ehrlich, Michelson, Lippmann, Haber, Willstätter, and Einstein.[9] Or in the esoteric and imaginative universe of mathematical invention, take note only of Kronecker, the creator of the modern theory of numbers; Hermann Minkowski,* who supplied the mathematical foundations of the special theory of relativity; or Jacobi, with his basic work in the theory of elliptical functions. And so through each special province of cultural achievement, we are supplied with a list of preeminent men and women who happened to be Jews.

And who is thus busily engaged in singing the praises of the Jews? Who has so assiduously compiled the list of many hundreds of distinguished Jews who contributed notably to science, literature, and the arts—a list from which these few cases were excerpted? A philo-Semite, eager to demonstrate that the Jews have contributed their due share to world culture? No, by now we should know better than that. The complete list is found in the thirty-sixth edition of the anti-Semitic handbook by the racist Fritsch. In accord with the alchemical formula for transmuting in-group virtues into out-group vices, he presents this as a roll call of sinister spirits who have usurped the accomplishments properly owing the Aryan in-group.

Once we comprehend the predominant role of the in-group in defining the situation, the further paradox of the seemingly opposed behavior of the black out-group and the Jewish out-group falls away. The behavior of both minority groups is in response to the majority-group allegations.

If blacks are accused of inferiority, and their alleged failure to contribute proportionately to world culture is cited in support of this accusation, the human urge for self-respect and concern for security lead some of them *defensively* to magnify each and every achievement by members of the race. If Jews are accused of excessive achievements and excessive ambitions, and lists of preeminent Jews are compiled in support of this accusation, then the urge for security leads some of them *defensively* to minimize the actual achievements of members of the group. Apparently opposed types of behavior have much the same psychological and social functions. Self-assertion and self-effacement become devices for seeking to cope with condemnation for alleged group deficiencies and condemnation for alleged group excesses, respectively. And with a fine sense of moral superiority, the secure in-group looks on these curious performances by the out-groups with mingled derision and contempt.

---

*Obviously, the forename must be explicitly mentioned, else Hermann Minkowski, the mathematician, may be confused with Eugen Minkowski (who contributed so notably to our knowledge of schizophrenia), or with Mieczyslaw Minkowski (high in the ranks of brain anatomists), or even with Oskar Minkowski (discoverer of pancreatic diabetes).

ENACTED INSTITUTIONAL CHANGE

Will this desolate tragicomedy run on and on, marked only by minor changes in the cast? Not necessarily.

Were moral scruples and a sense of decency the only bases for bringing the play to an end, it would continue its run indefinitely. In and of themselves, moral sentiments are not much more effective in curing social ills than in curing physical ills. Moral sentiments no doubt help to motivate efforts for change, but they are no substitute for hardheaded institutional arrangements designed to achieve the objective, as the thickly populated graveyard of softheaded utopias bears witness.

There are ample indications that a deliberate and planned halt can be put to the workings of the self-fulfilling prophecy and the vicious circle in society. The sequel to our sociological parable of the Last National Bank provides one clue to the way in which this can be achieved. During the fabulous 1920s, when Coolidge undoubtedly caused a Republican era of lush prosperity, an annual average of 635 banks quietly suspended operations. And during the four years immediately before and after The Crash, when Hoover undoubtedly did not cause a Republican era of sluggish depression, this zoomed to the more spectacular average of 2,276 bank suspensions annually. But, interestingly enough, in the twelve years following the establishment of the Federal Deposit Insurance Corporation and the enactment of other banking legislation, while Roosevelt presided over Democratic depression and revival, recession and boom, bank suspensions dropped to a niggardly average of twenty-eight a year. Perhaps money panics have not been exorcized by legislation. Nevertheless, millions of depositors no longer have occasion to give way to panic-motivated runs on banks simply because deliberate institutional change has removed the grounds for panic. Occasions for racial hostility are no more inborn psychological constants than are occasions for panic. Despite the teachings of amateur psychologists, blind panic and racial aggression are not rooted in human nature. These patterns of human behavior are largely a product of the modifiable structure of society.

For a further clue, return to the instance of widespread hostility of white unionists toward black strikebreakers brought into industry by employers after the close of the very first World War. Once the initial definition of blacks as not deserving of union membership had largely broken down, black workers with a wider range of opportunities no longer found it necessary to enter industry through doors held open by strikebound employers. Again, appropriate institutional change broke through the tragic circle of the self-fulfilling prophecy. Deliberate social change gave the lie to the firm conviction that "it just ain't in the nature of the Nigra" to join trade unions.

A final instance is drawn from a study of a public biracial housing project, one of the first to be established in this country.[10] Located in Pittsburgh, the community of Hilltown is made up of 50 percent black families and 50 percent white. It is not a twentieth-century utopia. There is some interpersonal friction here as elsewhere. Still, in a community made up of equal numbers of the two races, fewer than a fifth of the whites and a third of the blacks report that this friction occurs between members of *different* races. By their own testimony, it is largely confined to disagreements *within* each racial group. Yet only one in every twenty-five whites initially *expected* relations between the races in the community to run smoothly, whereas five times as many expected serious trouble, the remainder anticipating a tolerable, if not altogether pleasant, situation. So much for expectations. Upon reviewing their actual experience, three of every four of the most apprehensive whites subsequently found that the "races get along fairly well," after all. This is not the place to report the findings of this study in detail, but substantially these demonstrate anew that under *appropriate institutional and administrative conditions,* the experience of interracial amity can supplant the fear of interracial conflict.

These changes, and others of the same kind, do not occur automatically. *The self-fulfilling prophecy, whereby fears are translated into reality, operates only in the absence of deliberate institutional controls.* And it is only with the rejection of social fatalism implied in the notion of unchangeable human nature that the tragic circle of fear, social disaster, and reinforced fear can be broken.

Ethnic prejudices do die—but slowly. They can be helped over the threshold of oblivion not by insisting that it is unreasonable and unworthy of them to survive but by cutting off the sustenance now provided them by certain social institutions.

If we find ourselves doubting the human capability to control society, if we persist in the tendency to find in the patterns of the past the chart of the future, it is perhaps time to take up anew the wisdom of Tocqueville's century-old remark: "I am tempted to believe that what we call necessary institutions are often no more than institutions to which we have grown accustomed, and that in matters of social constitution the field of possibilities is much more extensive than men living in their various societies are ready to imagine."

Nor can widespread, even typical, failures in planning human relations between ethnic groups be cited as evidence for pessimism. In the world laboratory of the sociologist, as in the more secluded laboratories of the physicist and chemist, it is the successful experiment which is decisive, not the thousand-and-one failures which preceded it. More is learned from the single success than from multiple failures. A single success proves it can be done. Thereafter, it is necessary only to learn what made it work. This, at least, is what I take to be the sociological sense of those revealing words of Thomas Love Peacock: "Whatever is, is possible."*

*This concluding sentence should perhaps be amended. For during the third-of-a-century since it was first put into print, I have been periodically asked to indicate *where* Peacock stated the epigram. The question has grown more embarrassing with every repetition. The facts of the case, so far as I am able to reconstruct them, are these: In my youth, I became strangely addicted to Peacock's satiric novels, with their graceful language, acute wit, and often alliterated titles (*Crotchet Castle, Headlong Hall, Maid Marian,* and *Gryll Grange*). In due course, I put away these eccentric conversational pieces. But when I was searching for a way of summing up the reasons for believing that the self-fulfilling prophecy can be institutionally controlled, I evidently dredged up a seeming memory trace which had Peacock stating in playful and pithy style what I wanted to say. And so I emerged with the aphorism I ascribed to him: Whatever is, is possible. Later, when I found myself repeatedly asked to cite the precise source in Peacock, I paid the price of not having recorded the reference. Once again, my bedtime reading was devoted, with somewhat less pleasure than before, to Peacock's considerable writings. To no avail. The experience has begun to give me pause. Perhaps Thomas Love Peacock never delivered himself of this philosophical and sociological epigram; perhaps I am the victim of a false memory. Perhaps it was some other novelist or poet or philosopher.

Indeed, a colleague of mine, William J. Goode, learning of my failure to locate the aphorism in Peacock, became persuaded that it was originated by James Thurber. He accordingly wrote to Thurber's widow only to be told that she had never read this "law" in any of her husband's many works, that she had never heard him state it in conversations and, to close the matter once and for all, that it "really doesn't sound like him."

But if not Peacock and not Thurber, another possibility springs to mind. Perhaps I had engaged in a kind of retroactive ghostwriting. Once having hit upon the existential theorem that "whatever is, is possible," perhaps I had unaccountably (though surely not mischievously) ascribed it to that youthfully favorite novelist of mine. If so, it was a substantively inept ascription. For if Peacock had originated—or, to keep the door open, if he did in fact originate—the epigrammatic theorem, he would surely have meant it in a sense remote from my own. I had introduced it to argue that, however fanciful or repugnant a social innovation may seem to some, if it has succeeded even once, then it demonstrates that the seemingly impossible is quite possible. "A single success proves it can be done. Thereafter, it is necessary only to learn what made it work."

But Peacock would scarcely have drawn this sociological moral. His life long, he resisted innovation, social and other. All his graceful conversational novels—not least, his last, long-postponed and summational novel, *Gryll Grange*—vigorously express his hearty distaste for science and its technological offshoots.

Since the third part of a century has gone by since I assigned the theorem to Thomas Love Peacock, and since neither he nor anyone of his presentday fans has risen up to document that ascription, perhaps the statute of limitations governing intellectual property has run its course. Perhaps I should amend that concluding sentence to incorporate this short tale of its history by having it say: ". . . those revealing words which I once ascribed to Thomas Love Peacock: 'Whatever is, is possible.' " (Note appended 1982.)

NOTES

[1]The counterpart of the self-fulfilling prophecy is the self-defeating (or "suicidal") prophecy which so alters human behavior from what would have been its course had it not been made, that it *fails* to be borne out. So it is that in occasional elections where large numbers of constituents come to believe that their candidate is bound to win, sizable fractions fail to vote and the prophecy destroys itself. This important class of consequential prophecies is not considered here. On it, see R.K. Merton, "The Unanticipated Consequences of Purposive Social Action," *American Sociological Review* 1 (1936):894–904, especially pp. 903–904, reprinted in Merton, *Sociological Ambivalence* (New York: The Free Press, 1976), pp. 145–155, especially pp. 154–155. For examples of both types of social prophecy, see Robert M. MacIver, *The More Perfect Union* (New York: Macmillan, 1948).

[2]Gunnar Myrdal, *An American Dilemma:* The Negro Problem and Modern Democracy (New York: Harper and Row, 1944)—editors' note.

[3]Two Southern congressmen in the 1940s known for their extreme racist views—editors' note.

[4]Donald Young, *American Minority Peoples* (New York: Harper, 1932).

[5]Robert S. Lynd and Helen M. Lynd, *Middletown* (New York: Harcourt Brace, 1929).

[6]On Lincoln as culture hero, see the perceptive essay, "Getting Right with Lincoln," by David Donald, *Lincoln Reconsidered* (New York: Alfred A. Knopf, 1956), pp. 3–18.

Though Lincoln nominally remains, of course, the symbolic leader of the Republicans, this may be just another paradox of political history of the same kind which Lincoln noted in his day with regard to Jefferson and the Democrats.

"Remembering, too, that the Jefferson party was formed upon its supposed superior devotion to the personal rights of men, holding the rights of property to be secondary only, and greatly inferior, and assuming that the so-called Democrats of to-day are the Jefferson, and their opponents the anti-Jefferson, party, it will be equally interesting to note how completely the two have changed hands as to the principle upon which they were originally supposed to be divided. The Democrats of to-day hold the liberty of one man to be absolutely nothing, when in conflict with another man's right of property; Republicans, on the contrary, are for both the man and the dollar, but in case of conflict the man before the dollar.

"I remember being once much amused at seeing two partially intoxicated men engaged in a fight with their great-coats on, which fight, after a long and rather harmless contest, ended in each having fought himself out of his own coat and into that of the other. If the two leading parties of this day are really identical with the two in the days of Jefferson and Adams, they have performed the same feat as the two drunken men."

Abraham Lincoln, in a letter to H.L. Pierce and others, April 6, 1859, in *Complete Works of Abraham Lincoln,* John G. Nicolay and John Hay, eds. (New York, 1894), Vol. V, pp. 125–126.

[7]See William Ryan, *Blaming the Victim* (New York: Pantheon Books, 1971)—editors' note.

[8]Bronislaw Malinowski, *Argonauts of the Western Pacific* (London: Routledge and Kegan Paul, 1922).

[9]A monograph on the Nobel prize in science finds that, as of 1972, Jews constituted about a fifth of all 286 laureates and about a fourth of the 89 laureates in the United States. Harriet Zuckerman, *Scientific Elite* (New York: The Free Press, 1977), p. 68. (Note appended 1982.)

[10]R.K. Merton, Patricia S. West, and Marie Jahoda, *Patterns of Social Life* (New York: Columbia University Bureau of Applied Social Research, 1951); R.K. Merton, P.S. West, M. Jahoda, and H.C. Selvin, *Social Policy and Social Research in Housing* (New York: Journal of Social Issues, 1951).

INDEX OF NAMES

Index of Subjects